Pacific Possessions

Pacific Possessions

The Pursuit of Authenticity
in Nineteenth-Century
Oceanian Travel Accounts

CHRIS J. THOMAS

The University of Alabama Press   Tuscaloosa

The University of Alabama Press
Tuscaloosa, Alabama 35487-0380
uapress.ua.edu

Typeface: Adobe Caslon Pro

Cover images: William Torrey, from the frontispiece of *Torrey's
Narrative: Or, The Life and Adventures of William Torrey*; "Our
Home in Fiji," from the frontispiece to Constance Gordon-
Cumming's *At Home in Fiji*
Cover design: Michele Myatt Quinn

Cataloging-in-Publication data is available from the Library of
Congress.
ISBN: 978-0-8173-2094-2
E-ISBN: 978-0-8173-9358-8

Contents

List of Illustrations   vii

Acknowledgments   ix

Introduction   1

1 George Vason's Tongan Tattoos   12

2 A Häolé's Hawaiian Hula   36

3 Constance Gordon-Cumming's Fijian Cannibal Fork   64

4 Robert Louis Stevenson's Gilbert Islands Photographs   102

Notes   143

Works Cited   159

Index   167

Illustrations

1.1. Frontispiece to James Orange's *Narrative of the Late George Vason of Nottingham* 13

1.2. *A weroan or Great Lorde of Virginia* (1590) 14

1.3. "Portrait of Jean-Baptiste Cabris" 18

1.4. John Rutherford 19

1.5. Frontispiece to *Torrey's Narrative* 31

2.1. "On Guard" 48

2.2. "Children's Dance" 54

2.3. "Native Man—Mode of Sitting" 60

2.4. "Native Female—Mode of Sitting" 61

3.1. Front cover of Constance Gordon-Cumming's *At Home in Fiji* 65

3.2. Frontmatter note to Constance Gordon-Cumming's *At Home in Fiji* 73

3.3. Objects from Fiji 78

3.4. "Cannibal Forks" 79

3.5. "Our Home in Fiji" 98

3.6. "A Chief's Kitchen" 99

4.1. Penguin Classics cover (1998) of *In the South Seas* 103

4.2. "Stevensons in company with Nan Tok' and Nei Takauti, Butaritari" 104

4.3. "Moipu and Paaaeua as the past and the present in Atuona" 119

4.4. "'Disbelief': Removing False Teeth" 123

4.5. "Nan Tok' and Nei Takauti" 125

4.6. "Butaritari—Maka and Mary Maka, Kanoa and Mrs Maria Kanoa—Hawaiian missionaries of the American Board of Missions, Honolulu" 127

4.7. "Stevenson's Camp at Apemama. 'Equator-Town'" 130

4.8. "King Tembinoka writing the 'History of Apemama' in an account book" 134

4.9. "Tembinok[a], King of Apemama" 136

4.10. "The manner in which the King is carried about" 137

4.11. "King Tembinoka with his adopted son—standing in front of wives" 137

4.12. "Mr Stevenson being mesmerized under devil-work tree by notable devil-man named 'Terutaki'" 140

Acknowledgments

First and foremost, I am grateful to Christoph Irmscher, who believed in this project from the beginning. Throughout the writing process, Christoph commented on countless drafts, and his keen insight helped shape this project. I could not have asked for a more supportive mentor and a better model of scholarly generosity. I am thankful, as well, for insightful feedback on my writing from Lara Kriegel, Richard Nash, and Nick Williams.

Several institutions have allowed me to reproduce material from their collections, including the British Museum, Edinburgh Museums and Galleries, and the City of Edinburgh Council. Edinburgh Museums' digitization of Robert Louis Stevenson's photographs made chapter 4 possible. Thank you to Nicolas Tyack for helping parse through that collection. And thank you to Carla Manfredi for providing generous direction and guidance about the Stevenson photographic archive.

A version of chapter 1, "Clothed in Tattoos: Cultural Fluidity in George Vason's Authentic Narrative of Four Years' Residence at Tongatahoo," was published in *Studies in Travel Writing* 19, no. 2 (2015):109–26. I thank the journal editor, Tim Youngs, and anonymous reviewers for their revision suggestions, many of which have been incorporated into the current version of this chapter.

I would also like to thank the staff at University of Alabama Press, especially Dan Waterman and this book's acquisitions editor, Wendi Schnaufer, who patiently guided me through the publication process. I am especially appreciative of the anonymous reviewers that Wendi sought out to read my manuscript. Both reviewers provided valuable and welcome advice. In particular, I am grateful to one of those anonymous reviewers for directing me to ways I could better engage with Pacific Islands scholars, as well as to better represent the Oceanian culture—both historical and present—to Americanist and Victorianist scholars.

Finally, I express my thanks to the many Oceanian scholars whose work helped me to better understand, and hopefully represent, Oceanian cultures. Two of these brilliant scholars recently passed away: Paul Lyons, whose work *American Pacificism* served as a foundation for me to think more critically about Western representations of Oceanian cultures; and Tracey Banivanua-Mar, whose work was fundamental to my understanding of how missionary discourse shaped ideas of Fiji as "savage" and how Fijian people resisted and spoke back to that discourse, as seen in chapter 3. Like the travelers about whom I write, I have had to critically encounter my privileged assumptions, seeking to learn and understand more about the Oceanian world. This has been the most meaningful part of this writing process.

Pacific Possessions

Introduction

Nineteenth-century Pacific travel accounts formed a sort of Island mystique, a legacy that extends to our present moment. This mythology around a supposed authentic experience of the "exotic" Pacific lives on in vacation sites such as TripAdvisor. User-generated reviews of Hawaiian spaces abound with references to the alleged authenticity of their experience. For example, the user HotelFanDeLuxe writes about what she calls the "most authentic Hawaiian experience ever." Her stay at the Lodge at Koele, she writes, was "perfection in every way: spacious, perfectly laid out, sumptuous bathrooms, glorious views. The restaurant offered delicious options, the pool setting was serene and calming." Since well-constructed bathrooms, breathtaking views, delicious restaurants, and swimming pools are common fixtures of many places around the globe, one wonders what made this such a distinctly Hawaiian experience. Perhaps recognizing this oversight, HotelFanDeLuxe adds that the "front porch and Hawaiian pillows added a special touch." With this out of the way, she gushes that "the golf course [was] smashing" before concluding that "the Hawaiian crafts offered as an activity were fun and unusual." Hawaiian authenticity, for this reviewer, is defined not by the experience as a whole but by the "special touch[es]" of Hawaiianness.

HotelFanDeLuxe is far from alone in framing their expertise on Hawaiian authenticity on TripAdvisor. Quite often, however, such expertise is filtered through something more specific than just a "special touch." For the majority of reviewers, it is the Hawaiian luau that determines the authenticity of their experience. User Allan Y insists that "a visit to Hawaii without the experience of a Luau would be like going to Paris and not seeing the Eiffel Tower." In setting up this analogy, Alan Y frames the Hawaiian luau as a semiotic sign for Hawaii itself. And yet descriptions of the luau as an exotic Hawaiian experience are curiously interspersed with familiarity, even a sense of ownership. Titling a review of the Mauna Lani shopping center version of the

Hawaiian luau "authentic and free," user jcarmello recommends that visitors "dine at Ruth's Chris and ask for a seat overlooking the stage." The image of a tourist watching a supposedly authentic luau while sitting in a chain restaurant, a choice cut of prime rib in front of them, would surely be amusing to nineteenth-century travelers like Henry Augustus Wise, who, in the 1850s, was disappointed to find Honolulu a "town of strangers, with shops, stores, and warehouses" (*Los Gringos* 362). Perhaps even more so for pseudonymous author of *Sandwich Island Notes* (1854), A Häolé: he had to travel far off the beaten track, "where foreigners seldom or never go," to see an authentic Hawaiian hula ceremony (283). Even still, A Häolé struggled to distinguish between performance and cultural practice, between watching a performance and being part of one.

The contradiction between performance and authenticity, likewise, underlies many of TripAdvisor's reviews of luau. Commenting on the Mauna Lani shopping center luau, one user happily asserts that "performers really get into the act, and seem to have an amazing time. You can take pictures with the performers after the show." This reviewer's use of the terms "performers" and "act" is revealing. We often think of "performance" and "acting" as antithetical to authenticity, yet for this reviewer they seem to work as validation of the luau's authenticity. Further, the reviewer's tentative assertion that the performers merely "seem" to be enjoying themselves suggests an incipient awareness of the falsity of these performances. In the absence of the real thing, one settles for "seeming" to have a good time, the performance of authenticity. Thus, the reviewer concludes by mentioning that he or she "caught a glimpse of the Luau at the Marriot, [which] looked pretty pale in comparison." The same criterion is applied by the user Levi F, though it leads him to the assessment that "Kauai's Best Luau" was "Very Underwhelming." The dancers "were stiff and did not seem to enjoy the performance," Levi F grumbles, from the Marriott Hotel. Rather than seeing performance and authenticity as distinct, both reviewers curiously yoke the two together. For them, authenticity appears to mean "convincing": if the performers "seem" to be enjoying the "act," then the performance must be authentic.

I begin this book on nineteenth-century Pacific travel narratives by engaging with twenty-first-century digital travel reviews to emphasize that Westerners continue to traffic in nineteenth-century definitions of Pacific authenticity.[1] These online reviewers typify the central concerns of *Pacific Possessions*: authenticity and possession. Despite demonstrating limited firsthand knowledge of Hawaiian culture, these reviews frame the quality of the writers' experiences through an arbitrary standard of what constitutes authentic Hawaiian culture. And, as user jcarmello's comparison to Paris's Eiffel Tower suggests, a particular cultural marker often stands in for the whole. However, it is important to note the slippage in this analogy. The Eiffel Tower, a quintessential object of European tourism as a whole, is just that, an object. It can be taken in as an architectural marvel that can be admired without any consideration of what makes it uniquely French. The luau, however, is a practice and an embodiment of cultural identity. And as such, it is, as these examples show, varied and subject to various interpretations. No one, however, questions the authenticity of the Eiffel Tower; it stands impassive. One might react with awe or, conversely, with disappointment upon seeing the tower, but those reactions have little bearing on tourists' notions of French culture more broadly. Even as it stands as a semiotic marker of France, it does not come to represent the whole French culture and people. Tourists will encounter many more elements of French culture and likely engage with a variety of French locals. But the luau, as TripAdvisor reviews show, tends to *be* Hawaii for the majority of tourists.

For these reviewers, then, the luau functions as a narrative possession, a cultural signifier around which they define Hawaiian culture as a whole, and one through which they will define the authenticity of their own experience. In designating the luau—as I do with other cultural markers of Oceanian authenticity throughout this work—a narrative possession, I mean to suggest that it becomes the imaginative property of a Western audience. Modern travelers to Hawaii arrive with preformed expectations about the Hawaiian luau, and their engagement with it becomes part of their own narrative. Lulled into the comfort of touristic familiarity, the prefabricated performance of cultural authenticity comes across as exotic. The "special touch," to return to Hotel-FanDeLuxe's phrase, becomes the place itself.

Pacific Possessions takes shape around such "special touches" of Oceanian culture. Of course, the nineteenth-century texts that I analyze are not quite as glib as the above sampling of TripAdvisor reviews. Edward Perkins, a travel writer who toured the Pacific in the early 1850s, provides a more complex version of these contemporary special touches: agreeable disappointments. Surprised by the "neatness" and "regularity" of the town, Perkins declares himself "agreeably disappointed," as "but for the distant landscape, one would fancy himself at home, or what would be nearer the truth, in an English or American colony" (112–13). Perkins's agreeable disappointment serves as an apt framework for understanding the Western traveler's pursuit of Pacific authenticity in the nineteenth century. On the one hand, colonialism rendered the Pacific accessible and familiar (agreeable); on the other hand, such familiarity necessarily came at the expense of the more authentic Pacific world they sought (disappointing). As a result of this disappointment, nineteenth-century Western travelers turned to more agreeable versions of Pacific Islands authenticity.

These agreeable versions of Pacific authenticity are what I term Pacific possessions: cultural signifiers around which Western travelers come to define
various Pacific cultures. In other words, Oceanian cultural practices become
narrativized for Western audiences, turning into their imaginative property.
As Noelani Arista puts it in *The Kingdom and the Republic*, "the distance between Hawai'i and the American and European worlds was not just one of
nautical miles; it was an imaginative space enlarged by the projection and production of Hawai'i and Hawaiians as objects of knowledge by New England
merchants, missionaries, visiting transient explorers, and ship captains" (7).
While one might contend that such logic applies to any colonial site, Oceania,
I argue, is uniquely bound up in a contradiction wherein it is at once imagined *as* Western possession while also representing the antithesis of Western
society. This is another way of thinking about what Paul Lyons has termed
"American Pacificism," which in his book by the same title he defines as "the
double logic that the islands are imagined at once as places to be civilized
and as escapes from civilization" (27). This double logic informs the way that
nineteenth-century travelers read the Pacific world. Indeed, their pursuit of
Pacific markers of authenticity represents its own sort of civilizing process for
Western observers, a means of embracing Pacific exoticism while still maintaining their Western sensibilities.[2] This is not to say, however, that such interpretations are a purely colonial imposition. Nineteenth-century travelers
were, of course, subject to the colonial and imperial ideologies of their time,
even if their travelers were not explicitly colonially motivated; however, their
desire to understand Oceanian cultures seems, by and large, sincere. I thus
read these cultural markers as part of a complex discourse, one that simultaneously privileged various Oceanian islands' unique cultural identity while at the
same time writing over them, in turn generating a Western version of Pacific
authenticity.

Pacific Possessions navigates the space travel writing creates between cultural
exchange and Western invention, between interchange and imposition. In
this way, I see my work as building most explicitly on the influential work of
Oceanian historian Greg Dening. Recognizing the limitations of postcolonial
readings of Euro-Pacific contact, Dening sought to show that such encounters
were not one-way streets, that Islanders influenced their European visitors just
as much as Europeans influenced their islander hosts. Focusing primarily on
eighteenth-century encounters, Dening, in *Mr. Bligh's Bad Language*, uses "the
beach"—the unique site of Pacific first encounters—as a guiding metaphor for
his analysis. The beach, he argues, "is a marginal space, where neither otherness nor familiarity holds sway, where there is much invention and blending
of old and new" (179). The beach, in contrast to Mary Louise Pratt's contact
zone, then, is not a site of European cultural imposition but instead a vibrant

site of cultural exchange. Dening's work has inspired a subfield of rich readings of eighteenth-century Oceanian encounters, reconceiving this moment in a way that gives voice to both indigenous and Western perspectives.[3] In other words, in preferring the concept of exchange over a purely postcolonial model, such scholarship has empowered Oceanic perspectives in the history of eighteenth-century encounter.

Nineteenth-century Oceanian travel narratives, however, have been read far less imaginatively.[4] Most critical accounts of nineteenth-century Oceanian travel have focused on a narrow canon of popular authors: Herman Melville, Robert Louis Stevenson, and, moving into the early twentieth century, Jack London. Consider, for example, David Farrier's *Unsettled Narratives: The Pacific Writings of Stevenson, Ellis, Melville, and London* (2007).[5] As the subtitle suggests, these authors themselves form the body of Pacific writing. Vanessa Smith's *Literary Culture and the Pacific* (1998) invokes a similar pattern, dedicating a chapter each to the beachcomber and missionary literary traditions, and then focusing three chapters—and an afterword—on Robert Louis Stevenson.[6] In this way, Stevenson alone comes to represent the nineteenth-century Pacific travel narrative.[7] Such an approach ignores a wide corpus of nineteenth-century Oceanian travel accounts, accounts that, though less conventionally literary than their canonical counterparts, were nonetheless widely circulated, read, and well reviewed at the time. What we are left with is an incomplete—and literary elitist—understanding of a genre that was well recognized and popular at the time.[8]

In short, these travel narratives are more or less ignored in scholarly communities because they do not easily lend themselves to a particular critical paradigm. They are, that is to say, not readily definable as narratives of exchange—"the beach" had been washed over—and their relationship to colonialism remains ambiguous as well. Moreover, distinctions between British and American travel writers are often blurred by their shared conceptions of the Pacific, conceptions more Western than nationalistic. The authors of Oceanian travel narratives are difficult to pin down: their fascination with Pacific Island cultures is both inspired by colonialism and driven by a desire to reclaim a precolonial Pacific. The varied and ambiguous nature of their travels can be seen through a sampling of their introductory justifications for writing.[9] Henry Augustus Wise published his Polynesian travels, *Los Gringos*, "merely to compile a pleasant narrative, such as may perchance please or interest the generality of readers" (vi). Constance Gordon-Cumming traveled to Fiji because "a cruise in the South Pacific ha[d] been one of the dreams of [her] life" (12).[10] Edward Perkins first considered "a geographic, historic, and descriptive account of the various localities visited . . . but the absence of either library or work of reference precluded its adoption, and at the hazard of the imputation of egotism, a narrative of personal adventures was concluded upon" (iii). John Coulter's *Adventures in the Pacific* had something for everyone: "Being strictly authentic, the senior reader may feel an interest . . . and the junior be amused by the shooting, fishing, and sailing excursions, with the exploring rambles on uninhabited islands" (v). For each of these authors, their personal experience motivates their accounts. This is not to suggest that they were uninfluenced by and subject to the ideologies of their time. Indeed, my argument focuses very much on how they were. Yet, even as they arrived with their own expectations, these travelers remain open to negotiating the differences between European and Pacific Island cultures. Their interactions with missionaries and colonial merchants were likewise varied, sometimes condemning their restrictive practices, at others championing European influence. Their narratives depend on this negotiation with a multitude of different perspectives.

Recovering these forgotten works allows us to reconceive of nineteenth-century Oceania as a vibrant cultural hub, a space brimming with cultural interchange. *Pacific Possessions* thus seeks to recapture the polyphony of voices that enlivened this space, focusing on both British and American travel writers, while also paying attention to their Oceanian interlocutors.[11] Each of my chapters centers around a distinct Pacific cultural markers: the Tongan tattoo; the Hawaiian hula; the Fijian cannibal fork; and, finally, Robert Louis Stevenson's cache of South Seas photographs. Focusing both on how Westerners formed narratives around these objects and what those objects meant within nineteenth-century Oceanic cultures, *Pacific Possessions* argues that these critically neglected travel narratives served to shape a version of Oceanian authenticity that remains persistent today. The "possessions" within my title speaks to the way Westerners sought to repossess and narrativize these objects, focusing on how they wrote Pacific culture back to their Western audiences. At the same time, these Western writers are often forced to reconsider their own literary-informed notions of the Pacific Islands. Their narratives, then, also unravel their audience's expectations of the Pacific. This literary crafting and uncrafting of Oceania ultimately informs contemporary issues of cultural representation, tourism, and globalization.

Each chapter is built around two complementary narratives. Broadly, I want to tell the story of the exchange between Pacific cultural markers and Western interpretations of them. But such a story cannot be told in broad terms alone. It is for this reason that I centralize each chapter around one particular author. In doing so, I emphasize individual authors' complex and evolving understanding of their Oceanian surroundings. In other words, I reclaim these travel accounts *as* narratives. I treat these texts, then, not merely as cogs in the service of a larger postcolonial argument but rather as stories worth hearing. While I tell the story of how these authors structure their narratives around their experience with these markers of authenticity, I also unfold the ways that these markers challenge and unsettle their expectations.

Taken as a whole, these individual narratives form a more expansive narrative, one that charts Western travelers' increasingly nostalgic—and Western-inflected—pursuit of Pacific authenticity, as colonialization continues to render the Pacific world more familiar. I thus begin this study by analyzing Romantic-era beachcomber narratives: firsthand accounts of sailors' willing and unwilling assimilations into Oceanian societies. These texts, with their emphasis on the authenticity of their accounts and engagements with, variously, Polynesian, Melanesian, and Micronesian culture, set a standard of exotic romanticism that informs nineteenth-century travel writing. Disappointed when the colonialized Pacific failed to meet their romantic expectations, travelers fixated on representations of the precolonial. They sought, to borrow from Jonathan Culler's "The Semiotics of Tourism," "an escape from the code." But, Culler continues, "this escape is coded in turn, for the authentic must be marked to be constituted as authentic" (165). Applying Culler's logic to the Pacific, then, the very idea of escaping the colonial Pacific in favor of something purer and more authentic becomes a trope itself. It turns into a convention of Western travel rather than an escape from it.

For George Vason, the focus of the chapter 1, "George Vason's Tongan Tattoos," Tongan tattooing, indeed, seemed to offer an escape from Western society. Vason arrived on the island of Tongatapu, the main island of the Tonga in the Pacific Ocean, in 1797, abroad the *Duff*, which transported the London Missionary Society's first troupe of Tongan converters. But it was not long before Vason became a convert to Tongan culture, a conversion that dramatically culminated in his tattooing. Vason initially conceives of his tattooing as authenticating his immersion into Tongan society. Despite this embodied conversion, Vason is disappointed by the limits of his assimilation. Yet upon returning home, Vason's tattoos unsettle his European identity. Though Vason's *An Authentic Narrative of Four Years' Residence at Tongataboo* (1810) was published under the framework of Christian reclamation, as the story of a "missionary seduced abroad and reclaimed at home," I argue that his travel account in fact seeks to imagine an identity unbound by any culture. For while Vason looks at his Tongan tattoos as a form of clothing, scholars have dismissed this as a means of justifying his tattoos to a European audience. I suggest, however, that Vason regarded his tattoos as a productive amalgamation of Tongan and European values. For Vason, Tongan tattooing allows cultural values to be embodied in a way that European clothes cannot, effectively uniting body and culture.

By the middle of the nineteenth century, experiences like Vason's became increasingly scarce. Such unexpected encounters are replaced by an emerging tourist industry, which curated travelers' experience of Polynesia in particular. Chapter 2, "A Häolé's Hawaiian Hula," thus turns to the most rapidly colonized of Polynesian spaces, Hawaii, to examine the origins of the sightseeing impulse in the Pacific, which I trace through accounts of the Hawaiian hula. Despite the fact that the hula has become the most ubiquitous symbol of authentic Hawaiian life, as we have seen from the TripAdvisor accounts, scarcely any critical work has been done on nineteenth-century literary representations of it.[12] My work seeks to redress that, showing how mid-nineteenth-century travel writers helped to shape perceptions of the hula. My primary focus in this chapter is the once widely read but now forgotten *Sandwich Island Notes* (1854), by the American writer "A Häolé" (the author's pseudonym means "foreigner" in Hawaiian). I argue that travelers' interest in the hula stems from its forbidden nature: to see the hula is to see a supposedly authentic Hawaii hidden away from Western eyes. However, upon coming into contact with the hula, travelers like A Häolé are quick to turn away, assuring their reader that it is "too lascivious to bear description." These early accounts of the hula thus epitomize the complex paradox of Pacific authenticity, wherein the precolonial is at once celebrated and written over. The Pacific tourist wants to be both within and without the Polynesian world, even as they idealize a more fluid engagement with its culture.

Traveling to the geographic border of Polynesia and Micronesia, chapter 3, "Constance Gordon-Cumming's Fijian Cannibal Fork," revolves around the Fijian cannibal fork, which, I argue, came to signify both the proud achievement of colonial intervention and a nostalgic reminder of a complex precolonial Pacific culture. This contradiction is built into the title of this chapter's main text, the Scottish-born travel writer Constance Gordon-Cumming's *At Home in Fiji* (1881). As a "lady traveller," Gordon-Cumming's engagement with Fijian culture is particularly revealing, demonstrating the extent to which, by the latter part of the nineteenth century, the once-threatening Fiji had been rendered safe, turned into a more exotic version of home. Gordon-Cumming's fixation with the Fijian cannibal fork encapsulates this narrative. Accounts of the cannibal fork, I argue, form part of what Gannath Obeyesekere terms "cannibal talk," fictionalized tales produced through Anglophone and Oceanian accounts of cannibalism that crystallized into "fact" for Victorian travel writers. The cannibal fork provided a tangible representation of this sensational discourse. Far from being just a dutiful collector, Gordon-Cumming's engagement with Fijian culture is complex and revealing. Her representations of Fijian cannibalism can never be easily defined as purely colonially motivated savagism or overinflated literary Romanticization. In this way, Gordon-Cumming's depiction of cannibalism represents an important moment in the history of Oceanian travel narratives: she is simultaneously content with colonial achievement ("At Home") and wistful for a supposedly more authentic Fiji.

In the final chapter, "Robert Louis Stevenson's Gilbert Islands Photographs," I turn the Pacific possession on its head, focusing on Robert Louis Stevenson's unpublished South Seas photographs, primarily those taken in the as yet fully colonized Gilbert Islands (Kiribati). While the authors in the previous three chapters sought to understand Pacific authenticity through indigenous practices, the central writer in the last chapter, Robert Louis Stevenson, turned to a distinctly Western practice to represent Pacific authenticity. Reading Stevenson's photographs alongside his posthumously published travel account *In the South Seas* (1896), I show how Stevenson saw his work as providing an objective—and therefore more authentic—account of the South Seas. By shifting to a canonical author in the final chapter of this book, I emphasize that Stevenson saw his work as directly responding to—and correcting—the less obviously sophisticated literary accounts that preceded him. Photography, he thought, would enable him to move past the romanticized South Seas clichés of previous writers. Despite his ambitions, however, Stevenson remained dissatisfied with his project: his narrative would not be published until after his death, and the photographs, which he saw as essential complements to it, have remained buried in the archives. I contend that far from demonstrating distance and objectivity, Stevenson's photographs reveal his own clichéd notions of Pacific authenticity. I focus not just on the photographs themselves as objects of exchange but also on Stevenson's *use* of photography as a medium of cultural negotiation. Tracing Stevenson's photographic endeavors, I demonstrate that it is not until the final part of his trip, in Kiribati, that Stevenson begins to abandon his own ideas of authenticity, arriving instead at a genuine interchange between himself and Oceanian peoples.

By now, the reader has surely noticed that I use a number of different terms to define the geographic site of my analysis: Polynesia, the South Seas, the Pacific, Pacific Islands, and Oceania. These are not interchangeable terms, as the Tongan-born Fijian scholar and poet Epeli Hau'ofa has pointed out. Following Hau'ofa's lead in "Our Sea of Islands," I generally use the term "Oceania" when I am referring to the place, people, and culture *outside* of the context of the nineteenth-century authors I am analyzing. However, when referencing nineteenth-century conceptions of the space, I tend to use the term "Pacific Islands," "Polynesia," or "South Seas." Hau'ofa provides a compelling rationale for distinguishing between these two sets of terms. The term "Pacific Islands," he argues, suggests "dry surfaces in a vast ocean far from the centres of power," emphasizing the "smallness and remoteness of the islands." The term "Oceania," however, "denotes a sea of islands and their inhabitants"; they are not "islands in the sea" but rather a "sea of islands" (31–32). Oceania, as Hauʻofa conceives it, lends to the space an interconnectedness, both with other islands and with the ocean itself. Yet this act of shifting denotation is also a political act of decolonizing language. The term "Pacific Islands" fundamentally altered indigenous perceptions of Oceanian space, "erecting boundaries that led to the contraction of Oceania, transforming a once boundless world into the Pacific Island states and territories we know today" (34). These terms, in other words, are active, and they create political facts.

Thus, when using the terms "Pacific Islands," "Polynesia," and "the South Seas" in my work, I treat them as nineteenth-century constructions, which, like the focus of my chapters, become imagined Western possessions. The Pacific Islands—like Oceania—encompass three different subregions: Polynesia, Micronesia, and Melanesia. Polynesia, the main focus of my study, is a Western geographical construction, a colonial binding together of more than one hundred small islands in the central and south Pacific region, most notably Hawaii, the Marquesas, Samoa, and Tonga.[13] The lumping together of these islands on the basis of shared cultural traits and racialized categorizations was, of course, as much an imaginative construction as it was a geographic certainty or anthropological discovery. Among the three subregions, Polynesia was the one most subject to Western romanticization; hence this is precisely the area to which most of my readings gravitate. Polynesia, a popular eighteenth-century geographic construction, is what readers in England or America most often thought of when they heard the term "the South Seas." A vague and nebulous term, "the South Seas" fell out of use in the nineteenth century, when mapping became an empirical science. Yet even as it ceased to be used as a geographic specifier, it retained its cachet in a literary context, often used to invoke the region's romantic and picturesque qualities, its authenticity, in other words.[14] It seems only fitting, then, that Stevenson's late-nineteenth-century travel account is titled *In the South Seas*,[15] for, as he rhapsodizes, "no part of the world exerts the same attractive power upon the visitor, and the task before me is to communicate to fireside travelers some sense of its seduction" (5).

Indeed, the South Seas attracted and seduced British and American writers in equal measure. For this reason, my archive consists of English-speaking writers from a broader Anglo-American and transatlantic context. This reflects my sense that what unites George Washington Bates (A Häolé) and Constance Gordon-Cumming—a shared Western, European-inflected framework—is, for the purposes of my study, more important than what separates them. For one thing, the writers I have chosen, by virtue of being travelers, conceived of their own identities as rather fluid and not constrained by their cultural origin. Constance Gordon-Cumming, for example, spent extended periods of time in India, Australia, New Zealand, and the United States, as well as in the South Seas and was read (and rather vigorously criticized) by American readers such as Henry Adams, as well as in England. Second, *Pacific Possessions* is less invested in the specific differences that separate Anglo-American travel writers than in the cultural difference they encounter and try to normalize and appropriate during the time they spent in the South Seas. This is a book about travel and travelers' experiences, written and researched, it seems important to acknowledge at this point, for the most part while land-locked in southern Indiana. And that has, of course, imposed some limits on methods and material. When I first began this project, I conceived of it as a strictly literary one, a project that would analyze Pacific travel accounts, such as Herman Melville's *Typee*. I quickly realized, however, that I had to think critically about my own assumptions about the Pacific. My expertise is primarily in literary studies, but I have also sought to engage thoughtfully with Oceanic history and scholarship. At the same time, my somewhat circumscribed position—that of an outsider imagining how other outsiders have imagined what the inside of another culture looks like—has its advantages. My work, like the works that are the focus of *Pacific Possessions*, has been a process of exchange, a metaphorical beach encounter. But it also maintained its distance from the lure of possessiveness that has marked the encounters I write about. Distance breeds a respect for specificity, or, in my case, for individual island traditions. I hope that, in writing about these encounters performed by men and women from another period, I have begun to open up more imaginative avenues for thinking about the worlds we make when we travel, in real life or, holding a book or a laptop, in our armchairs.

1

George Vason's Tongan Tattoos

The frontispiece of the 1840 edition of George Vason's narrative features an engraving of a fully tattooed Vason looming proudly over the Tongan landscape, with the caption "A Chieftain of Tongataboo" (figure 1.1). In the illustration, Vason is visually defined by his assimilated "savage" characteristics: his headdress, his bow and arrow, and, most importantly, his tattoos. This striking frontispiece was not part of the first edition of Vason's narrative, published in 1810 under the title *An Authentic Narrative of Four Years' Residence in Tongataboo*. Further setting itself apart from the earlier publication, the title of the 1840 edition, *Narrative of the Life of the Late George Vason of Nottingham*, attempts to reclaim Vason from his Tongan experience and to restore him to his English home—he is, after all, "of Nottingham." But in a way—at least if we look at the frontispiece—the republication seems designed to come across as even more authentically exotic than the original. The editor appears to want to have it both ways: while the title recasts Vason as "civilized," the engraving once more affirms his "savage" identity.[1]

In framing Vason as "savage," this latter version repurposes the construct of authenticity set up in the 1810 edition, *An Authentic Narrative of Four Years' Residence at Tongataboo*: it is Vason himself, and not just his account of Tonga, who is advertised as "authentic." The popularization of the ideal of "authenticity" is often traced back to Jean-Jacques Rousseau,[2] who, as Charles Lindholm notes, was "influenced by travellers' accounts of simple native cultures" and contrasted their primitive purity with the corruption of modern society. As Lindholm articulates in *Culture and Authenticity*, Rousseau held that the more closely modern life resembles that of the original state of society, the more authentic it is (8). Given this context, the frontispiece depiction of Vason offers an ironic comment on the "noble savage" trope. It is, in fact, Vason's descent into "savagery," his devolution, that renders him authentic in Rousseau's sense of the term. Vason's frontispiece, perhaps not coincidentally, does

Figure 1.1. Frontispiece to James Orange's *Narrative of the Late George Vason of Nottingham*. Engraving by H. Wilkins. Derby: Henry Mozely, 1840.

bear a striking resemblance to one of the more famous depictions of the "noble savage," Thomas De Bry's "A weroan or Great Lorde of Virginia" (1590) (figure 1.2).[3] The very resemblance of the two images serves to undermine the validity of the concept of authenticity. In seeking to authenticate Vason's "savage" identity, the text effectively turns Vason into a type. Johnathan Culler, in "The Semiotics of Tourism," suggests that the paradox of the authentic is that while "the authentic sight requires markers," our *notion* of the authentic is always "unmarked" (64). In presenting Vason in his Tongan context, his tattoos "marking" his authenticity, the narrative frames him as merely a *version* of authenticity. His tattoos recede in significance, blending in with the other markers of "savage" authenticity.

The contrast between the title and the frontispiece foregrounds the fundamental contradiction of Vason's narrative: any attempt to define his identity

Figure 1.2. *A weroan or Great Lorde of Virginia* (1590). Engraving by Thomas De Bry, based on watercolor by John White.

constantly comes up against the awareness of how he does *not* fit in. His Tongan conversion has rendered him too "savage" for his Christian reconversion to be anything but conditional; and yet, by his own account, however much he assimilated into Tongan culture, he was never not seen as an outsider. But, as this chapter will show, Vason himself continues to invest his tattoos with meaning, even as the narrative framework pushes against such thinking. While Vason's description of Tongan tattoos as a form of clothing has often been read as a means of justifying his tattoos to a European audience, I suggest instead that Vason reads his tattoos as a productive amalgamation of Tongan and European values. For Vason, Tongan tattooing allows cultural values to be embodied in a way that European clothes cannot, effectively uniting body and culture.

In analyzing Vason's narrative as representing a meaningful interchange of cultural values, I am building on Greg Dening's concept of "the beach" in *Mr. Bligh's Bad Language*, which fostered a paradigm shift in Oceanian critical discourse. Dening defines the beach as a "space where neither otherness nor familiarity holds sway, where there is much invention and blending of old and new" (179). The concept has been most influentially furthered by Jonathan Lamb, Vanessa Smith, and Nicholas Thomas, who, in the introduction to their anthology of South Seas textual encounters, *Exploration and Exchange*, argue that while narratives like Vason's "might invoke the moral, political, and religious, and literary certitudes of home," their authors were also "subject to the risks of encounter, and their narratives are motivated by the consequences (terrifying or pleasurable) of chances being taken" (xvii).[4] For these critics, such cross-cultural encounters, full of risk for both sides, resist a purely postcolonial reading. While I do read Vason's narrative in this spirit, I also highlight the limits of "exchange" experienced by the traveler upon recrossing the beach, that is, when he returns back home. I want to read "encounter" and "exchange" as a process that continues long after the traveler has left the beach. For Vason, narrating his story after his return is also a way of *re*encountering the beach, of laying claim to the end product of the exchange that occurred in that space. Vason brings the beach home with him.

EXCHANGE AND CONVERSION

George Vason arrived on the island of Tongatapu, the main island of Tonga in the Pacific Ocean, in 1797, abroad the *Duff*, which transported the London Missionary Society's first group of Tongan converters. Their mission was as much cultural as it was spiritual, calling on these young men to both preach the word of God and teach practical skills. Vason was thus chosen not simply on account of his fervor for the cause but also because of his background as a bricklayer.[5] This early missionary foray into the Tonga islands was largely a failure: the Tongan people remained clueless as to why the missionaries had come there. William Mariner, who, a few years after Vason's escape, fell into Tongan captivity when the crew of his ship (the *Port au Prince*) was massacred, reported that "the King and several other chiefs at the Tonga islands appeared quite surprised when [I] informed them that the object of the missionaries had been to instruct them in the religion of the white people. They had thought that the latter came to live among them merely from choice, as liking the climate better than their own" (25). And yet, the London Missionary Society debut expedition turned out to be not entirely useless: Vason would come to serve as an example of why young men should not be left alone to evangelize the "seductive" Pacific Islands. While his fellow missionaries either abandoned the mission or were killed in the midst of the Tongan civil war, Vason grew closer to the Tongan way of life, adjusting both physically and culturally to the island.

Traveling to the Tongan Islands, Vason and his fellow missionaries "encouraged each other; and amid tears of doubt and hope, sang the Hymn that often cheered us in our voyage (22)."[6] Upon arriving in the islands, however, each man was left on his own. The modest crew of fewer than thirty young men was spread out across the islands,[7] with each individual taking responsibility for his own portion.[8] Away from the encouragement and unifying hymns of his missionary brethren, Vason found himself drawn to the way of life he was sent to reform. "Modesty," Vason confesses, "lost with me its moralizing charm; and it was not long ere I disincumbered [sic] myself of my European garment, and contented myself with the native dress" (108). Stripping away and exchanging clothes is, for Vason, a symbolic act of discarding values such as modesty and morality. The moralistic tone he employs, though, is deceptive and part of what Vanessa Smith identifies as the "conflicted" nature of Vason's narrative (*Literary Culture in the Pacific*, 37). It is a peculiar characteristic of Vason's narrative that the structure of Evangelical reform does not consistently act as his own narrative's overarching framework. Instead, this framework seems to function merely as a means of dressing up Vason's narrative. Vason's editor suggestively writes that he "only arranges his thoughts, and *clothes* them with language" (vii; my emphasis). I see this metaphor of "clothing" as especially significant to Vason's narrative: his narrative is "clothed" by its evangelical framework, but that clothing often seems ill-fitting.[9] While Vason's account of initially shedding his clothes is carefully attired in the language of guilt, his enthusiastic retelling of when he is later tattooed resists such clothing over.

Embodied Values: The Tattoo as a "Cuticle Vesture"

The tattoo figures as the most potent symbol of cultural transgression throughout beachcomber narratives (i.e., firsthand accounts of European sailors' willing and unwilling assimilations into Pacific culture). Perhaps the most famous case in point is an intended tattoo, a tattooing that never came to fruition. Herman Melville's narrator Tommo, in his semiautobiographical *Typee* (1846), quips that undergoing Marquesan tattooing would prevent him from being able to "have the *face* to return to my countrymen" (219). For Tommo, being tattooed would be equivalent to having no *American* face at all. Unlike Tommo/Melville, John Coulter, in his *Adventures in the Pacific* (1845), does subject himself to Marquesan tattooing. But after seeing his reflection in the water, he, too, is convinced that his "friends at home would scarcely know [him]" (215). The sense of anxiety exhibited by both Tommo and Coulter exemplifies how the tattoo was often seen as a threat to one's reassimilation upon returning home, a rewriting of identity. Yet the tattoo also offered a form of acceptance within the various Oceanian communities that nothing else could. As Coulter later attests, his tattooing "enabled [him] to pass the time more agreeably, having the full confidence of the people" (216).[10]

To be tattooed, as Coulter here suggests, is to become a confidant. Coulter's tattooing[11] is characteristic of most beachcomber tattooing accounts: he reluctantly (but bravely) acquiesces to be tattooed, as he has no other choice but to "protect [his] life" (207).[12] Vason's narrative does not easily fit into this generic pattern, nor does it seem quite fair to simply suggest that Vason "goes native," which is in itself an unproductive way of understanding both Pacific culture and the Pacific beachcomber. Where Coulter and Melville's narratives seek to generalize the tattoo as a "marking" that alters their European identity, Vason's account of his tattooing shows a much greater concern for the implications of the tattoo within Tongan society.

Polynesian tattooing was integral in constructing both social and individual identities, as Alfred Gell's seminal study *Wrapping in Images* (1993) shows. Taking his title from the Marquesan term *pahu tiki*, Gell defines the Polynesian tattoo as "a skin over skin, a wrapping for the person which is not separate but integral" (32). This "wrapping," Gell argues, is formed not only by the tattoo itself (the "images") but also by the process through which it is made. That is to say, the pain endured during one's tattooing is a constitutive element of the tattoo. According to Gell, the combination of this pain and the visible traces of that pain form a sort of "armour" for the wearer (38). Although Gell's overarching project is meant to provide a general theory of Polynesian tattooing, he also carefully examines how tattoos differ from one place to another, both stylistically and symbolically, offering their own unique "metaphoric possibilities" (23).

Building on Gell's study, I suggest that Vason's tattoos ought to be understood as an amalgamation of Tongan and European "metaphoric possibilities." Vason's tattoos were specifically Tongan, a simple fact often overlooked in critical studies of his narrative. Gell notes that Tongan tattooing and Marquesan tattooing (from which Gell takes his term "wrapping in images") existed on opposite ends of the spectrum: where Tongan tattooing was "the most stylistically conservative" form found in Polynesia (312), the Marquesan version was "the most elaborate and extensive" (163). Returning to the frontispiece image of Vason with those distinctions in mind, one notices the relative uniformity of design on Vason's body—he is fully covered, but unique "images" seem to be the variation rather than the norm. Vason's tattooing stands in stark contrast to Jean-Baptiste Cabri's Marquesan tattoos (figure 1.3)[13] and John Rutherford's Māori tattooing (figure 1.4).[14] Tongan tattooing, it seems, was more concerned with the "wrapping" of the body than with the "images," focusing primarily on coverage rather than design.

Before being tattooed, Vason's casting away of English garments only more dramatically (and quite literally) exposes his cultural difference. Despite Vason having partaken in the Tongan civil war, his fellow warriors nonetheless

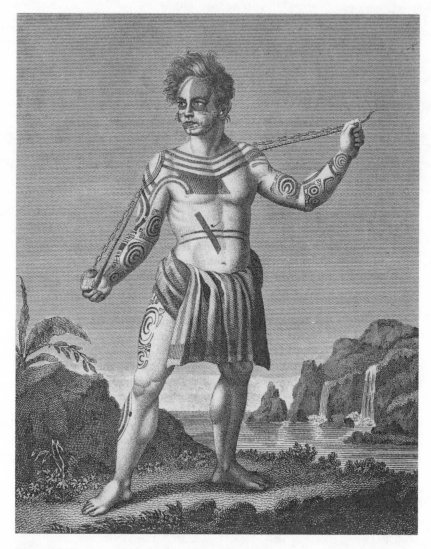

Figure 1.3. "Portrait of Jean-Baptiste Cabris," from Georg von Langsdorff, *Voyages and Travels in Various Parts of the World, during the Years 1803, 1804, 1805, 1806, 1807* (1813).

persist in viewing him as an outsider: "Whilst going from place to place, on these triumphant excursions of pleasure, I was frequently exposed to the reflections and sarcasms of the young people, especially in the hour of bathing, which generally recurred three times every day, for being destitute of that cuticle vesture, which modesty has taught the South-Sea islanders to throw around them as an excellent imitation and substitute for garments; I mean the Tatoo. On these occasions, they would raise a shout of merriment and call

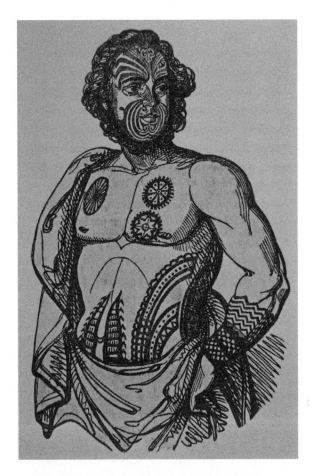

Figure 1.4. John Rutherford, from George Craik, *The New Zealanders* (1830).

me by opprobrious epithets, such as Ouchedair, &c. I was at length determined no longer to be singular and the object of ridicule" (178–79).[15] Rarely is the language of Vason's narrative as poetic and expressive as it is in this declaration that he was "destitute of that cuticle vesture." Here, the tattoo is described not as a marking but instead as a sort of embodied piece of clothing: clothing embedded into the skin.[16] While Vason concludes by saying that he did not want to continue to be "an object of ridicule," he prefaces this assertion by marvelling about what "an excellent imitation and substitution for garments" the tattoo is. Gell points out the "logical fallacy" in Vason's equating of clothes and tattoos, arguing that "modesty in the Judeo-Christian sense is not what the Tongan tattooing was all about. Exhibitionism would be nearer the mark" (103–4).[17] But while Vason's Eurocentric view of tattoos as a form of clothing may be misguided, what seems most important in the context of his narrative is his recognition of the tattoo as meaningful. In focusing on

Vason's misapprehension, we neglect to consider the powerful symbolic implications of Vason's self-conception. To be permanently outfitted in someone else's "clothes" is no small gesture. In describing the tattoo as a "cuticle vesture," Vason attempts to unite the body (the self) and clothes (culture). Tattoos, as Vason describes them, do not cover the body; they coalesce with it. In becoming tattooed, Vason embodies and formalizes the Tongan cultural values he has come to embrace.

He desires to "no longer be singular," opting to instead have his most distinguishing feature among the Tongans (his whiteness) clothed over by tattoos. The Tongan tattoo, as Gell notes, was distinct from other Polynesian tattoos in that it seemed to be obtained more "as a matter of individual enterprise, undertaken in adulthood or adolescence," as opposed to being "quasi-initiatory" (102). As with indigenous Tongans, Vason takes the initiative to become tattooed. So, while he comes to Tonga as an outsider, his tattooing is not necessarily the tattooing of an outsider.[18] The process, in his mind, renders him "no longer singular," authenticating his status within Tongan society in a way that even fighting alongside his Tongan companions could not.

The willingness to be tattooed was often perceived, by European and Pacific Islander alike, as the foremost return of cultural exchange. Greg Dening, in *Mr. Bligh's Bad Language,* persuasively argues this point through the example of *Bounty* mutineer Peter Heywood's tattooing: "His was not a discovery of the Noble Savage or of the Primitive. It was much more simple and less a culturally centered image than that. It was a realization that their hospitality and generosity were genuine, that he could not find the limits of them, that the greatest gift he could give them in return was to let them make him like themselves—to endure the pain of the tattoos, to speak their language, to know the subtleties of their thinking" (258). To be tattooed, Dening contends, is to go beyond simply appreciating the culture; it is to accept and embrace its meaning to that culture. There is little indication, though, that Vason's motivations are like those that Dening discerns in Heywood. But this is not because Vason does not have those feelings of respect, admiration, and even love. For example, Vason fights alongside his host [Mulkamaair] and, upon the latter's death, laments, "I gave up all for lost, and was ready almost to lay myself down by his side, and die with him" (170). His narrative reveals a deep affection for both the Tongan people and the Tongan culture. Nevertheless, it does not adhere to the same simple and predictable pattern that Dening locates in Heywood's experience, where exchange is merely a token of respect. Heywood, as Dening sees it, endures the pain of the tattoo at the hands of the Tahitians not because he believes in its value but only because he believes in its value *to them.* Exchange in this sense implies a favor, a concession to Tahitian customs and ways of thinking. Framing Heywood as active—"the gift he could *give them*" (emphasis added)—Dening affords Heywood primacy in this exchange. Even while being tattooed, Heywood is "giving" rather than receiving.

Like Heywood, Vason is overwhelmed by the islanders' generosity, but it is his own feelings of inadequacy rather than thankfulness that inspire his decision to endure both the process and permanence of tattooing. He requests the tattoo because he wants *to be part* of what the tattoo means, not simply "to know" what it means. In this way, Vason's narrative is unique among beachcomber narratives. He does not become tattooed as a favor to his islander hosts, nor does he do it because he has no other choice; he does it because he wants the values associated with the tattoo to be embodied within him, to "no longer be singular." For Vason, the tattoo, a "cuticle vesture," is not merely representative of Tongan values but instead constitutive of them.

Even in looking back upon his tattooing, Vason shows none of the guilt that surrounds his initial exchanging of clothing; instead, his reflections exude pride and an almost wistful exuberance.[19] While the initial act of shedding his clothes to conform to Tongan custom causes Vason "turpitude and guilt," his later decision to become tattooed is recounted heroically. He recalls that the pain was so great that it could be performed only every third day; even then, the process was "so exhausting" that "large tumours" developed and remained when he returned for his next session. While Vason, when it comes to the exchange of clothes, is merely "contented . . . with the native dress," here he ruminates upon the results of his tattooing gleefully, triumphing that he "was very much admired by the natives, as the European skin displays the blue colour, and the ornaments of the tattooing to very great advantage: I looked very gay indeed in this fancy new covering" (179).[20] Juniper Ellis in *Pacific Designs in Print and Skin* uses this passage to argue that "vanity (rather than the modesty he claims) motivated his choice" (122). Michelle Elleray in "Crossing the Beach" interprets Vason's reflection even more critically, suggesting that "it is his Englishness that makes his tattooed body a superior aesthetic object, since his whiteness highlights the intricacy of the *tatatau* in a way that the Tongans' brownness cannot" (170). Yet Vason's language in this passage never quite represents his whiteness as having an "advantage" *over* the complexion of the Tongans. That is to say, his whiteness, in fact, makes his tattooing, and, in turn, his conversion, even more legible. His assertion that they "admire" him seems to be suggestive more of feeling embraced rather than being singular. Vason positions himself as neither equal nor superior in this passage; he simply likes and takes pride in both his enduring the process of tattooing and the results of that process. More important, it is easy to forget the initial act of tattooing was a surrendering of his whiteness. Rather than reading this passage as a reflection of racial superiority, I read it as an endorsement of the superiority of the tattoo as a form of "clothing." It works *with* his body, simultaneously revealing and clothing it. In the context of Vason's narrative, the tattoo, dramatically put on display on his white body, establishes him as an authentic part of Tongan culture, allowing him to take on the position of chief.

Tattooed in Body Only: The Limits of European Tattooing

But while his tattooing makes Vason more accepted and thus more comfortable within Tongan society, it does not, as he seems to desire, make him indistinguishable from indigenous Tongans. His escape back home is significantly precipitated by a moment of exposure, of being recognized as still other. A Tongan fisherman immediately recognizes Vason as European in spite of his tattooed body and fluency with the language, "discerning a difference of tone and accent." Identifying Vason as belonging to a different world, he informs him that "a ship of your's [is] here" (196). Only moments later, Vason is then comically misrecognized by European sailors as "a native, who had picked up some European phrases" (197).[21] This double misrecognition suggests that, despite Vason's original hopes, only Europeans could perceive Vason as "authentically" Tongan. The tattoo may be, as Juniper Ellis suggests in *Pacific Designs in Print and Skin*, a "form of social registry" (3), but Vason's registry can never be the equivalent of the indigenous Tongan's registry. Being tattooed seems to engender respect and confidence from the Tongans, but it does not lead to a full assimilation; it does not create authenticity.

Far from simply marking Europeans as authentic, the tattoo often only reinforced the differences in cultural perspectives. Robert Louis Stevenson, in his *In the South Seas* (1896), provides further anecdotal evidence of the limitations of Polynesian tattooing on European bodies. Stevenson recounts the story of an old beachcomber who proposes to his Marquesan lover, only to be told that she would never marry an untattooed man, as he "looked so naked." Undeterred, the man then undergoes the process of tattooing. This does not have the desired effect, as, Stevenson writes, from then on the Marquesan woman "could never behold him from that day except with laughter," even though Stevenson "could never see the man without a kind of admiration" (50). What is laughable to the Marquesan woman is laudable to Stevenson. Stevenson's story follows familiar tropes of the tattooing narrative: the white man demonstrates his courage, his "greatness of soul," by enduring the pain of the tattooing, pain that, as Stevenson remarks, even the high chief himself is unwilling to endure; and yet, for all his endurance his tattooing makes him even more singular than he was before he was tattooed. The man may have previously seemed "naked" to the woman, but he was nevertheless himself. After he has been tattooed, he becomes an object of ridicule, because his tattoos remain at odds with what the woman sees as his authentic identity. His tattoos do not clothe him in the way that either he or she expects. Instead, his is a naked body incongruously marked. His resolve, however much Stevenson admires it, does nothing to change the way that he is perceived by the Marquesan woman. The problem for her, then, was not that he was not tattooed; it is that he never could be *tattooed*. This scenario enacts Culler's claim in *Framing the Sign* about the paradox of authenticity: "The authentic sight requires markers but our notion of the authentic is always unmarked" (164). The Marquesan woman cannot see the tattoos as anything but "markers," disproving their authenticity precisely by calling attention to it.

Both Stevenson and the spurned lover in this story make the mistake of equating the tattoo's meaning with the pain and sacrifice of enduring the process. They assume the lover's endurance should guarantee his acceptance, because they assume that tattooing is a process that, once completed, transforms the individual. But what this story suggests is that the tattoo is an auxiliary to an already defined identity, not simply an add-on that allows anyone to embody this identity. Though he endures pain that even a high chief is unwilling to endure, his full tattooing still means less than the high chief's partial tattooing. Stevenson, through this man's story, conceptualizes the tattoo only as a marker of endurance.

James O'Connell's *A Residence of Eleven Years in New Holland and the Caroline Islands* (1836) similarly emphasizes the pain of the tattoo in order to praise his own masculine endurance. While stranded on the island of Pohnpei, part of the Caroline Islands, O'Connell and a companion were, according to O'Connell's account, forced to be tattooed. In recounting his tattooing, O'Connell frames his reserve against his companion's ravings: "I summoned up all my fortitude, set my teeth, and bore it like a martyr," while his friend "swore and raved without any attention to rule." His companion is from then on teasingly referred to as a coward, whereas O'Connell is labeled "'Jim Aroche ma coo mot,'—Jim Chief brave!" (115). O'Connell focuses on the respective epithets that the Pohnpeians give the two tattooed white men, reveling in the validation. But what O'Connell reads as validation is really only another way of making him singular. The Pohnpeians, as he retells the experience, see him as brave—which is what is most essential to O'Connell's heroic framework. However, his "bravery" is actually a way of marking O'Connell as singular among the Pohnpeians; he says nothing of how the tattoos themselves made him any more a part of the culture than his comrade was. He is, by his own account, labeled a chief when they praise him, but this does nothing, in his narrative, to change the fact that he is a white man tattooed.

The manner in which O'Connell frames his tattooing offers an apt counterpoise to Vason. Where Vason initiates his own tattooing in hopes of becoming a more authentic part of Tongan society, O'Connell actively repels the collectivizing potential of the tattoo. The Pohnpeian tattoo, the *pelipel*, as

David Hanlon explains in "Beyond 'the English Method of Tattooing,'" "identified an individual's lineage and recorded in symbolic form the clan and other relational histories and associations that marked one's identity. In a real sense, Pohnpeians wore their histories on their bodies" (20). O'Connell's tattoos, then, would have had a great deal to say about his social standing among the Pohnpeians. In this way, his tattoos would not only identify his belonging but also, more importantly, define the nature of his belonging. They would individuate him within the context of the larger social structure.

Significantly, O'Connell admits that he "never learned to read their marks" (163),[22] a comment that prompts Juniper Ellis to observe that O'Connell "remains imprinted with patterns whose meanings he cannot understand" (2). But it is important to add that O'Connell doesn't seem to *want* to understand them. Because he cannot read the values inscribed onto him, he ascribes meaning solely to the *process* of being tattooed.[23] His tattoo*ing* is more significant than his tattoos. O'Connell can easily signify the process of being tattooed in familiar terms: he is "brave" and a "martyr." Like Vason, he emphasizes the fortitude he displayed in undergoing the tattooing, but unlike Vason, O'Connell is incapable of conceptualizing tattooing in any other but already familiar terms. Far from reflecting upon how "gay [he] looked in this fancy new covering," O'Connell notes that while he is tattooed on most of his body, his friend, quips O'Connell, "escaped with a few stripes" (119).[24] Instead of reading the tattoo as an indicator of cultural assimilation, O'Connell seeks to assimilate the tattoo to his preexisting cultural values.

Thus, after he has been tattooed, O'Connell is quick to reassert his own singularity: "At night we were pointed towards some mats and informed that we must sleep there. As Logic says in the play, ours were any thing but rose blankets; and we had the farther gratification of reflecting that they were fixtures of this tattooing hospital, and had probably encased the limbs of at least two generation of Indians. I refused at first to accept the embraces of *such* clothing; but not quite used to going nearly naked, I was fain to seek protection among the mats from the bamboo floor" (117). O'Connell refuses "*such* clothing" as the blanket because it has already "encased" generations of "Indians."[25] While his refusal initially might seem like something akin to modern germaphobia, his references to the wearers as "Indians" and his refusal of "*such* clothing" can be read as an attempt to detach himself from the culture of which the tattooing has so literally made his body a part. He may be tattooed, but he will not willingly put on "*such* clothing" as has been worn by the Pohnpeians who have undergone the tattooing process. He refuses to allow the process of his tattooing to become a shared process. Where Vason regards himself as clothed in tattoos, O'Connell sees himself as "nearly naked," holding fast to his rejection of the indigenous culture's clothing.

O'Connell thus both willfully and naively misinterprets the tattoo, and his attempt to reassimilate the tattoos' meaning to his own values is mirrored when the Pohnpeians attempt to (quite literally) embody European values:

> The natives noticed our devotion to the books and shared in it; they supposed printing was the English tattoo. . . . At length, upon an unlucky day, after the books had been with me nearly two years, I was careless enough to leave them exposed while I went upon some excursion. When I returned, the leaves were torn out and sewed into blankets, under which half a dozen women were strutting in all the pride of peacocks. In addition to the beauty which the article thus manufactured possessed as a "lagow," (blanket), it had another charm in tattooing. The wearers imagined themselves connected with the English chiefs while thus wearing the white man's tattoo. . . . Their gratification was, however, soon turned to vexation, and then my turn to be pleased came. Situated so near the equator, rains are frequent and violent upon the Carolines. The Jane Porter bedecked belles were surprised in a shower, and their new garments washed off their backs. They were very much chagrined at this, and protested that the white man's tattoo was good for nothing, it would not stand. That the islanders' tattoo will stand, my body is witness. (112)

Recognizing the value that O'Connell places on the books, the Pohnpeian's in turn attempt to re-direct this significance into the language of their own values, *wearing* the books as if they were tattoos. In claiming that this makes the islanders feel "connected with the English chiefs," O'Connell seems to want to emphasize that what they are exhibiting is a desire to be as *powerful* as an English chief. But what their actions suggest is that they long to find a way of experiencing from an English perspective. They are trying on Englishness. This desire connects to Hanlon's description of *pelipel* as "wear[ing] their histories on their bodies." The Pohnpeian islanders want to know what it would be like to have Englishness embodied in the same way that they feel their tattooing might embody their own identities. What both the Pohnpeians and O'Connell conclude is that "the white man's tattoo will not stand." Their attempt to identify as English is ephemeral, susceptible to simply being washed away. O'Connell himself recognizes the superiority of the tattoo on the basis of its longevity: "The islanders' tattoo will stand, [his] body is witness."

Vason's narrative, however, suggests that while the tattoo itself is permanent, what it "stands" *for* is constantly in flux. As he bathes on the shores of New York, before finally returning home, Vason's tattoos become subject to the interpretive gaze of passersby: "I went on shore in the evening and plunged into the water to refresh myself with bathing. Some people not far off, who saw me enter the water, supposing that I was swimming in trowsers, came near to look at me. I remained in the water til they had walked away, but a boy of fifteen stayed til I came out: he looked at me with great surprise, as though he could not believe his own senses, and upon coming nearer, exclaimed, 'I thought you had some clothes on.['] Others upon hearing him began to approach, and had I not put my clothes on, their curiosity, it is probable, would have discovered equal cause for surprise" (179–80). Unlike the pages of O'Connell's books as worn by the Pohnpeians, Vason's tattoos withstand the water in which he bathes. The tattoos remain, but, to American eyes, they leave no trace of their original meaning. Here, the tattoo figures as a peculiar approximation to clothing and as a symbol of Vason's strangeness. It does not serve to authenticate his Tongan identity; instead, it functions as part of his multifaceted identity. As a signifier of Tongan identity, his tattooing is unconvincing, yet his tattoos remain authentically exotic to outsiders' eyes. The tattoos that fail to stand for his Tongan authenticity do stand to trouble his European authenticity.

Here, again with the tattoo taking center stage, the narrative reaches an uncharacteristically high peak of enthusiasm and even playfulness. In this scene, near the end of his narrative, Vason is finally viewed in the way he desired the Tongans see him: as defined by his tattoos just as the Tongans are. That is, he almost is: while the tattoos signal his uncertain status as European, they do not give him a new identity. Vason is at once familiar and unfamiliar, not quite authentic as either Tongan or European. His elaborate tattooing is initially seen, by American eyes, as a pair of "trowsers." Like Vason himself earlier in the narrative, the young boy in this scene can interpret Vason's tattoos only as a form of clothing.

In the frontispiece illustration to his book, Vason's entire body is covered in tattoos, a problematic choice, as John Martin helps us understand. A doctor who took a special interest in tattooing from a surgical perspective, Martin provided the narrative framework for William Mariner's account (1817) of the Tonga islands. Martin notes, on the basis of Mariner's experience, that in Tongan practice the tattooed parts of the body "are from within two inches of the knees up to about three inches above the umbilicus" (396).[26] This description, of course, contrasts the full body tattooing seen in Vason's frontispiece. It seems unlikely, then, that the frontispiece accurately represents Vason's tattooing. With that in mind, we might read the frontispiece not as realistic depiction but rather as an exoticized exaggeration, in which the tattoos serve only as indiscriminate markings of Vason's transgressions.

Martin's description of Tongan tattooing illuminates Vason's bathing scene, in particular why Vason would have likened his tattoos to "undergarments" and "trowsers." While the tattoos function as the most obvious marker of his

Tongan identity, this public act of bathing is also a remnant of the Tongan values adopted by Vason. The scene recalls Vason's earlier reference to his participation in Tongan bathing, when the Tongans ridiculed his nudity. Now, on the shores of New York, despite being removed from his Tongan environment, Vason still feels clothed—and thus comfortable in taking a public bath. After all, Tongan tattooing spared no space on the lower body, according to Martin, including "the penis and the verge of the anus" (396). Having left Tonga, Vason's tattoos maintain their dual function as clothing, at once covering his body and revealing the cultural values the tattoos embody. The bodily nakedness in this scene is further mirrored at the narrative level, as the "clothing" of the reform narrative is stripped away. This moment of bodily nudity is fittingly a moment of narrative nudity as well. The tone of this passage, lighthearted and self-amused, seems to suggest that Vason revels in the challenge his clothes/tattoos present to his Western audience—both the audience in this scene and, in turn, his readers.

CLOTHED BY THE NARRATIVE: THE EDITORIAL REFRAMING OF VASON'S TATTOOS

The confusion between clothing and tattoos extends to the level of narrative. Juniper Ellis, in *Pacific Designs in Print and Skin*, resorts, perhaps inadvertently, to a clothing metaphor when she remarks that "Vason relates his story wrapped in English clothes and the English language" (123). But just as his tattoos are liable to peek out from under his clothes, so, too, can the Tongan values associated with them slip out into the otherwise "English" narrative. Vason's narrative constantly pushes up against its stated goal that "some backsliders should be roused, immediately to return, from a fear of death and perdition in the midst of sin, of which I was so often in danger" (225). There is plenty of moralizing in Vason's text, but many other passages reveal an unadulterated enthusiasm: the pleasure he takes in his tattooing, the comedy surrounding his inscrutable identity, his "burn[ing] for the fight" during the war (164). Initially, upon his return home, his story *becomes* his identity: "After the novelty of amusing myself and them by relating the events that had befallen me had subsided; I felt an insuperable reluctance to return to the confinement of one particular spot, and the labours of weekly employment" (221). It is not just the listeners who are amused; Vason himself takes pleasure in telling his story. Like Coleridge's Ancient Mariner, he is compelled to retell his story; but if the Mariner is possessed by his story, Vason seeks *to possess* his story.

Vason's account serves as a means of escape from the confinement that his return to England will inevitably produce. Upon his death, though, Vason's story would become the possession of another evangelical editor. When, thirty years later, the Reverend James Orange (himself of Nottingham) republished Vason's narrative,[27] he framed it as the story of a man who "assumed the revolting customs of savage life" (v).[28] Orange's version was released two years after George Vason's death, but it claimed to be the more "authentic" edition, insisting that the previous publication was "crowded with gross mistakes, &c., and in many respects incomplete" (vi). This new version Orange produces thus seeks to redefine the earlier narrative, to inform his readers of how the narrative should be read, thus adding, as it were, another layer of cultural clothing. The most significant alteration to Orange's edition is the inclusion of a brief biography of Vason's life upon returning to Nottingham. And yet, as much as Orange wants this narrative to be read as a story of reform, he has little interest in a "civilized" Vason. He admits to "compressing" the story of Vason's return to respectability, claiming that Vason's "private documents supply many anecdotes of considerable interest, yet they are commonplace, and would lose much by comparison were they placed in juxtaposition with those constituting the body of his narrative." A clothed Vason is uninteresting in comparison with the tattooed "body" that constitutes his narrative. As Paul Lyons suggests, it was the job of editors like Orange to "market texts that could at once pass for authentic and fulfill increasingly inflated desires for exoticism" (32). Orange thus simultaneously condemns and promotes Vason's "exotic" identity, ultimately rendering his reformation the matter of least "interest" to this narrative.

What little information Orange does provide, though, seems more suggestive of resignation than reformation. The details of Vason's respectable marriage, employment, and position within the community are offset by the description of Vason himself as "subject to nervous irritability, by which he was at times betrayed into unbecoming bursts of passion" (218). The "bursts of passion" that enlivened his life in Tonga are now read as "unbecoming" signs of "nervous irritability." Vason's dress, now "remarkably neat and clean," covers his tattoos, but the values associated with his tattooing sneak out from under his respectable dress.

Before his death, one of the parts of Vason's body that is devoid of tattooing becomes significantly "marked" in a different way, rendering him once again socially unfit: he is "seized with erysipelas in his face, attended with the most agonizing pain, which so fearfully affected his brain, that it overthrew and laid prostrate his reason; his manner was then the violence of madness" (218). The physical markings (redness and rashes) of erysipelas coincide with Vason's "madness."[29] His malady causes him to lose his "reason" and his "manner"; in other words, he loses those qualities that are most essential to a "civilized" life. Such an end is bitterly poetic—and Orange must have been aware of this. In the context of Orange's biography, Vason's condition of erysipelas is, at the very least, suggestive of the consequences of his tattooing. John Coulter makes this connection in his account of tattooing, relating that "often erysipelas is produced; but those are rare cases, all generally getting clear with the ordinary inflammation" (212). Orange thus seems to frame Vason as ultimately unable to escape the consequences of his Tongan lapse.

Reflecting on Vason's "madness" and Orange's assertion that Vason never again made a public profession of his faith, Vanessa Smith concludes in "Falling from Grace" that "the period of easy communion he achieved in Tonga thus retrospectively figures, despite the aims of his confessional project, as a state of innocence before his lapse into redemptive shame" (160). But while Vason's narrative is certainly rich with examples of "easy communion," this does not represent the totality of his experience. Vason's faith, however much he abandons it, seems to prevent him from ever being completely comfortable with himself or others. Moments of innocence and communion are disrupted throughout by unwanted intrusions of conscience: "I endeavoured to forget that I once called a christian" (122); "I wished to forget myself" (151); "amid all these interchanges of ease and indulgence, employment, and amusement, I could not prevent the intrusion of uneasy reflections. I enjoyed no true peace and happiness" (156). And while it may be tempting to suggest that Vason's restlessness is merely another function of his reform narrative, it seems hard to imagine Vason at peace—surely he at least never forgot the image of seeing his fellow missionaries killed amid the Tongan civil war. His discomfort upon returning home is not a new symptom, one that develops upon returning; rather, it originates in Tonga and *remains* with him upon returning home. Vason does not fully belong in either place.

Vason's narrative does not suggest that he wishes he could return, or even that he feels his life in Tonga was objectively better than his life in England; instead, his narrative reveals an anxiety about his identity having to be defined by one or the other. Vason embraces his tattooing, but he refuses to present himself as defined by those tattoos, unlike O'Connell, who would use his tattoos to attain status as a "freak" for P. T. Barnum.[30] Vason seems to want his identity to be fluid, to be composite, but his reform narrative insists that his Tongan past be reduced to a cautionary tale so that "some [other] backsliders should be roused" out of sin (225). Such a framework, imposed after the fact, indeed makes it difficult to reconstruct Vason in all his multifacetedness.

THE DISSEMBLED CUCKOO CLOCK: NARRATIVE AND THE RECONSTRUCTION OF IDENTITY

Vason's own preoccupation with the construction and reconstruction of identities is best illustrated in a mini-narrative from his account in which Vason reflects on his inability to put back together a cuckoo clock taken apart by a

Tongan prince. The Tongans assume that because the clock is from Vason's culture, he must know how to reassemble it. His obvious incompetence excites "great laughter" and "ridicule" from the Tongans. In an uncharacteristic critique, Vason declares that the Tongans are "naturally very conceited, and this circumstance much encouraged their vanity; and now they prided themselves in the idea, that they were as skilful and cleaver [*sic*] as we" (78). Vason's criticism seems to have been caused by feelings of embarrassment and by his realization that he has as little claim to this cultural technology as the Tongans do.

In the context of Vason's narrative, the disassembled cuckoo clock can be read as a metaphor for the way cultural affiliations are made and unmade: while it is easy to deconstruct them, they can never be reconstructed or fully restored to the way they were. Like the clothes he eventually sheds, the cuckoo clock represents that part of Vason that has been preconstructed by his culture. Vason's anxiety about his failure to restore the cuckoo clock foregrounds his anxiety about being able to re-create his identity through the story he wants to tell about himself. His narrative tasks him with the same impossible challenge that the disassembled cuckoo clock presents to him, requiring him to reassemble his fractured identity. In writing his narrative, Vason must use the disassembled parts of his experience and reformulate how he felt at that time. But while Vason's narrative requires him to piece his experience back together, the reform narrative that frames his text limits how the reader is allowed to think of him. It provides a template for reconstruction, but the parts do not fit; his "clothing" bursts at the seams. His tattoos, to return to O'Connell's term, "stand," both on his body and in the body of his narrative. But they serve to authenticate neither his Tongan identity nor his "exotic" status. Instead, they challenge the very notion of authenticity, the very idea that one must be this or the other but not both. Vason does not seek to write over the tattoo; instead, he writes with it.

Coda: Writing with Tattooed Hands, William Torrey's *Torrey's Narrative* (1848)

Written about forty years after the original publication of Vason's *Authentic Narrative*, William Torrey's *Torrey's Narrative* provides a compelling contrast to Vason's narrative of tattooing, one suggestive of shifting perceptions of the tattoo. If Vason's narrative is about writing *with* the tattoo, then Torrey's narrative is focused on writing *over* the tattoo. *Torrey's Narrative* is *advertised* as being "written by himself" and "illustrated with engravings of his own sketching." The title page thus emphasizes that Torrey alone is responsible for the content of the book.

While, on a more basic level, this highlights Torrey's freedom from any kind of editorial control—the very thing that creates the oft-conflicted voice

William Torrey.

Figure 1.5. Frontis-
piece to *Torrey's Nar-
rative: Or, The Life and
Adventures of William
Torrey* (Boston: A. J.
Wright, 1848).

in Vason's narrative—it also, more significantly, foregrounds the author's control over his story; it allows him to take control of the body of his text in a
way that he cannot take control of the body "marked" by his tattoos.

In stark contrast to Vason's narrative, Torrey's frontispiece (figure 1.5) features a portrait of the author after his return, fully clothed in European attire.
The hardened and sunken features visible in Torrey's face form the illusion of
a tattoo, but they are markings of a different sort: of weariness and experience.
His hands, which bear Torrey's only visible markings, peek out from under
his billowy white shirt, the lone part of his body that cannot be covered by a
traditional European outfit. His tattooed hands seem to rest uncomfortably, as
if aware that they are, and always will be, on display—or, as if knowing where
the viewer's eye will inevitably be drawn. Torrey's tattooing was limited to his
hands and therefore less extensive than Vason's. But despite how minimal the
tattooing is, he is, ironically, tattooed on one of the few places (the face being
the other, more prominent, place) that everyday European attire does not con-
ceal. His hands, which serve to write his narrative, cannot be hidden.

Torrey arrived on a more remote island in the Marquesas under desperate
circumstances, making his way to the island after his ship, the *Doll*, foundered.
The reception for Torrey and his fellow survivors was, by his own account,

sympathetic, as the Marquesans[31] "immediately set themselves about amelio-
rating our condition and rendering us as comfortable as possible, giving us
to eat of such as they had—bread fruit—bananas—raw fish, &c." (113). Like
Vason's troupe of missionaries, Torrey's group of survivors was split up, though
in this case into groups of two and at the hands of the Marquesans. While
Torrey and his companion Noyce lived comfortably early on, they were eventually faced with the decision to be tattooed, a decision that, according to Torrey, "there was no alternative to, save death and leaving the island" (125–26).
While it is, of course, impossible to know how much autonomy Torrey had
in this decision—his treatment beforehand does not seem to suggest that
such a threatening demand would follow—he certainly would not have been
the first beachcomber to exaggerate the stakes of his tattooing as a defense
against criticisms from his European readership. As Joanna White notes in
"Marks of Transgression," beachcomber narratives often depict their tattooing as an "outcome of pressure from indigenous communities," to "play down
their own personal volition in an attempt to avoid alienating their readership."
John Rutherford claimed that he was forcibly tattooed over the course of four
hours, but, as White points out, we know that Maori facial tattooing could
have been accomplished only over the course of several days. Thus, beachcombers might have framed themselves as more unwilling participants in tattooing than they may actually have been, given that a tattooing extended over
several days would have been difficult to implement without the consent of
the to-be-tattooed person (87).

Torrey's narrative provides a description of tattooing absent of the valorizing
present in the accounts of Vason, O'Connell, and even Mariner. Instead, he
matter-of-factly accepts his tattooing as a necessary step to ensure his survival.
Being tattooed, for Torrey, does not mean becoming part of the culture, as
with Vason's involuntary tattooing; it means becoming subject to the tribe's
king. As Torrey further clarifies: "A person thus marked is considered as the
king's own private property, subject entirely to his control and disposition, and
when bearing this mark can never desert the tribe, for he would be as cruelly
treated by the tribe he wishes to join, as by the deserted one, should he be
taken, the penalty for which is death" (126). Rather than becoming part, Torrey becomes "property." In Torrey's interpretation, the tattooing offers him no
form of individuality.[32] The markings themselves are meaningless to him; their
only meaning is that he has been marked, and in being marked he has become
a "subject." Torrey finds value neither in his courageous endurance of pain (as
with Vason and O'Connell) nor in the beauty of the coloring against his white
skin (as with Vason and Mariner). Instead, he focuses on his tattooing from a

technical and anthropological standpoint. I quote at length here to highlight his almost tediously detailed account of tattooing at a general and depersonalized level:

> Consequently we were brought forward to be tattooed, which was done on the back of the hand, as seen in the Frontispiece.
>
> First an ink is made from the smoke of the *Amer nut*, which when ripe is about the size of a common filbert. These are strung on the stem of the cocoa-nut leaf, which when dry is hard and stiff. The larger end of this stem is placed in the ground, or in some manner so that it will stand erect, when the top end is lighted and burns freely. The stem of the leaf serves as wick. Over the blaze a piece of bark is held to collect the smoke. When a sufficient quantity is collected, it is put in water, thus forming ink.
>
> The figure to be made is then traced on the desired spot, with a stick dipped in the ink. An instrument made by fastening six or eight small sharp fish bones to a stick, which in shape resembles the gauge used in splitting straw, is dipped in the solution and driven into the flesh by means of a blow given with a short stick, thus forming a mark which cannot be obliterated. This was an operation indeed painful, especially so on the more sinewy parts of the hand. A long time elapsed before I could use my hands very much.

Torrey's account of the process, celebrated by Vason and emphasized over the course of more than three pages in O'Connell's narrative, is reduced to a few minimally descriptive sentences of the objective pain it inevitably produces. His mark "cannot be obliterated" and he cannot "use [his] hands very much" in the days afterward.

That this "mark which cannot be obliterated" should be on his hands seems significant in the context of Torrey's narrative, which emphasizes that both the writing and the illustrating were done by Torrey's own hands. His marked hands are thus employed in the process of re-marking himself as deserving of "patronage and sympathy for his sufferings when in bondage among those savages" (vi). Torrey, in his preface, takes pride in the fact that he is a seaman; throughout the book, he refers to himself and his fellow sailors as "hands."[33] This shorthand synecdoche for crew members defines sailors by what is most essential to their competency aboard a ship. In this context, having his hands tattooed has more suggestive connotations, symbolically implying that his very identity as a European seaman has been marked.

One of the most striking scenes in *Torrey's Narrative*, in fact, is itself suggestive of how "marked" hands come to invalidate one's cultural belonging.

Before his captivity, Torrey and his shipmates spend time in Fernando Po, where a group of "natives" flock aboard their ship to trade with them. Here, Torrey and his fellow crewmates are struck by an individual "with both hands cut off at his wrists." So struck by this man are Torrey and his companions that they bungle their way through signs in order to ask how this man came to be in such a condition, upon which they are informed, "if we rightly interpreted their signs, that he was a thief, and that was one of their modes of punishment. In wishing to come on board, he threw his arms around the hauling part of the fore sheet, (a rope hanging at the ship's side) which not being fast in-board gave way with his weight, and fell him into the sea. Not one of his fellows tendered him a helping hand. Some looked on without betraying the least emotion, while others with ribaldry and mirth saw the water close over him forever. He seemed to be an object of universal contempt. Whether his thieving propensities were coupled with other misdeeds I know not" (37–38). While doubtless Torrey records this event as both an interesting story and a remarkable example of cultural practice, the implications of this story to Torrey's personal narrative cannot be dismissed. Like this social outcast in this scene, Torrey's hands bear marks of experience that can only be speculated upon (Torrey admits that their interpretation of the man is contingent upon whether or not they correctly interpreted the signs of the natives). Rather than being cut off, Torrey's hands are *marked off* from the rest of his body. No longer possessing his own hands, the ill-fated man must rely on the "helping hand[s]" of his "fellows." But his "fellows," or countrymen, allow him to drown as they look on in laughter. It is an image that must resonate in Torrey's retrospect, as he too must rely on the "helping hands" of his countrymen to return and reintegrate. This man's hands represent a permanent marking, one that all of his fellows know how to read. Torrey's final admission that he does not know "whether his thieving propensities were coupled with other misdeeds" suggests a certain anxiety about a marker coming to define a person and to take control of one's personal narrative. He seems to hope that there are "other misdeeds" that earned the man the disdain of his mates, fearing that he, like this man, will be judged and punished on the basis of just one thing. The whole of who this man is is swallowed up by the markings of past experience. Torrey's anxiety represents a central concern of the tattooed beachcomber: that these surface markings allow their countrymen to define and interpret their origin and that such interpretations can invalidate one's cultural status.

To write his story, then, is to take control over his narrative, to assure his reading public that no "other misdeeds" can be read in his tattooing. His narrative does not seek to establish his identity but only to acquire "patronage and sympathy for his sufferings when in bondage among those savages." Torrey, through his narrative, asks that his markings not be read as his; rather, he asks that they be read as a record of his victimization and subjectivity. The central irony, as seen in Torrey's frontispiece, is that his hands, unlike every part of the body besides the head, are visible to the viewer. Unable to clothe over his tattoos, Torrey thus seeks to write *over* them. Torrey's tattoos are part not of his identity but only of this particular experience. The distinction between Vason's and Torrey's presentation of their tattooing experiences is, I think, suggestive of a shift in narrative modes of thinking about residence in Oceanian spaces.[34] Writing about Oceanian peoples becomes continually more concerned with writing *over* rather than with writing *alongside*, as Vason does.[35] Rather than seeking to don the garments of a different culture, writers increasingly seek to dress up the Oceanian world in a manner that best conforms to their audience's expectations. Cultural exchange becomes a commodity and the individual remains largely unchanged, taking what he or she can but giving little in return.

2

A Häolé's Hawaiian Hula

This chapter takes us from the beach to the Pali (Hawaiian for cliffs), from the shore to the edges. Wearied by the westernization of Hawaiian culture and eager to break free from the structure of his missionary-sanctioned tour of Hawaii, the author of *Sandwich Island Notes* (1854), pseudonymously identified only as "A Häolé," is "urged to visit the Palis on the assurance that foreigners seldom or never went there" (283). The Pali, a range of cliffs in the Hawaiian island of Molokai, were, in other words, off the proverbial beaten track. For the author, "the Palis" stand as a marker of a more authentic Hawaii, one uncontaminated by colonial presence. Here, he will see a hula ceremony: for native Hawaiians, a traditional dance performed in synchronicity with chanted or sung poetry (mele) and rhythmic drumming (pahu); for local missionaries, a heathen dance charged with sexuality. By the middle of the nineteenth century, the hula was already all but forbidden, practiced only under missionary supervision—or, better yet, out of sight. One can imagine, then, the tantalizing appeal for travel writers of seeing a hula, having had their *Typee*-tinged expectations disappointed by increasingly westernized Oceanian spaces.

Attending a hula ceremony, for A Häolé, is a chance to "see all [he can] of native character." Seating himself at a safe distance from the participants and casually smoking a cigar, he "patiently await[s] the drama." However, the author quickly realizes that he is in for more than he bargained for, as the dance gradually moves toward him. When A Häolé is eventually called into the dance, he promptly flees, determining that "for [him], it was the last act in the drama" (283–84). The language of performance here ("drama," "act,") and elsewhere in A Häolé's description of the hula ("scene," "performing," "performance") is not incidental. Rather, it speaks to how the authors of mid-nineteenth-century Polynesian travel narratives such as *Sandwich Island Notes* imagined their travels: as a neatly unfolding script in which all participants (the traveler, the "natives") would assume their assigned roles. When A Häolé is asked to join the dance, his role as a passive observer is challenged and the scripting illusion is broken. It is, then, not an authentic performance that he is interested in but a performance of authenticity.

Upon its publication, *Sandwich Island Notes* was quite popular among the reading public and divisive among reviewers. Among the negative reactions was the review published under the title "Sandwich Island Notes" in the conservative *New Englander*, a scathing, seven-page vitriolic rant. Most of this outrage can be attributed to the reviewer's moralistic, pro-missionary bent. But the reviewer also seems to have been aware of the strongly performative nature of the account given by A Häolé. "The whole style of the book," the reviewer wrote, "is dressed up with the cast off garments of the writer's school-boy days, and made to swell with the pompous inanities of Fourth of July speeches." Indeed, A Häolé gives us a "dressed up" account, but the costume he wears is that of the Pacific literary tradition of Herman Melville— and a poorly fitting one it is. But this is not the only guise he wears. He is also costumed in a new way, by virtue of the pseudonym that he has adopted: A Häolé. This pseudonym (Hawaiian for "foreigner" or "outsider") is suggestive of his own role in the "drama."

Although the author of *Sandwich Island Notes* has been identified as George Washington Bates, I have retained the self-effacing pseudonym A Häolé precisely because of its implications.[1] His choice of pseudonym certifies both his expertise in Hawaiian culture (he knows enough to identify himself in the Hawaiian language) and his distance from it, suggesting at once both cultural exchange and Western detachment. This, I argue, is a defining characteristic of the mid-century travel narrative. In titling this chapter "A Häolé's Hula," then, I mean to play on the multitude of "haoles" who engage with the Polynesian world similarly. As much as this chapter revolves around George Washington Bates as a particular haole, it is also about the figure of the haole more generally.

Sandwich Island Notes marks a crucial shift in the genre of the Polynesian travel narrative genre, as spectatorship begins to replace the participant-observer model of earlier texts like Vason's narrative. Accounts of the hula, which occur throughout popular mid-century Hawaiian travelogues, are particularly representative of this shift. While tattooing (the topic of the previous chapter) was an almost unavoidable zone of contact for Romantic-era travelers, the hula was actively sought out by mid-nineteenth-century travelers. And whereas the tattoo left a permanent trace, the hula allowed travelers to experience it while keeping their distance from that experience. Hence, A Häolé can safely flee the hula the moment he becomes too implicated in it. The hula is a sight to be seen but never a site of cultural exchange. What we see in these texts is a new set of parameters being put into place. While they invoke the language and scenarios of earlier sailors and explorers, they also promote a new kind of visitor: the tourist.

In this chapter, I am interested in the connection between sightseeing and the search for authenticity, which Dean MacCannell has discussed in both his groundbreaking *The Tourist: A New Theory of the Leisure Class* (1976) and, more recently, in *The Ethics of Sightseeing* (2011). Taking his cue from Erving Goffman's *The Presentation of the Self in Everyday Life*, MacCannell, in *The Tourist*, divides the quest for touristic authenticity into front and back regions. In searching for authenticity, tourists fetishize the "back regions," which MacCannell defines as spaces that "in their mere existence intimat[e] their possible violation . . . the putative 'intimate and real' as against 'show'" (94). The appeal of the "back regions" is that they offer a sense of intrusion: they are not ready-made sights meant for the eyes of tourists but rather the "real" sights hidden away. In other words, to see these sights is to transcend the role of mere tourist.

And yet, MacCannell suggests that this, too, is a form of "staged authenticity," a carefully curated performance designed to meet the tourists' preconceived expectations about what constitutes authenticity. This "staged authenticity" works in a slightly different way in the texts I analyze, as the staging is not yet directly facilitated, of course, by the tourism industry. Instead, these travelers seek to restage the idealized authenticity of the literature that inspired them.

While their dissatisfaction with the "staging" of Hawaii's front regions leads them to seek a more authentic experience, their forays into the "back regions" remain guided by a conventional set of expectations about what constitutes Polynesian otherness. To return to Jonathan Culler's formulation, "the authenticity the tourists seeks is at one level an escape from the code, but this escape is coded in turn, for the authentic must be marked to be constituted as authentic" (165). In other words, the pursuit of authenticity presents a paradox, as its pursuit necessarily implies that it, too, has been marked. Within this framework, the hula comes to represent the type of premarked authentic otherness that has become scarce in Hawaii, thanks to the literary treatment it has received by an earlier generation of travelers.

I begin by analyzing how the tourist's gaze follows from the traveler's gaze, focusing on how this second wave of travelers' expectations was informed by their literary predecessors. Though *Sandwich Island Notes* is the primary focus in this chapter, I also draw connections across a variety of similar "häolé" accounts. My discussion of the hula is thus initiated by first examining the disappointment that these travelers felt upon arriving in a Polynesia more westernized than that of their literary predecessors. It is this feeling of disappointment that informs the accounts of the hula at the center of this chapter, and it is through the hula that I distinguish the traveler's gaze from the tourist's gaze. While the traveler's gaze is about interpreting what he or she sees—however imperfectly—the tourist's gaze focuses on the seeing itself. That is to say, seeing comes to take the place of experience, of interpretation. The tourist gaze, as John Urry and Jonas Larsen argue, "is a performance that orders, shapes, and classifies, rather than reflects the world" (2). Unable, as cultural outsiders, to understand the hula, these proto-tourists instead seek to "classify" it. Gazing at the hula from the perspective of an outsider, the hula is persistently defined through Western ideologies of sexuality and, accordingly, deemed illicit—too graphic, even, to describe to readers back home.

While there is no shortage of criticism related to the literary beachcombers of the late eighteenth and early nineteenth centuries, among the late-nineteenth-century to early twentieth-century travelers who arrive "after the fact," and even the often tedious missionary narratives of the mid- nineteenth century, there has been hardly any sustained criticism of mid-nineteenth-century travelers still looking for the authentic South Seas. Further, when this group of travelers does appear in criticism, they often function as little more than cogs in service of an argument, brief examples of a more general cultural discourse. David Farrier's *Unsettled Narratives: The Pacific Writings of Stevenson, Ellis, Melville, and London* (2007) is indicative of the typical focus of Pacific studies: Melville is the beachcomber (modelling his narrative after earlier beachcombers), William Ellis is the missionary, and Stevenson and London are the late travelers inspired by earlier literary accounts.[2] Mid-nineteenth-century travel writers occupy an uncertain space within this critical context: they come to Polynesia to write about their experiences, but their works lack traditional literary merit, and while their thinking is implicitly shaped by Western ideology, their motive for traveling is not explicitly colonial. Such uncertainty provides for more ambiguous accounts, rich in both nuance and contradiction. These mid-century narratives both significantly react to beachcomber narratives and, in ways that have not yet been recognized, shape Western perceptions of Oceania that remain in place even today.

It is worth emphasizing that mid-nineteenth-century travel writers, when they arrived in Polynesia, were readers first and foremost, with Herman Melville captaining their journeys. Much has been made of the indebtedness of Robert Louis Stevenson and Jack London, among other early-twentieth-century travelers, to Melville and the Romantic tradition that preceded him. Farrier writes that narratives "of missionaries and sailors who jumped ship . . . so gripped Stevenson's imagination that he was impelled to travel to the South Seas himself" (19). In the South Seas anthology *Exploration and Exchange*, Vanessa Smith titles the section on Stevenson "Belated First Contact," arguing that Stevenson's "search for the exotic is doubly nostalgic: he elegizes not only the Hawaiian heroes of old but equally the visitor's first privileged experience of objectification within the Hawaiian metaphoric imagination" (300). Similarly, Paul Lyons, in *American Pacificism*, calls his section on "cannibal tours" in the early twentieth century "Desperately Seeking Herman" and proposes that, for Jack London, "the whole of the Marquesas is unalterably [Melville's] Typee" (128–29). But mid-nineteenth-century travelers to the South Seas had an even more intimate relationship with Melville and other early documenters of Polynesia. When Henry August Wise, author of *Los Gringos* (1849),[3] began his search for the cast of *Typee*, "without in the least designing to sully the enchanting romance" (339), the dust had hardly settled after the stir created by the publication of Melville's *Typee* (1846) and *Omoo* (1847). Edward Perkins, who, like Melville, had experience as a whaler, performed his own search for the cast of *Omoo* in his *Na Motu* (1854).[4] While he learns that Dr. Long Ghost "led a free-and-easy life for some time, and afterwards took his departure," he is able to locate both *Omoo*'s carpenter and the carpenter's Tahitian love interest.[5] Perkins, however, finds her unrecognizable, concluding that "whatever she might have been, her present appearance offered no criterion for judging. Add ten years to the existence, and time will leave its indelible trace on her features" (323). This reflection epitomizes the prevailing sentiment within these early touristic travel accounts: the Pacific world they encounter is recognizable, but time has left "its indelible trace on [its] features." But while these travelers lament what is lost to them, they also frame what comes after them and thus work to define Polynesia—and Hawaii in particular—as a touristic site.

Disappointed Arrivals: Seeking the Literary Pacific

When *Sandwich Island Notes* was published in 1855, the Hawaiian touristic experience was a relatively new phenomenon. Polynesia, at mid-century, while still popularly imagined as "exotic," was becoming a site of increasing familiarity—no longer solely the realm of paradise-seeking castaways, captive survivors, and imperiled missionaries. In fact, these travelers were well aware that Polynesia was quickly turning into a popular destination for tourists. Edward Perkins, whose account of his tour of Polynesia, *Na Motu*, was published in 1854, sounds much like a modern travel brochure when he observes that Tahiti "possesses many attractions for the tourist," insisting that the influence of missionaries and merchants will "render their sojourn agreeable." He goes on to assure potential Tahitian tourists that they will have no "reason to complain of want of civility, or lack of the ordinary courtesies of social intercourse from foreign residents" (441). In other words, tourists will encounter Tahitian people, but only in the "ordinary" sense; their experiences of the space will not be obscured by direct contact with the people who occupy that space. Perkins's configuration of the Polynesian tourist is that of someone who is at home while abroad. A Polynesian tourist can expect a well-curated authentic experience.

Perkins, a self-styled traveler, ironically resembles the tourist he purports to describe. The authentic world that these travelers ostensibly seek is often unpalatable, as Perkins himself demonstrates in quite literal terms. Commenting on his experience with Polynesian food, Perkins concedes that he "could eat taro fresh from the oven, for then there is something agreeable about it." However, witnessing how it is actually made turns his stomach: "After seeing John, sans culotte [sic], and girded with nothing but a malo, pounding away at it with a stone pestle upon an old board, with the perspiration streaming from his body, my stomach refused to encounter it" (96). Though satisfied with the product itself, Perkins cannot stand to "encounter" the production of it.[6] His repulsion underscores these travelers' reluctance to become too immersed in the Polynesian world they have come to explore. However much they desire to see the authentic Polynesian world—that which is unspoiled by the missionary—they often find such marks of authenticity to be less than savory. His reflection is an apt metonym for the general queasiness experienced by these travelers upon coming across that which is too authentic. Perkins and his contemporaries want to experience Polynesian culture in the same way that their literary predecessors did, and yet they remain unwilling to let go of their own cultural expectations.

Because these writers arrived in the Pacific as readers, they interpreted the world they saw as readers. For them, it was as much a fictional world as a literal space. S. S. Hill, one of the most published travel writers of the time, thus frames his pre-impressions of Hawaii through familiar published accounts. He admits in *Travels in the Sandwich and Society Islands* that before arriving he had "very little acquaintance with anything concerning these islands that related to a date subsequent to their epoch of their discovery, and that of the visits of Vancouver. Their very name was to me romance." Hill's vision of the Hawaiian Islands is frozen in time, permanently framed by romantic notions of first contact. Inviting his readers into what he reads as a collective sentiment, Hill relates, "The animated impressions we have all read of the intercourse that took place between our early navigators and the native inhabitants, I remembered only as we retain the impression of some of the leading features of the first work of fiction we peruse" (95). Despite its basis on firsthand accounts, Hill's Hawaii is nonetheless a fictive Hawaii, a romanticized Hawaii only tenuously held together by an "impression of some of the leading features."

The traveler's romanticized expectations, however, were often dashed upon arriving in a Hawaii much changed since the "epoch of their discovery," a

Hawaii seemingly equal parts Christian and exotic. Contrasting his prearrival impressions with his own first impressions, Hill is obliged to "confess [that he] was upon landing, somewhat suddenly awakened from the pleasing vision of societies of men fresh from the hand of our common mother Nature, which the imagination and memory of early reading had presented." Hill expects the Hawaii of his books, but his "pleasing vision" of the Polynesian noble savage is spoiled. And yet, despite his disappointment, Hill assures the reader that "it must not be supposed that we are about to see only the reverse side of the picture of these islands and their inhabitants so long engraven on most of our minds, and to contemplate that view alone which has too many European features to possess the charm of novelty we expect to find; for, although we shall presently tread the streets of a semi-European town, we shall subsequently see some genuine traits of the proper native life of the islanders" (96). In language resembling a pact or a contract, Hill insists that his narrative will work within the familiar confines of the tradition that inspired him: it will reinforce the picture he had formed before his arrival. Hill recognizes that his audience expects a certain script and that it is his responsibility to follow that script. To write of a Hawaii unlike that described by the travelers who preceded him would be to write of an experience neither "genuine" nor "proper." A "genuine" Hawaii is a picturesque Hawaii, as Hill's use of the word "picture" suggests. Moreover, Hill imagines himself as part of the literary legacy responsible for upholding this picturesque world, duty bound to provide a new chapter as filled with the "charm and novelty" as those of his predecessors. Even though the setting of the "semi-European town" is what allows Hill the privilege of touring, it is presented as an object of scorn, too close to home to provide the travel writer with a novel account of an exotic world.

Hill's conflicted sentiments are representative of the expectations of these mid-century travel writers: they wanted the Pacific to be touristically accessible but also to retain its "exotic" qualities. Paul Lyons, in *American Pacificism*, has defined this ideology as "the double logic that the islands are imagined at once as places to be civilized and as escapes from civilization" (27). Such contradictory feelings are succinctly exemplified by Edward Perkins, who upon arriving in Honolulu finds himself "agreeably disappointed" with the town of Honolulu, Europeanized and "regular" as it has obviously become (112). Through his paradoxical phrasing, Perkins simultaneously allies himself with the Romantic tradition of the Pacific while still conceding that the narrative of progress is equally important. From the perspective of an American concerned with the potential colonial integration of Hawaii, Perkins is pleased; as a travel writer, however, hoping to capitalize on the strange and exotic, he is disappointed.

In *Los Gringos*, Henry Augustus Wise, a US Navy lieutenant turned travel writer, ironically defines Honolulu as a "town of strangers, with shops, stores, and warehouses" (362). Unlike earlier accounts of Pacific encounter, Wise sees, to his great disappointment, very little that is culturally strange. For Wise, Honolulu is strange precisely because it is not strange at all. Its strangeness is its familiarity. Walking through these familiar streets, Wise is met by Hawaiians seeking to capitalize off of Hawaii's already bourgeoning tourism: "Again the quays are crowded with more miserable natives, with sprigs of coral, shells, calibashes [*sic*], or island ornaments in their hands, looking wistfully, and silently towards you; for they never use importunities, they are too indolent by half. And there is a market shed near by, where a fat woman will swallow a gallon of *poee-poee*, to show how the thing is done, provided it be paid for" (363). Although Wise imagines this scene as an illustration of the "indolent" avarice of "civilized" Hawaiians,[7] it more fully represents how the exotic has become commercialized and commodified. Much to the dismay of the writer publishing and monetizing an account of the exotic Pacific, the Hawaiian people are seeking to profit from the most prominent aspects of their culture. This irony is central to understanding the contradiction that shapes these texts: travelers expect to see the authentic but are not prepared for the possibility that that authentic culture might take a closer look back at them. Writing on the "Allure of the Authentic," Stacy Burton describes modernity as "a complex condition that produces the pursuit of representations and circumstances it Romanticizes as authentic even as it makes them scarce," adding that "travel's claim to provide firsthand experience of the world thus acquires a new urgency" (163). The "pursuit" of Wise and contemporary Pacific travel writers is, of course, what leads to such exploitation of the "authentic." That is to say, the more those markers of authenticity become romanticized, the more likely those things are to lose their authentic cachet (to become "scarce").

In the context of Polynesian travel, these "representations" take the form of scenes: familiar images ingrained in the minds of travelers based on romantic literary depictions. Throughout these travel narratives, their writers find that the scenes they come across do not fit with the scenes that they have read about. It is this disappointment that leads them to pursue the hula, as it comes to represent a more "genuine" scene hidden away from the eyes of their missionary counterparts. As part of the "back region," the hula is imagined as a precontact scene, a scene that befits their literary-infused expectations of Polynesia.

Locking Away the Literary in *Sandwich Island Notes*: A Changing of the Guard

In the review of *Sandwich Island Notes*, the *Albion* opines that "it is to be deplored that on the evidence of this apparently impartial writer, the inhabitants of *scenes* so highly favored by nature are so debased and degraded as a race" (my emphasis). As is customary with nineteenth-century reviews of travel narratives, the people being written about are as much subject to critique as the author. For the *Albion*, the Hawaiian people come across as almost unworthy of their scenery; they fail to blend with the landscape. What is implicit in the *Albion*'s critique is that the Hawaiian people, too, are imagined as sights; and as sights, they detract from the beauty of the scenery that surrounds them. Their behavior is incongruous with the "scenes" that surround them, putting them at odds with their picturesque setting. The reviewer thus adds that "the *pictures* drawn by [the author] of the horrible licentiousness generally prevalent are probably not over-charged, though they are dwelt on with painful and reiterated earnestness" (my emphasis). Once again, the review employs pictorial language to frame the written text. The author does not "relate anecdotes" or "document behavior," or even, as the title *Sandwich Island Notes* suggests, "take notes." Rather, he "draws pictures." Using this type of language, the *Albion* defines the general expectation of works like *Sandwich Island Notes*: they are to frame Hawaii as a space of sights, a place to be gazed upon rather than interacted with. In the beachcomber and sailor tradition (popularized by Melville, who borrowed heavily from earlier beachcombers), exchange and interaction were central. In the new tradition of travel writing pioneered by A Häolé, scenes take precedence over exchange and observation wins out over interaction. Fittingly, then, A Häolé's first tableau features a "drunken sailor" being forcefully jailed. This is, he writes, "the last marine animal I should have pictured to my own fancy." As he is carried away by "twenty ragged and dirty native police," the sailor "swore, and sternly threatened what he would do when he regained his liberty and felt like 'himself again'" (57–58). Despite his protests, the drunken sailor is locked away in a newly built jail. A Häolé's pleasant reflections on a romantic Hawaii are quickly upset by a very real image of European dissoluteness, leading him to reflect that "life is chiefly composed of incongruities, and not unfrequently do the beautiful and the sublime precede by but a single step the absolutely ridiculous." This drunken sailor is labeled only as "Jack," a commonplace name for a sailor and a title that the Hawaiians had adopted when referring to foreigners. In this scene, the boozy sailor acts as a character type, a representation of the sailor's current position on the island. To modern readers, the image likely does not come across as "absolutely ridiculous." In fact, there is something almost quotidian in the image of the town drunk being taken to jail. But the "incongruity" that the author points to is that this scene goes against Western perceptions of the Pacific as a space of license and freedom. Even the worst impressions of Polynesia as barbarous and uncivilized still adhered to a mythology of Pacific lawlessness. The opening scene witnessed by the author, however, is defined by its adherence to Christian law. The Hawaiian police, though "dirty and ragged," engage in subduing the barbarous European sailor. "Jack's" threats of what he will do when he becomes "himself again" thus assume a significant double meaning. In the literal context, "Jack" will be himself again when he sobers up, but in the context of the author's narrative, the sailor's words seem more suggestive than that. To be "himself again" is to occupy a position on the island that missionary presence will no longer allow. Threats that may have carried greater weight in earlier times now fall on deaf ears: it is "all unavailing." The voice of Jack, so influential in creating the mythology of the Pacific, is silenced. In *Typee*, Melville describes "Jack's" influential position within the Pacific world:

> Jack, who has long been accustomed to the long-bow and to spin tough yarns on a ship's forecastle, invariably officiates as the showman of the island on which he has settled, and having mastered a few dozen words of the language, is supposed to know all about those who speak it. A natural desire to make himself of consequence in the eyes of the strangers, prompts him to lay claim to a much greater knowledge of such matters than he actually possesses. In reply to incessant queries, he communicates not only that he knows but a good deal more, and if there be any information deficient still he is at no loss to supply it. The avidity with which his anecdotes are noted down tickles his vanity, and his powers of invention increase with the credulity of his auditors. He knows just the sort of information wanted, and furnishes it to any extent. (170)

Melville's critique is focused on Jack's dubious authorship of Pacific culture: Jack is motivated by "vanity" as he watches while "his anecdotes are noted down." This critique speaks to how important Jack was in creating the narratives of the Pacific that reached European audiences. Of course, Melville himself is "Jack" at the highest literary level—Melville is Jack par excellence.[8] It is Melville's "yarns" that inspire future travelers, and it is his "anecdotes [that] are noted down" in the memory of these travelers. In opening the narrative proper of his *Sandwich Island Notes*, the author's foundational story thus fittingly locks up the sailor. By locking up the sailor, the narrative announces a locking up of the romantic Hawaiian tradition, a tradition dominated by seafaring men like Melville and the imprisoned "Jack." Jack, too, is a casualty of the "civilizing" process. The perspective of "Jack" is replaced by the perspective of the Häolé. The Häolé takes on the role of showman—in a different way—and becomes the interpreter of Pacific culture.

For all the generalized praise A Häolé heaps upon the civilizing efforts of Hawaiian missionaries, his *Sandwich Island Notes* continually draws the reader's attention to scenes of native Hawaiians failing to fit into this new Hawaii. Even his seemingly forthright assertions concerning missionary progress often come across as attempts at convincing himself, such as when he asserts that "it is a self-evident fact, that, to a certain extent, the Hawaiians are morally and physically happier now than they were before the introduction of Christianity" (246). Beginning with emphatic authority ("it is a self-evident fact"), the author quickly lapses into equivocation ("to a certain extent"). The scenes depicted by the author lead us to question to what extent Hawaiians are better off. Before shutting away the drunken Jack from the reader, A Häolé encounters another unfamiliar version of a familiar Pacific literary figure imprisoned, this time in the form of a beautiful Hawaiian woman no longer of sound mind. Upon "hearing a shriek from the contiguous cell," the author finds "a native woman, in a deplorable state of insanity." A Häolé's description of this woman is worth citing in whole, as the manner in which he lingers, almost in soliloquy form, on this woman is as significant as the description itself:

> She was rather above the medium size of women, and apparently forty years of age. Her hair, which clung around her beautifully moulded head, in short, massive curls, was a black and glossy as a raven's wing. She was entirely nude, excepting a wreath of sea-grass, that answered the same purpose as Eve's fig-leaves. Her form, however, was perfect; and there lingered about her such distinctive traces of peerless beauty as would once have ranked her with the early women of creation, whose matchless perfection seduced the "sons of God" from their allegiance. In her violent moments she had dashed her head against the walls of her prison; and now her fine brow was bruised and bleeding. There was no couch, nor a single comfort in her cell; for the hard cold earth was her only bed. There she stood, a mournful smile playing around her lips, and a sort of half-dreamy, half-frantic light gleaming in her large black eyes. There she stood, a pitiful object to the gaze of every recreant stranger that might feel inclined to linger before her iron bulwark. Oh God! it was a distressing scene—that total wreck of beautiful humanity. She had once mingled freely with her own race, and cradled her infant to sleep on her beautiful bosom. . . . She had once laved her limbs in the clear blue waters of her native seas, and threaded the cocoa-nut grove around her dwelling with a dignity that would not have dishonored Milton's "*Eve.*" But, poor creature, she was mad now! (58–59).

Never one for subtlety, A Häolé clearly spells out the connection between this imprisoned Hawaiian woman and the biblical Eve, echoing a familiar literary refrain of describing Pacific women in Edenic terms. Tommo, in Melville's *Typee*, most notably, writes of Fayaway that she "for the most part clung to the primitive and summer garb of Eden. But how becoming the costume!" (87). Melville's description of Fayaway builds on an already established ideal, in which the Pacific woman's "primitive" beauty, seen through the lens of the male gaze, represents her oneness with nature. However, the Hawaiian Eve in this story could hardly be any farther from nature, as she is locked away and mad, still "beautiful," but now only as a "total wreck of beautiful humanity." She remains an "object" of the (male) gaze, but her altered state renders her an unbecoming object of fixation, a sight that only a "recreant stranger [the author himself, apparently] might be inclined to linger" upon.

It is fitting that A Hāōlé indirectly contrasts his "recreant" gaze with a visual memory of the Hawaiian woman having "once laved her limbs in the clear blue waters of her native sea," as no scene could better typify the male gaze in the Pacific. Mark Twain's *Roughing It* (1876), though written later than most of the texts discussed in this chapter, provides an illuminating illustration (figure 2.1). The engraving accompanying Twain's anecdote about watching "a bevy of female bathers" depicts the author lounging luxuriously on the beach, legs kicked up on a log, pipe in one hand, as his other hand "guards" the women's discarded clothes (519). Twain's nonchalant chivalry as he "guards" the bathers' clothes appears to presuppose that this gaze was often imagined as noble, as motivated by respect and admiration rather than objectification.

By contrast, Henry Augustus Wise provides a much less "guarded" interpretation, openly acknowledging the sexually voyeuristic motivation behind this gaze. For Wise, watching Hawaiian women bathing is a "sight to make a lover forget his mistress, or a parson his prayers" (354). His description invokes the pleasurable risk latent in this type of scene, as the bathing Hawaiian women threaten to unbridle Western conceptions of both beauty and sexuality. It is a moment of cultural exchange, but it is cultural exchange from a distance. Wise "spends his leisure hours beholding the beautiful panorama," observing the scene as an outsider, while he and his companions make "indifferent remarks as to what the good missionaries might think" (354). As suggested by his remark about what the missionary would think, this is a transgressive act, an act that hearkens back to the narratives of sailors before Christian missionaries became a dominant presence in Hawaii. For Wise, what seems to be most transgressive about this scene is not simply the subversion of Western beauty and sexuality but, more important, the reclaiming of this sight from local missionaries. Wise revels not just in the sight itself but also in his possession of the sight.

These travel writers register a resentment over missionary influence, particularly in terms of their access to Hawaiian women. But, as Noelani Arista points out in *The Kingdom and the Republic*, these restrictions originated from the Hawaiian chiefs (*ali'i*), and it is reductive to assume that it was *only* missionary influence that prompted them to make these changes. Arista points to

ON GUARD.

Figure 2.1. "On Guard," from Mark Twain's *Roughing It* (1872).

the 1825 kapu "forbidding Hawaiian women from going out on ships for the purpose of prostitution" as a turning point, "a reaction to the increased presence of transient sailors in the islands and as a measure of control over Hawaiian social interaction with foreigners deployed by the ali'i in their governance of the islands" (139, 155). Missionaries, of course, were enthusiastically supportive of these changes for their own reasons, though both missionaries and Hawaiian chiefs alike were quick to put the blame on the supposed licentious nature of Hawaiian women rather than on the sailors themselves. The kapu ultimately led to "heated clashes . . . between sailors, missionaries, and ali'i [that] were precipitated by the frustrated desires of sailors, who had been accustomed to having access to Hawaiian women for almost two and a half decades" (155). Henry Augustus Wise, a sailor before a travel writer, fittingly sees this access to Hawaiian women—even if from a distance—as a sort of reclaiming.

If we now return to A Häolé, we can see that his sentimentality about the imprisoned woman is equally sentimentality about what is lost to him. So while he nostalgically opines that "she had once freely mingled with her race," he also seems to lament what is a loss to him, as a tourist of Hawaii. Like Jack in the "contiguous cell" of the prison, the narrative shuts the Hawaiian woman away. In lamenting the fate of the woman gone mad, A Häolé evinces what Renato Resaldo terms "imperialist nostalgia," defined as the "paradox" in which "people mourn for the passing of what they themselves have transformed" (108). The power of the feeling of nostalgia resides "in its association with (indeed its disguise as) more genuinely innocent, tender recollections of what is at once an earlier epoch and a previous phase of life" (108). It is such "genuine innocence" that A Häolé can no longer encounter.

Similar instances occur throughout the author's *Sandwich Island Notes*, including a particularly haunting scene in which A Häolé notices being observed by an elderly, one-eyed Hawaiian man dressed only in a European-style vest, "buttoned up with the most scrupulous care," who "seemed to be totally ignorant of every other necessary appendage, such as unmentionables, &c., &c." With his one-eyed gaze directed at A Häolé and his companions, the man happily delivers to them the traditional greeting of "aloha," after which he "drew a long breath as though he had ridded himself of a serious responsibility" (146–47). Once again, the author depicts a native Hawaiian who seems incapable of comfortably existing within this newly European space. His European vest is "buttoned up with scrupulous care" while the lower half of his body remains completely uncovered—a fitting metaphor for the cultural incongruity present within this increasingly Christianized space. The "aloha" that the man continually discharges as if "ridd[ing] himself of a serious responsibility" suggests an awareness of what white travelers expect of him, an awareness that he has a role to fulfill toward these travelers. He must be both "civilized" and retain those qualities most admired by white visitors—in this case, friendliness.[9] These are not the scenes A Häolé expects. Haunted by the experience of loss and feelings of imperialist nostalgia, his desire to see a precontact Hawaii increases. And it is the hula, hidden away from the sight of missionaries, that offers him and other travelers such as Edward Perkins that opportunity.

Off the Beaten Path: The Hula as a "Back Region"

> Little Lani looked archly at us as we left the house, and,
> shaking her finger, said: "Ua iki au ko olua hile ana," (I know
> where you are going.) "Ilea' ka hewa" (what of it)?
> Returned Allaire, laughingly, as he closed the door.
> —Edward Perkins, *Na Motu*, 103

To see the hula was to see something off the beaten path. We find this cliché literalized in another contemporary narrative, Edward Perkins's *Na Motu*. His beachcomber guide Allaire navigates him through the "margins," along a "route that [Perkins] had never been" (103). Allaire, whom Perkins describes as "an Englishman [who] was qualified by birth and education to move in a higher sphere of social relations than that into which the chances of adventure had thrown him," provides Perkins with access to scenes restricted by his missionary hosts. This, for Perkins, is the primary appeal of the hula: it is an authentic scene, a scene devoid of Western influences. The hula is part of what Dean MacCannell defines in *The Tourist* as the "back regions," spaces that "in their mere existence intimat[e] their possible violation . . . the putative 'intimate and real' as against 'show'" (94). As their young host Little Lani's arched brow and finger wag suggest, seeing the hula is a violation. In fact, it is a double violation. In MacCannell's sense of the term, going to a hula is a violation because it is a sight that exists outside of the touristic gaze; therefore, to seek it out is to threaten its "back regions" status, to bring it nearer to becoming a tourist site. But, of course, for Little Lani, a young native Hawaiian for whom missionary presence has been a constant, to pursue the hula also represents a moral violation, as the hula was deemed illicit by both foreign missionaries and native Hawaiian leaders. Perkins himself straddles the line between these two violations, at once intrigued by the possibility of the "back regions" and aware of how getting too close to these "back regions" could be read as a moral indictment.

The respective behaviors of Perkins and Allaire offer a fitting contrast between beachcomber and tourist. Upon their arrival, Allaire is "recognized by all, to judge by the storm of salutations," while Perkins remarks, adopting the characteristic documentary language of the travel writer, that his "estimate of the quality and quantity of the assemblage had not been premature" (103). Allaire is immediately recognized as a participant, while Perkins settles into the role of observer. While it is hardly surprising that Perkins would feel less at ease than his more experienced companion, his detached nature contradicts his expressed desire to experience a more "authentic" Hawaii. Seeing the "back regions" is one thing, but being part of the "back regions" is, for him, a step too far. This desire to remain uninvolved also manifests itself in Perkins's reluctance to take part in the preparation of the 'awa root,[10] knowing that it has been tabooed by local missionaries.[11] However, Allaire assures him that "there is no kingdom in the world where appearances are more deceptive than in this" (104). In other words, Allaire is drawing attention to the difference between the "show" of Hawaii and the "intimate and real." When Perkins reluctantly drinks the 'awa ("the first and last time" he ever did so, he fastidiously assures his readers), he insists that "he could not perceive . . . that he was in the slightest degree affected by it." But Allaire, he continues, "whose libations had been copious, soon began to manifest symptoms peculiar to persons who are 'three sheets to the wind'" (106). Their respective post-'awa states provide an apt metaphorical contrast: Allaire imbibes freely, and, in his drunken state, loses himself amid the ceremony,[12] whereas Perkins remains un-"affected," firmly rooted outside the collective experience.

It is Perkins's description of the hula itself, however, that most clearly evokes his sense of detachment from the situation. In describing the hula, Perkins resorts to the type of evasive and nondescript language uniformly invoked by contemporary missionary and "historical" accounts of Hawaii. For example, Perkins relates that the "influence [of 'awa] was speedily manifested upon some of the girls, who assumed a variety of attitudes, and commenced a *húra*, or chant, that will not admit description" (105). As is so often the case in mid-nineteenth-century accounts of the hula, Perkins's description is articulated through language that purports to be descriptive without committing itself to details. The women, in his telling, express a "variety of attitudes." While "variety" suggests range and breadth to these performances, it, without any follow-up, remains nebulous. Deeming the hula as unfit for the eyes of his audience, he declares that it "will not admit description."

THE "LASCIVIOUS" HULA: THE ELUSIVE HISTORY OF THE HULA

Even today, the hula hardly "admits description"—at the least the historical version of it. While, ironically, the hula has become the most ubiquitous symbol of genuine "Hawaiian life," it remains familiar to non-natives *only* as a symbol. As Adria L. Imada writes in *Aloha America*, her analysis of the legacy of the hula in the first half of the nineteenth century, "Hawai'i has been personified by the figure of the female dancer during more than a century of American colonization" (4). The hula dancer now adorns car dashboards, clad only in a grass skirt and a coconut bra, her hands extended to her side as she makes the gesture that has come to stand for the hula. Of course, despite its kitschy appeal and its nostalgically inspired semiotics of exotic sexuality, this image has little in common with the historical hula. In fact, the side-to-side hand gesture that has become synonymous with the hula was hardly a significant part of the historical practice. As Adrienne L. Kaeppler writes, in her exhaustive study *Hula Puha*, most of the "arm movements neither allude to nor interpret the words of the texts . . . but instead enhance the lower body motifs by decorating them or by similar movements at a different level or different plane" (67). The "text" that Kaeppler refers to here is the *mele*, "chanted/sung poetry," accompanied by rhythmic drumming on *pahu*, "shark-skin-covered drums" (9). Presumably, it is the *mele* that Perkins, who does not recognize the elements of the performance as codependent parts of it, refers to as "a *húra*, or chant." According to Kaeppler, the "chant," or text, was intimately connected with the movements,[13] which function synchronously rather than serving as mere accompaniment. The classic version of the hula was, at heart, an interpretive process, in which the performance supersedes the product (8). Responding to the text through movement, the performer actively makes meaning. What is at stake in the hula is not "correctness" but significance, or "how skillfully the choreographer" has "made the text visible in a culturally satisfying way" (13).

This also means that the specifics of the historical hula remain, for the most part, out of our conceptual reach. Since traditions were passed on orally and through practice, "little is known . . . about the movements or choreographies performed." Kaeppler adds that "written records by Hawaiians in the Hawaiian language were made considerably later—after Christian missionaries had introduced writing systems, and in many cases after their writers had converted to Christianity" (1–2). By 1851, the hula was formally outlawed, as the first law "regulating public performances" was passed in 1851.[14] The most comprehensive "firsthand" account of the hula is Nathaniel B. Emerson's *Unwritten Literature of Hawaii: The Sacred Songs of the Hula* (1909), which was commissioned by the Smithsonian Institution Bureau of American Ethnology.[15] Emerson sought to order the variety and complexity of the hula, classifying nearly thirty distinct types of hula, sedulously reproducing musical lyrics in Hawaiian and English alike, and both describing and providing pictures of costumes and instruments. Lamenting that the hula's "introduction to us moderns" has been "unfortunate," Emerson asserts that it is "an institution of divine, that is, religious origins" and not the "riotous and passionate ebullitions of Polynesian kings and amorous posturing of their voluptuaries" (7–8).[16] And yet, for all these good intentions, Emerson's introduction smacks of the type of "liberal racism" that Paul Lyons argues defined most twentieth-century Oceanian histories (28). This "liberal racism" is best exemplified in Emerson's expressed hope that "if this book does nothing more than prove that savages are only the children of a younger growth than ourselves [then] the labor of making it will not be in vain" (8). So, while there is certainly value to Emerson's work, especially in his effort to retain the native language of hula, his translations are surely inflected by paternalism and Western modes of thinking. Emerson's work has also been called into question for its lack of proper accreditation for his Hawaiian sources. As both Noenoe K. Silva and Ku'ualoha Ho'omanawanui have pointed out, Emerson's later work *Pele and Hiiaka* (1917) was drawn mainly from [M. J.] Kapihenhui in *Voices of Fire*, "whom he neither credits nor names" (xxxiv).

More recent accounts, such as Amy Ku'uleialoha Stillman's *Sacred Hula: The Historical Hula 'Āla'apapa* (1998) and Dorothy B. Barrère's *Hula: Historical Perspectives* (1980), both published by Hawaii's Bishop Museum, have endeavored to distinguish both the ancient and modern forms of hula from the Western perceptions that have come to define it. Stillman differentiates *hula* 'ala'apapa (indigenous hula)[17] from hula 'auana (the modern or westernized hula). Some of these distinctions are simple: the westernized version's music is provided by guitar and ukulele, as opposed to the "double gourd *ipu*" percussion of indigenous practice. Others are more subtle: modern "hula movements and gestures" are characterized in *Sacred Hula* as "soft and languid," while ancient forms tended to be "vigorous in effort expended by the dancers" (2). This distinction is essential to understanding both A Hāolé's account of the hula as well as the descriptions—or nondescriptions—of the hula that inform his thinking.

In both historical and literary accounts, the adjective "lascivious" so consistently precedes "hula" that the two words appear almost to be one in the same. James Jackson Jarves's *History of the Hawaiian Islands* (1846) is perhaps the most prominent example of describing the hula in these terms. So influential was Jarves's *History* that the usually irreverent Mark Twain humbly refers to it in *Roughing It* as "Mr. Jarves' excellent history," apparently assuming his readers know the book to which he refers (466). As Edward Perkins will do eight years later, Jarves excuses himself from clearly defining the hula, writing only that hula dances "consisted in a variety of uncouth motions and twistings of the body, of too lascivious a nature to bear description" (35). Jarves's language is remarkably similar to that of Perkins. Here, too, the word "variety" is used to avoid description rather than expound upon it. The hula will not "bear" description for Jarves, just as it will not "admit" description from Perkins. Jarves, however, does clearly state what remains beneath the surface of Perkins's account—that the hula is "lascivious" and that it therefore cannot and should not be described to American audiences. As if to offset even broaching the unseemly topic of the hula, the corresponding illustration depicts a "children's dance" (figure 2.2). The illustration thus seeks to write over the historical hula by reinscribing Hawaiian dancing with a more comfortable and "innocent" depiction of dancing. Thus, while the history itself bespeaks of cultural oppression, the illustration insists that the spirit of the dance has been retained and, in fact, returned to a purer state. Jarves's *History* renders the hula as a thing of the past, defined by its absence rather than its presence.

Sheldon Dibble's *History of the Sandwich Islands* (1843) refuses to even mention the hula by name, instead generically labeling it as "the dance." Seemingly seeking to counter romantic impressions of the hula, Dibble, who came to Hawaii as a missionary, insists that "their motions were anything but graceful, and often very revolting." In this respect, Dibble's description accords with Stillman's assertion that ancient hula was not "soft and languid," the defining characteristics of later hula. For Dibble, though, to suggest that the hula lacks "grace" is to invalidate it, to show that it is devoid of the most defining element of dance. Further contrasting it to Western notions of dance,

Children's Dance,

Figure 2.2. "Children's Dance," from James Jackson Jarves's *History of the Hawaiian Islands.*

Dibble adds that "every variety of song was rehearsed and acted, even the most vile and lascivious, and the action, always corresponded with the sense" (119–20). But Dibble's use of the adjective "lascivious" spells out why this particular term continues to be used. His description emphasizes the (too) intimate relationship between song and dance, between content and form. The hula is not simply a set of moves performed with musical accompaniment but instead two elements that work together: by modeling a lewd form of sexuality, it arouses and induces sexual desire.

This distinction is made explicit in Hiram Bingham's *A Residence of Twenty-One Years in the Sandwich Islands* (1848).[18] Bingham struggles through a description of the hula, after dismissively and tersely defining it as "a heathen song and dance" (123). Unable (and probably unwilling) to capture the essence of the song and dance, Bingham continually tries to relate it to concepts more familiar to his American audience: the participants walk "precisely like the aborigines of North America"; they move "much like the Shakers"; and the simple melodies they use, in his perception, correspond to what American boys call "'Bean porridge hot'" (123–24). As far as Bingham is concerned, the practitioners of the hula are "wasting their time," time that could be better spent in a much less lively way, "attend[ing] schools and public lectures" (123). Bingham's complaint reveals the way missionaries justified the ban on the hula as pertaining to work ethic as well. In her article "Kanawai E Hoʻopau I Na Hula Kuolo Hawaiʻi: The Political Economy of Banning the Hula," Noenoe K. Silva convincingly argues that the ban of the hula had as much to do with economics as it did fears about its overt sexuality: "Exhortations against it were related to the problem of cheap labor needed for the plantations. . . . The puritan work ethic and disdain for traditional Kanaka Maoli practices dovetailed seamlessly with the attempts to exploit Kanaka Maoli labor" (32–33). As improper as they seemed to Bingham, then, hula performances in 1821 were already sanitized versions of precontact hula, which, according to Bingham, actively "promote[d]" lasciviousness and could not be allowed to "flourish in modest communities" (125). In adding the active verb "promote" to the traditional description of "lascivious," Bingham articulates his main concern: the problem is not what the *hula* is but what it can *do*.

A Häolé's Hula: "The Last Act in the Drama"

A Häolé's *Sandwich Island Notes* literalizes what is suggested by the works just discussed, as the author finds himself unable to see the hula without becoming part of it. Like Perkins, A Häolé views the hula as a "back region," performed in "the Palis," where "foreigners seldom or never" go. As the literal translation of Pali as cliffs suggests, this is a site at the edges. "The Palis" function metaphorically as a precipice, exhilarating precisely because of the risk of getting too close to the edge and falling. A Häolé is "resolved to observe all [he] could of native character" (283), even if it means jeopardizing his own moral character. His willingness to take this risk arises from his sense that he has not seen the authentic Hawaii.

This distinguishes A Häolé from his contemporaries. S. S. Hill, for example, is unwilling to even take this risk. He admits in *Travels in the Sandwich and Society Islands* that he would, "had [he] consulted his wishes, have requested that some of the girls dance," writing, "But we knew this to be tabooed by the missionaries, in opposition to whose influence we did not, after the manner of many of the white inhabitants in town, wish to set ourselves, however we might have disagreed with them concerning a part of the means employed to accomplish their ends" (215). While Hill recognizes the unjust "means" by which missionaries re-appropriated native *taboo* in order to stifle the hula, he also knows what he stands to lose by seeing the hula. The "white inhabitants" Hill references are presumably non-missionary beachcombers. In seeing the hula, he risks getting too close to the native culture, too close to becoming an "inhabitant" rather than a visitor. And in doing so, he risks losing the security of his missionary-sanctioned tour. Fittingly, Hill's initial reaction upon landing in a more remote area near "Karakakooa Bay" (Kealakekua Bay), where Captain Cook was famously welcomed and later killed, is one of nostalgia. Likely reflecting on Cook, their reception recalls to him "the time when the boats of our celebrated navigators' ships cautiously approached the shores of newly discovered lands, while the natives who lined

the beach stood stupefied, as full of doubt concerning the strangers, as the
Europeans were concerning the character of the reception they might meet"
(213). Hill's sentiments bring to mind Dening's definition of "the beach" in
Mr. Bligh's Bad Language as a "space where neither otherness nor familiarity
holds sway" (179). But the notion of exchange is immediately silenced; the
"risks" of encounter prevent Hill from acting on his initial impulse. Of course,
this impulse itself is already mediated. He thinks of "requesting" the dance
only because he already knows of it, because he has read about past explorers
seeing the dance.

For travelers like Hill, Polynesian dances offered travelers a more legitimate experience, a genuine encounter with Pacific culture. In Tahiti, Henry
Augustus Wise exerts all his "persuasive eloquence" to "induce the young la-
dies to delight us with a *hevar*." Wise likely would have known about *hevar*
from Herman Melville, who refers to it as "a genuine pagan fandango" and
later as a "jolly heathen dance" (*Typee* 62; *Omoo* 45). While different from the
Hawaiian hula, Tahitian dance occupied a similar space in the Western imagination.[19] Likely recalling Melville's experience, Wise does what Hill was only
tempted to do and actually asks that the dance be performed, lamenting that
he has never "witnessed a legitimate native dance." This emphasis on legiti-
macy suggests that Wise feels his Polynesian travels have so far been less than
authentic, that he cannot possibly say he has been to Tahiti without having
native women dance for him. But in this instance, it is the Tahitian women for
whom the risk is too much.

Instead of obliging Wise's request, one woman insists that she is "*mikonaree
all ovar*" [presumably 'missionary all over']; at the same time making a graceful
manipulation of her hands, from head to foot, to add strength to her assertion"
(353). Conceptualizing the dance as embodied, the woman suggests that the
dance no longer resides within her, that she has, as her gesture invokes, been
transformed. This does not mean, however, that she has been Christianized.
Hers is a change that cannot be adequately translated, hence Wise's decision
to quote the actual word she uses, "mikonaree." There is an interesting double meaning to this phrase: yes, she is suggesting an embodiment of values,
but the phrase is also suggestive of a Foucauldian form of surveillance—she
knows that missionaries are constantly watching her. Wise, certainly, seems
to doubt that this is anything more than a superficial change, as he desists in
his quest for experiencing a legitimate dance after noticing that the Tahitian
women, allegedly such a "pious and virtuous a coterie," did not find it incom-
patible with "their morality to sit down, with renewed zest, to cards" (353).
For Wise, the women refuse not because they are changed but rather because
they do not trust him.

A Häolé, however, gains access to the hula precisely because his appearance contrasts with that of missionaries. Earlier in his narrative, A Häolé, clad in his "Sandwich Island Suit"[20] is mistaken by a group of Hawaiian workmen as a foreman, prompting the "idlers" to return to their work (126).[21] But as he approaches the scene of the hula, he seems "uncouth enough to be taken for a runaway sailor" (283). Seen as a sailor rather than a merchant or missionary, A Häolé is granted access to a scene outside the scope of the traditional Hawaiian touristic experience. Runaway sailors, like those discussed in chapter 1, tended to be much more liberal than their merchant and missionary counterparts, for whom cultural traditions like the hula represented a threat to the implementation of Western values. A Häolé occupies a new, liminal space between the two, willing to see what missionaries refuse to see but unwilling to be part of the beachcomber's realm of experiences. Though not directly engaged in an imperial project, like a foreman overseeing new construction, A Häolé is nonetheless implicitly engaged in one, as he is "resolved to learn all he can of native character" (283).

But while his clothing gives him access to this scene, it also subjects him to risk, making him *part* of the scene rather than simply an observer of it. Thus, his ambitious goal of "learn[ing] all he can" is quickly discarded when it is the author himself who becomes an object of interest. Instead of giving him unfettered access to the scene, his appearance leads his would-be objects of study to "manifest every possible freedom" in their interactions with him, "especially the women." This moment stands in stark contrast to A Häolé's early soliloquy on the imprisoned Hawaiian woman, who, even in her abjection, the author regards as a sexualized object. Surely expecting to take in a "legitimate native dance," to return to Wise's term, A Häolé, to his surprise, finds the tables turned. The women "desirous[ly]" rifle through his pockets before finally being stopped by the author, who fears that they "would have soon left me minus my nondescripts" (283). Searching through his clothes puts A Häolé's body at risk; he himself has suddenly become the object of "desire." The author's body becomes subject to the gaze of the native Hawaiians; it is now his "native character" that the Hawaiians seek to see.

Unwilling to engage with the scene around him, A Häolé thus seeks to reposition himself as a detached observer. Much like Wise upon being spurned in his advances to see a "legitimate native dance," A Häolé turns away to smoke a cigar. For both authors, this seems to be a means of distancing themselves from the Hawaiian people, a means of reasserting superiority after being made to feel vulnerable. Perhaps turning to smoke a cigar can be read as a dramatic reassertion of detached otherness in response to having their attempt at being "inside" rebuffed. Smoking his cigar, A Häolé "patiently await[s] the rest of the drama." But the scene resists the "dramatic" structure the author might have hoped for, as his gaze encounters a naked young woman but surely

not of the kind he was expecting. The young woman is "covered with a syph-
ilitic eruption," with her hair "hanging down in tangled and filthy masses"
(283–84). She is both nude and covered, an object of desire that resists his in-
trusive gaze—not out of modesty, however, but because she is already marked
with the visible consequences of sexual desire. The scene calls upon the author's sympathy, but he can only react with "disgust." He is compelled to redi-
rect his gaze, to "look another way." This time, his gaze falls upon "several parties . . . performing comic acts which should never be performed only behind
the thick curtain of night." The sexuality latent in the tourist's gazing upon
the hula is made explicit in this scene, much to the author's discomfort. There
is no "drama" or performance here, and the author is surprised to find that "his
presence in the light of day had not the least influence on their motives and
actions" (284). His sense of anxiety is representative of a touristic contradiction: he expects to witness authentic "native character," and yet he becomes
uncomfortable when that presentation is not catered toward his expectations.

When the hula finally begins, A Häolé provides a familiar account of it,
declining to mention anything specific about it. The author displays typical
ethnographic detachment, stating that "three of the younger women placed
themselves in a state of nature, and commenced dancing the *hula hula* to the
music of native flute and drum" (284). But the moment the hula becomes
more than simply a sight—that is to say, the moment it is put into action—A
Häolé confesses that "their intricate gyrations I can not attempt to describe,
for I possess not the talent of a dancing master, nor could any form of written language assume sufficient modesty to attempt a description of that scene.
Its results, however, were to excite the animal passions to the highest degree
beyond endurance" (284–85). In accordance with other written accounts of
the hula, A Häolé cannot really capture the hula dance in words. While he
initially—and more convincingly—cites his lack of dancing talent as the primary impediment to describing the dance, he quickly reinforces that it is the
"immodesty" of the dance that stymies him. But while he cannot describe the
dance, he is more than happy, "however," to comment on "its results." Rather
than simply defining the dance as "lascivious,"[22] the author more directly
spells out the implications of the term, asserting that the dance was meant to
"excite the animal passions beyond all endurance." In this way, A Häolé per-
petuates the idea presented by Hawaiian "historians": the performers are not
in control of the hula, but, rather, it is in control of *them*. The dance "excites"
them, acts on them, and causes them to lose their humanity, as they "succumb
to their animal passions."

This "excitement" removes the would-be-ethnographer from the privileged
position of spectator. Expecting simply to watch, the author instead becomes
enveloped in the hula, relating that, "a *danseuse* advanced toward me, and

before I could repel the movement, she had taken a seat on my shoulders, precisely as a horseman would mount his saddle" (285). It's difficult not to laugh at the image of the author bravely maintaining his presence within this forbidden scene, desperately jotting down his "notes," furiously trying to repel the woman's attempt to make him *play* the horse in this "drama." This is a moment of risk for A Häolé and, potentially, a moment of exchange between insider and outsider: in mounting the author like a horse, the dancer presumably breaks from the deeply closed-circle nature of the hula, in turn asking A Häolé to break from his closed-off role as spectator. The Hawaiian dancer refuses, to borrow a phrase from Adria L. Imada in *Aloha America*, to be "a passive commodit[y] in the constraining order of empire" (64). A Häolé could read this as an acceptance of him as outsider—that is, so long as he, in turn, accepts that he is being invited into someone else's script. Or, of course, he could read it as a threat, a means of imposing dominance. A Häolé reads it as the latter, determining that, for him, "it was the last act in the drama." Seemingly attempting to re-inscribe his dominance, A Häolé mounts *his* horse and rides away (285). Endeavoring merely to "*see* native character" (my emphasis), he is instead forced to *encounter* "native character." Without the privilege of the gaze, he is unable (and unwilling) to be part of the scene.

While A Häolé's trip to this "back region" is certainly as authentic as he could have hoped, it resists being framed merely as an authentic scene. A Häolé, it turns out, does not really desire unfettered access to Hawaiian experience; what he wants is an easy way to classify it. His gaze, to return to Urry and Larsen's definition, seeks to "order, shape, and classify, rather than reflect the world." A Häolé's notion of "native character" itself falsely suggests that culture is orderly and readily observable, that the author need only infiltrate the inner circle to understand it. "Meaning," as Clifford Geertz remarks in *The Interpretation of Cultures*, "can only be stored in symbols" (127). For A Häolé and his contemporaries, the hula continually resists the symbolic framework they seek to impose upon it. Its "intricate gyrations cannot be described." The hula is constantly in motion, constantly engaged with sub-texts of music, history, mythology, and poetry, and, as a result, constantly eluding being framed simply as a touristic sight.

If A Häolé, frustrated in his desire for unfettered access to authentic Hawaiian experiences, ultimately relinquishes authority, his book *Sandwich Island Notes*, as a whole, does not cede control. Helped by the illustrations, it rather seeks to re-frame the hula, rendering the participants of this scene not as active, vibrant, and varied people but instead as mere types. Significantly, the text's most interesting passage of cultural interplay is bordered by pictures depicting something diametrically opposed to this interplay: specimens of native types (figure 2.3 and figure 2.4). As readers make their way through

NATIVE MAN—MODE OF SITTING.

Figure 2.3. "Native Man—Mode of Sitting," from *Sandwich Island Notes*.

the author's evasive account of the hula, attention is drawn to pictures labeled "Native Female—Mode of Sitting" and "Native Man—Mode of Sitting." While the Hawaiians, in A Häolé's account, at least have agency, even if it is expressed in terms of a desire to dominate him, that agency is reframed by these illustrations, which depict them as specimens, their eyes vacant and their postures docile and unassuming. The still-framed images could hardly be any more discordant with the motion and energy of the hula performance. At the moment in which the author cedes control and privilege, the editor reasserts the inferiority of the Hawaiians, turning them into the type of classificatory examples of "native character" that the author had initially hoped to record. In so doing, the text reasserts the cultural dominance that author had ceded. The hula proves to be a scene that cannot be framed, and thus the book in its entirety not only renders the hula invisible but also shifts attention away from it, offsetting its vibrancy with these stereotypical still-frames.

And thus, the author, too, ultimately reframes his encounter with the hula, emphasizing his successful infiltration into this native scene. In a self-congratulatory tone, A Häolé reflects on the scene as "having taught [him] a

NATIVE FEMALE—MODE OF SITTING.

Figure 2.4. "Native Female—Mode of Sitting," from *Sandwich Island Notes.*

species of philosophy, [that] the only mode of properly testing native character is this: A man must not go among them with a ministerial suit of clothes,
nor a ministerial deportment, as missionaries do." The failure of missionaries,
he suggests, is their detachment, externally represented by their clothing. To
gain access to the scenes, he advises: "Let a man—any man—put on a rough
suit, and put *off*, to a certain extent, his stoical gravity; let him go and sit on
their mats, share in their food—if nature will permit him—and smoke with
them, and indulge in a little *tête-à-tête*, and in one tour over the group he
will see more than many a permanently located missionary will see in twenty
years" (285). The author, in what he perceives as a rather ingenious discovery, contends that to understand "native character" one must put aside one's
own cultural reserve; one must actively engage rather than passively observe.
Putting on a "rough suit" and "sitt[ing] on their mats," A Häölé imagines
himself as a sort of proto–participant observer. His "test of native character"
anticipates his Pacific successor Bronisław Malinowski's "imponderabilia of

actual life and typical behavior," as articulated in *Argonauts of the Western Pacific* (1922), which "cannot possibly be recorded by questioning or computing documents, but have to be observed in their full actuality" (20).

But much like Malinowski's posthumously published *A Diary in the Strict Sense of the Term*, A Häolé's practice of engagement runs counter to his philosophy.[23] Despite his assertion that he saw "what the missionaries, as missionaries, never saw, and can never see" (286), the language of his experience hardly differs from the accounts given by missionaries. He "sit[s] on their mats," but he does so passively, unwilling to directly engage with anything that offends his own "stoical gravity." In this way, A Häolé engages in what Christopher Herbert calls "the complementary fictions of the bigoted missionary and the enlightened modern ethnographer," in which the latter "fictionalize their predecessors and rivals in 'the field' (both senses) in order to reinforce their deeply equivocal fictional image of themselves as both scrupulously 'objective' professionals and as bearers of the gospel of liberation—as missionaries" (155). A Häolé imagines that because he is willing to "see" something that missionaries are unwilling to see, he therefore is able to understand something they cannot. And yet, his "objective" account of the hula only reinforces the accounts of his missionary predecessors.

A Häolé's narrative, too, highlights the way that so-called concerns about the hula's sexuality often masked deeper political concerns. What is ultimately most upsetting to A Häolé is a recognition of the hula's potential for resistance, for pushing back against its Western audience's desire to possess it. Indeed, during the reign of Kalākaua (1874–1891), the hula became a symbol of nationalism, pushing back against American imperialism. This resistance, however, was short-lived, with the hula ultimately becoming the quintessential tourist marker of Hawaii. Where the hula once had been "political script in the islands," writes Imada, "hula performers were now unwittingly catapulted into being cultural ambassadors for their nation" (62–63). What the hula looked like, and who it appealed to, was a central conflict in the American colonization of Hawaii.

THE GRACEFUL HULA: THE HULA FOR AMERICAN EYES

By the time the next wave of Hawaiian travelers arrived, the classic hula had become Americanized. When Mark Twain arrived in Hawaii in the 1870s, he did not have to seek out the hula; the hula came to him. It had become a carefully curated performance. Nevertheless, Twain still conceptualizes the hula through the language of previous writers, referring to it by the familiar moniker: "the lascivious *hula hula*." Before experiencing this new version of the hula, Twain provides the reader with his own history of the classic hula—likely influenced by Jarves's *History*. Though Twain describes the classic hula with characteristic humor, that humor is not, as is usually the case with Twain, laced with irony: "The demoralizing *hula hula* was forbidden to be performed, save at night, with closed doors, in the presence of spectators, and only by permission . . . and payment" (477). Playing on the hula's forbidden but not quite forbidden status, Twain piles on qualifier after qualifier, culminating in one final post-ellipses qualification: payment. Through this final qualification, Twain likens the precontact hulas to prostitution. And like the accounts that inform his description, Twain does not use the word "hula" without an appropriately condemnatory adjectival chaperone, this time "demoralizing." Like "lascivious," this term emphasizes not what the hula was but what it did, what it caused. In Twain's account, the hula caused the Hawaiian people to lose their morality. Twain's use of "lascivious" and "demoralizing" suggests that it was not the Hawaiian people who controlled the dance but, rather, the dance that controlled *them*.[24]

This was no longer the case with this new version of the hula, stripped of both its political potential and its sensuality. In direct contrast to the vigorous motion, which travelers read as a lack of control, of precontact hulas, the new version emphasized grace, not power. Recounting his own hula-viewing experience, Twain marvels at the "perfect concert" of motion between all body parts, finding it "difficult to believe" that hula performers "were not moved in a body by some exquisite piece of mechanism" (476–77). If the classic hula threatened to incite energy, this version of the hula sought to pacify it. The vigorous motion so unfamiliar to American observers as a feature of dance and performance is replaced with the sensibilities of Western dance, in which the performers remain in step with each other.

The de-eroticized version of the hula came as a distinct relief to Twain's contemporary, the Victorian lady traveler Isabella Bird, who, like Twain, visited Hawaii in the 1870s. Bird ironically regarded Hawaiian dancers as having perfected European dance modes. Indirectly invoking the "lascivious" nature of precontact hula, Bird asserts in *The Hawaiian Archipelago* (1875) that "Hawaiians are a dancing people, and will dance or else indulge in less innocent pastimes." Whereas before the dance controlled the Hawaiians, leading them astray, now the dance acts as a means of keeping them in check. Instead of the hula, "the Sisters have taught them various English dances, and I," Bird gushes, "never saw anything prettier or more graceful than their style of dancing" (254). For Bird, these dances are the perfect synthesis of European formality and Hawaiian gracefulness. As Bird's enthusiastic endorsement of Hawaiian dancing indicates, the hula,[25] emptied of its "lascivious" content, had become just what the tourist ordered: a sight to see, safe even for a "lady traveller." Bird can watch the hula without feeling that she is part of it.

3

Constance Gordon-Cumming's Fijian Cannibal Fork

Western accounts of the hula allowed the reader to take a step back from indigenous experience and to take comfort in the fact that whatever darker meanings might reside in that practice could be easily controlled. Readers of *Sandwich Island Notes* or Isabella Bird's *The Hawaiian Archipelago* would have been in for a surprise had they gone to pick up a copy of Constance Gordon-Cumming's *At Home in Fiji* (1881). Reviewing the new book, the *Athenæum* warned that "cultivated and devout people will suffer a rude shock at the first sight of Miss Gordon Cumming's book, with its great 'cannibal fork' facing them on the cover."[1] It could have been worse. Tantalizing her readers in a prefatory note, Gordon-Cumming explains that some chiefs "had forks eighteen inches long, of dark polished wood, with handles richly carved." The Fijian cannibal fork represented on her volume's slender cover, she counsels, is but a "fair average specimen," implying that she had seen far more shocking versions of the implement (preface).

The book's cover (figure 3.1), combined with Gordon-Cumming's prefatory note on its "cannibal fork," seeks to authenticate Western tales of supposed Fijian savagery. Unlike sailors' yarns and even the slanted accounts of missionaries, the cannibal fork is a historical artifact. Or so it would seem, at least. But this image and its accompanying note are as much a crafted piece of storytelling as a sailor's yarn. Gordon-Cumming calls attention to the authenticity of her own cannibal fork, even as she notes its own limitations, its status as a mere "fair average specimen." She insists that this is not an imaginative illustration but rather a "facsimile" of an actual cannibal fork, presumably one in her possession. It is not "pictured" or "depicted" on the cover but rather "represented," the way one would document an exhibit in a museum. Obviously, Gordon-Cumming's strenuously scientific language aims to authenticate the

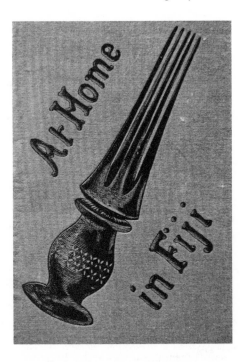

Figure 3.1. Front cover of Constance Gordon-Cumming's *At Home in Fiji.*

cannibal fork and, in turn, to authenticate her own travels. Yet, these words also call attention to the *merely* representative nature of this cannibal fork. Like René Magritte's pipe, *ceci n'est pas une fourche cannibale.*

In choosing this particular "representation," Gordon-Cumming's cannibal fork plays on the boundary between familiar and exotic. The Fijian cannibal fork—sometimes also dubbed by Westerners as a flesh-eating fork—both fascinated and horrified nineteenth-century travelers. Gordon-Cumming succinctly sums up the Western perception of the cannibal fork as being "used exclusively for human flesh, this being the only meat that might not be touched with the fingers" (102). The cannibal fork presented on Gordon-Cumming's cover is familiar in form but exotic in purpose. At first glance, the base of this cannibal fork almost looks like the base of a candlestick. Even the lower portions of the prongs are so compact as to reinforce this impression. It is not until we move our eyes upward, tracing the prongs, that the object takes shape as a fork. This elongation of the prongs serves as a dramatically legible semiotic marker. The tines at once mark the fork as familiar (a fork) to Gordon-Cumming's audience and foreign (but not like *our* forks). Gordon-Cumming's cannibal fork is defined by these elongated prongs, as if to say: with a fork like this, one can really dig in. In other words, the fork on the cover is legible: it tells a story to its readers. Westerners who never witnessed cannibalism could easily imagine this tool being used to tear into human flesh, just as they used their own—less imposing—forks to tear the flesh of the animals at their own dinner tables. The reader has to do minimal imaginative work to conceive of the purpose of the fork; they must merely extend their understanding of the object to a grotesque level. What might otherwise look like a familiar household fork becomes something grotesque because of the cannibal fork's elongated tines. This elongation thus serves to distance Gordon-Cumming's readers from their own association with this fork. Unlike European forks, the Fijian fork, they imagined, was "savage," an instrument of degeneracy rather than civilization.

Fittingly, the title of Gordon-Cumming's narrative frames the object on its cover. Like the fork itself, the title of Gordon-Cumming's book is part home, part Fiji. The cannibal fork cuts through the volume's title, leaving the words "At Home" curiously perched atop it, as the second half of the title, "in Fiji," is almost tucked away below. In this way, the words "At Home" seem to render the cannibal fork a harmless object; it is domesticated. By displaying the Fijian cannibal fork on the cover of her book, Gordon-Cumming makes the once-threatening exotic object come across as little more than the European domestic tool that it resembles. Nicholas Thomas argues that the juxtaposition between title and object represents the "paradox" at the core of Gordon-Cumming's work: that she "accentuate[s] both the negative and positive dimensions of her story." For Thomas, the cannibal fork is portrayed as a "horrifying variant upon a harmless domestic implement and almost an emblem of Fiji at the time" ("Quite Alone in a Mountain Village" 293). While the domestic connection between household forks and cannibal forks is important, it seems to me that this construction should be reversed: the title serves to domesticate the object more than the object exoticizes the title. The cannibal fork is indeed a Western "emblem of Fiji at the time," but the title, combined with the fork being put on display, renders it *merely* an emblem, depriving it of its former fear-instilling potency. In other words, Gordon-Cumming's title takes the bite out of the cannibal fork.

The cannibal fork, as Gordon-Cumming represents it, is an ideal Western marker of Pacific authenticity because of its ability to be repossessed, both literally and symbolically. In contrast to unwieldy tribal clubs and spears—likewise symbols of savagery, in the minds of Europeans—the fork is compact and easy to transport, to bring home. And where distinct Fijian objects like *tabua* (necklaces made from sperm whale's teeth) and ceremonial *yaqona* bowls were portable, their cultural significance did not easily translate. Decorative hair combs and Fijian mourning dresses (*liku*) were familiar, but too much so to be exotic. As Gordon-Cumming's personal sketches reveal, all of these other Fijian objects drew her attention as well, but it was the cannibal fork that was chosen to act as the first sight of Fiji for Gordon-Cumming's readers. Its literal dimensions enable it to fit to scale on the book's cover, and it tells a cultural narrative that is at once easily accessible and appropriately distant. Put into conversation with the authentic cultural markers of the previous chapters, the cannibal fork is ideal as well. Where the tattoo (see chapter 1) is inscrutable, the cannibal fork is legible; where the hula (see chapter 2) is hidden and eludes representation, the cannibal fork is portable and recognizable.

But while nineteenth-century writers often regarded the cannibal fork as the most objective evidence of Fijian cannibalism, I argue that it in fact functions as a narrative tool rather than an ethnographic object. More than any other Pacific "curiosity," the cannibal fork highlights the relationship between objects and stories in Pacific travel narratives. In framing the cannibal fork as authentic, late-nineteenth-century Anglophone writers do not represent authentic Fijian culture but rather produce an Anglicized version of it. That is to say, the cannibal fork (and the stories that form around it) is part of a Western narrative rather than of Fijian history. Thus, when telling the story of the "cannibal fork," and the supposed "savagery" it reveals, I tell the story of a Western invention, focusing primarily on the ways Western travelers projected their own ideas onto the object.

Far from being an authentic marker of Fijian cannibalism, the cannibal fork is surrounded by fiction and narrativization: stories coalesce around it. In support of this claim, the second half of this chapter will put the cannibal fork into conversation with what Gannath Obeyesekere terms "cannibal talk": the fictionalized tales produced through Anglophone and Oceanian accounts of cannibalism that crystallized into "fact" for the Victorian-era travel writers. The cannibal fork, I will argue, mobilizes this type of cannibal talk, functioning as a narrative accoutrement.

Representations of cannibalism—seen in both the cannibal fork (the object) and "cannibal talk" (the discourse)—demonstrate the way that late-nineteenth-century travel writers sought to retain and reproduce what they saw as an authentic precolonial Fijian identity.

In making this argument, I focus particularly on Gordon-Cumming's *At Home in Fiji* for how her narrative brings to the forefront this connection between the object and discourse of cannibalism. While scholars—both anthropological and literary—have noted how Western discourses of cannibalism sought to validate the need for missionary and colonial conversion, the cannibal fork, as both object and symbol, has mostly gone unexamined. To understand the discourse of cannibalism, we must understand the object that informs that discourse. Gordon-Cumming's engagement with the cannibal fork is both exemplary and representative. As much as the cannibal fork on her book's cover seeks to authenticate assumptions of Fijian savagery, it also acts as a way of authenticating her own travels. Unlike the female writers in Fiji who came before her, Gordon-Cumming traveled to Fiji for her own pleasure. It is not "every lady," as she reminds her readers throughout, who could enjoy such an experience (153). Indeed, in putting the cannibal fork on display in her cover, Gordon-Cumming gestures toward the authenticity of her experience. Collecting curiosities like the cannibal fork, Nicholas Thomas argues in *Entangled Objects*, was "not so much about what could be said or done with the specimens collected but the way the collected material attested to the fact of having visited remote places and observed novel phenomena" (141). Thus, the cannibal fork does not so much attest to Fijian savagery as it corroborates Gordon-Cumming's place within this "savage" world.

In her seminal *Victorian Lady Travellers*, Dorothy Middleton set a precedent for conceiving of Gordon-Cumming's writing as dull compared to her contemporary Isabella Bird, quipping that Gordon-Cumming's books are "alas, unreadable, so informative are they" (5). Claudia Knapman, following Middleton's lead, maintains that Gordon-Cumming merely "belonged to a large band of Victorian women . . . with high intellectual and moral standards . . . who wrote, botanised, missionised and above all, collected information as a duty" (98). Far from being just a dutiful collector, Gordon-Cumming's engagement with Fijian culture is complex and revealing. Her representations of Fijian cannibalism can never be easily defined as purely colonially motivated savagism or overinflated literary Romanticization. In this way, Gordon-Cumming's work marks an important moment in the history of Pacific travel narratives: she is simultaneously content with colonial achievement ("At Home") and wistful to be in a more authentic Fiji. The cannibal fork offered her the best of both worlds.

A Curious History: Collecting the Cannibal Fork

Before considering the cannibal fork as a marker of authenticity, it is important to understand its status within the broader context of Pacific curiosities. Ethnographic objects have a long history within narratives of Pacific travel, beginning with Captain James Cook's landmark voyages between 1778 and 1781. These voyages brought back to Britain more than two thousand ethnographic objects, including Hawaiian wooden images, Tahitian mourning dresses, and Tongan tattooing needles. This collection of artifacts was vast and unique—and also unprecedented. At the time of Cook's voyages, the ethnographic object was generally regarded as trivial. As Adrienne Kaeppler puts it in *"Artificial Curiosities,"* ethnographic specimens were "for the most part unimportant appendages to the great collections of specimens of natural history, which for centuries had been sought to adorn the 'cabinets of curiosities' of the leisured" (37). By the mid-nineteenth century, however, ethnographic objects had supplanted natural history specimens as the primary curiosity.

Unlike natural history specimens, these "artificial curiosities" were both easily obtained and simple to preserve. One needed no expertise to acquire and maintain these objects, and, as Kaeppler notes, Oceanians were not shy about gifting cultural possessions to visitors.

In early-nineteenth-century Fijian culture, the primary object of exchange was fittingly something of a cross between the natural history specimen and the ethnographic object: sperm whale's teeth (tabua). For native Fijians, these were not only a valuable commodity but also an ornamental item, meticulously polished and strung through coconut fiber to form necklaces. Tabua were an integral part of Fijian social exchange, fulfilling functions ranging from validating marriages to settling debts.[2] But these sperm whale's teeth would also become an important part of a much larger cross-cultural exchange. Early settlers such as David Whippy, Charlie Savage, and William Cary infamously introduced the musket into Fiji, significantly altering Fijian warfare and making their services a valuable commodity. In exchange for such services, these beachcombers were often paid with tabua. While settlers were able to appreciate the general aesthetic and cultural value of these objects, they could not understand—or even conceptualize—their value within Fijian culture. "Western ontological categories," Edward D. Melillo points out, were "inadequate . . . for understanding the symbolic depth of Fijian exchanges. Tabua were not reducible to currency; they represent a vast array of social interactions across human and non-human realms" (461). Their significance, in other words, was not portable; their meaning did not translate. To Westerners, these objects were curious, to be sure, but nothing more—for what story is there to tell about an object so culturally removed? In contrast, the cannibal fork was not only literally portable but ontologically portable as well: Westerners had no trouble imagining the cannibal fork's meaning and purpose.

However, Westerners' understanding of the cannibal fork was just that: imaginative. Nicholas Thomas sees this impulse as reflective of a distinctly nineteenth-century relationship to the Oceanian ethnographic object. Marking a shift between eighteenth- and nineteenth-century conceptions of Oceanian objects, Thomas argues that representations of the former period "implied a relationship between exotic object and knowing subject that was profoundly hermeneutic—a thing could not be considered a curiosity without reference to the knower's intellectual and spiritual desire." In other words, one could not properly take possession of a cultural object without also understanding its cultural story. Eighteenth-century Oceanic objects were curious in that they inspired a desire to know more. But Thomas argues in "Objects of Knowledge" that as interest in Oceanian objects grew, the willingness to understand Oceania's cultural history dissipated. For Thomas, this loss of cross-cultural generosity can be seen in the way nineteenth-century accounts "tended to objectify tribal specimens as expressions of a savage condition" (106). In the nineteenth century, objects were curious merely because of their novelty—they became "curiosities." As Thomas conceptualizes it, then, nineteenth-century narratives demonstrate how the connection between person and object becomes subsumed by the desire for a symbol of exoticism more generally. Or, to return to Greg Dening's language, "the beach," that space of risk and exchange, gets washed over.

For Gordon-Cumming, the cannibal fork is so far removed from the space of cultural exchange that she gets one not from a "former cannibal" but rather from her friend and curiosity-trading partner Baron Anatole von Hügel. Von Hügel, an aristocrat of mixed Austrian and Scottish descent, assembled an extensive collection of Fijian curiosities during his two and a half years in Fiji. In part because of both his vast collection and his intimate knowledge of those artifacts, von Hügel would later become the first curator of the University of Cambridge Museum of Archeology and Anthropology. Von Hügel's collection was born out of a desire to redress the differently flawed types of collecting done by missionaries and settlers. Nicholas Thomas notes in *Entangled Objects* that unlike missionaries who "grounded 'idols' and other things in narratives of social change," von Hügel "had no interest in singularizing the things he collected" (169). But as Thomas further argues in "Von Hügel's Curiosity," von Hügel also reacted against "such souveniring as planters typically engaged in— their dining rooms usually featured a few clubs or implements that stood as proof of the extreme savagery of the local people" (300). Von Hügel sought to understand these objects in terms of how they represented parts of the complex fabric of Fijian culture. However, this well-meaning desire was incidentally the motivating force behind the rise of the curiosity industry in Fiji. As von Hügel puts it, "curiosity of this kind [was] contagious," inspiring newly appointed Fijian governor Arthur Gordon and his entourage, which included Gordon-Cumming, to assemble their own collections. From here, "the trade in 'curios,'" von Hügel writes in an 1875 journal entry, became "so flourishing that one small business . . . expanded its premises, and blossomed forth as a 'curiosity shop' of fashionable resort." And, in the few months after von Hügel began collecting, "the price of 'curios' also rose tenfold" (105).

In the context of this commercialization of curios, no object was more sought after than the cannibal fork. Where tribal specimens like clubs and spears often served as generic—and not altogether culturally distinct— signifiers of Pacific savagery, the cannibal fork was distinct and culturally specific. Fiji was not the only "cannibal culture," but it was the only one wherein that cultural act could be so compactly represented by a single object. And if Pacific Islanders were typically generous about gifting their possessions to

Western travelers, the cannibal fork was an exception. Early in his stay, von Hügel laments that he has been able to procure just one cannibal fork during his first two months of collecting. It was not for lack of effort, though. In a June 1875 journal entry, von Hügel writes, "The people, though quite willing in general to give information concerning any of their possessions, show great reluctance to speak of these forks: to any questions with regard to them a native will either turn an entirely deaf ear or shrug his shoulders and say in a baffling, almost interrogative manner, 'Oh yes, Sir, a fork!'" (36). One could read this reticence in two different ways. On the one hand, the Fijian shoulder shrugging might reflect genuine confusion. In this reading, the "interrogative" "yes, Sir, a fork" would mean "yes, it's a fork—what's the big deal?" On the other hand, we might read this reluctance as performative. From this perspective, "yes, Sir, a fork" reads as evasive, insisting that Westerners are mistaken in assuming the object to be anything more than a simple fork: "Move along, nothing to see here." Read this way, this performative reticence is about not letting outsiders in on a cultural secret. This second interpretation seems to be corroborated by a similar account from Berthold Carl Seemann, a German-born botanist turned British government naturalist. Seemann, in his 1861 government mission account *Viti*, notes that "there was the greatest reluc-tance to part with [cannibal forks], even for a handsome equivalent, and when parted with displaying them was objected to." Initially, Seemann assumes that their dismay at parting with these items is because they are essentially heirlooms and to trade away a family heirloom would be disgraceful. Such an interpretation, however, is dispelled when Seemann shows his fork to "parties who could know nothing of the transactions." Seemann finds them equally horrified, going so far as to suggest that his "handling [cannibal forks] seemed to give them as much pain as if I had gone into a Christian church and used the chalice for drinking water" (182).

Seemann's analogy identifies the cannibal fork as occupying a sacred role in Fijian culture. Seeing an outsider handle it, oblivious to its cultural function, is akin to sacrilege: their cannibal fork is no more a curiosity than a Christian chalice is a drinking basin. Giving away a cannibal fork, as Seemann interprets it, is thus not merely a personal loss but a cultural loss. If we assume Seemann's interpretation is credible,[3] one can see why the Fijians von Hügel encountered some fifteen years later would have pleaded ignorance. Transferred into the hands of an outsider, the cannibal fork is divested of its cultural value—it becomes a curiosity for the sake of a curiosity.

The cannibal fork that Gordon-Cumming receives from von Hügel is presented in just such terms. Gordon-Cumming flippantly describes it as a "funny old cannibal fork" (242–43). She never elaborates on what makes this particular fork "funny" rather than, say, "horrifying"—a term that she applies, every so often, to Fijian cannibalism. In describing the fork as "funny" (likely meaning curious rather than comical) and "old," Gordon-Cumming frames the fork in the same way that the book's cover does: an interesting, and ultimately harmless, symbol of Fijian culture. Indeed, the coupled adjectival phrase "funny old" works as a term of endearment. For Gordon-Cumming, then, the cannibal fork is a curiosity because it is "interesting from novelty or strangeness" (as the *Oxford English Dictionary* defines it). In this sense of the term, curiosity both starts and stops with strangeness. Von Hügel, in a corresponding journal entry, writes that, upon receiving the cannibal fork, Gordon-Cumming's "delight was visible in sundry jumps before we had to set sail again" (436). The image of a proper Victorian lady leaping joyfully, cannibal fork in hand, offers a fitting counter-figure to the "shocking" cannibal fork on the cover of *At Home in Fiji*. Obtaining the fork seems to mean more to Gordon-Cumming than that fork itself. In this way, Gordon-Cumming's reaction speaks to the domestication of the cannibal fork: this once wildly unpredictable artifact is rendered harmless. It becomes an item to collect rather than something to reflect on.

Fijians capitalized on the popularity of the cannibal fork among Western travelers like Gordon-Cumming. Why give away the real thing when you could make new versions, versions designed not for any sacred Fijian practice but instead manufactured for rapacious Western collectors? In 1901, James Edge Partington, writing for the Royal Anthropological Institute of Britain, notes that "as the number of collectors of ethnographical specimens increases (as it is evident that it does, to anyone who attends the sale-rooms) so also does the supply of objects." This increased demand, Partington suggests, has led to a proliferation of forgeries. Partington cites Basil Thomson, a British colonial administrator in Fiji in the early 1890s, who writes about stumbling upon an old house with "rows and rows of clubs and spears suspended from the roof." Seeing so many Fijian weapons in one place, Thomson assumes he has discovered a plot against the British government. However, after talking with the "aged crone" inside, Thomson learns that these weapons are being made not for warfare but for "the white tourists in Suva." Fijian weapons were a popular choice for tourists, but the "most common forgery," Thomson insists, "is the cannibal fork." In *The Fijians, A Study of the Decay of a Culture* (1903), Thomson writes that the "genuine forks have all been removed from the country, and those offered for sale in the group are forgeries" (109).[4] Not cannibal forks, but *representations* of cannibal forks.

Representing the Cannibal Fork

Yet even before these forgeries, the cannibal fork was already a product of the European imagination, starting with its very name. The prefatory note (figure 3.2) to Gordon-Cumming's *At Home in Fiji* reads much like a museum label,

NOTE.—CANNIBAL FORK.

THE Cannibal Fork represented on the binding of this book is a facsimile of a fair average specimen. Some of the chiefs had forks eighteen inches long, of dark polished wood, with handles richly carved.

With reference to the vegetables specially reserved for cannibal feasts, Dr Seemann describes the Boro dina (*Solanum anthropophagorum*) as a bushy shrub, seldom higher than six feet, with a dark glossy foliage, and berries of the shape and colour of tomatoes. This fruit has a faint aromatic smell, and is occasionally prepared like tomato-sauce. The leaves of this plant, and also of two middle-sized trees (the Mala wathi, *Trophis anthropophagorum*, and the Tudano, *Omalanthus pedicellatus*), were wrapped round the *bokola*, and baked with it on heated stones.

Figure 3.2. Frontmatter note to Constance Gordon-Cumming's *At Home in Fiji*.

with the words of the title, "CANNIBAL FORK," printed in all caps and bold lettering. This stark, unadorned note offers a contrast to the book's cover, with its highly stylized font and ornate cannibal fork, marking a clear tonal shift. If the cover conjures the cannibal fork as whimsical, the prefatory note conveys a sense of authenticity. This note seeks to create context for the object on display; it serves to offer more objective identification of the fork than the image on the cover. But the note, too, is a narrative construction, an inevitable fact in the context of representation. As James Clifford argues in "On Collecting Art and Culture," "The objective world is given, not produced, and thus historical relations of power in the work of acquisition are occulted. The *making* of meaning in museum classification and display is mystified as adequate *representation*" (220). Gordon-Cumming's note seeks to "make meaning" of the cannibal fork for her readers, but this is mere representation. Instead, museum display and classification, rather than being objective, is a way of narrativizing the world. Gordon-Cumming's note thus tells a story, even as it purports to provide an objective and culturally neutral description of the cannibal fork.

Even the translation "cannibal fork" itself can be read as narratively motivated. What European travelers called the cannibal fork Fijians referred
to as iculanibokola. The original Fijian word was a complex compound. The
"i" functions as possessive preposition; "cula" as a verb meaning "to pierce";
"ni" designating either possession or an honorific singular. The final portion,
"bokola," is more complicated. Arthur Capell,[5] a Sydney-born linguist commissioned by the British government to compile *A New Fijian Dictionary*
(1941), tersely defines it as many nineteenth-century writers did: "the dead
body of an enemy, etc., to be eaten" (14). Indeed, Capell, in listing sources,
acknowledges mostly accounts of, and correspondence with, European missionaries in Fiji: Reverend David Hazelwood, who compiled the first Fijian-
English dictionary ninety years earlier; the notes of Wesleyan missionary
Reverend Frederick Langham, and so on. Capell also glancingly thanks indigenous Fijians "who have shown a keen interest and afforded willing help
on the correct reading of their language" (vi). However, Fijians' understanding of certain words, too, would inevitably be inflected by missionary contact.
Capell's dictionary embodies, then, the accumulated knowledge of the entire
missionary era of translation. His definition of bokola is thus based on years
of missionary tradition. Of course, there is—as always—something lost in
translation. But it would be a mistake to assume that these losses in translation are passive. In fact, such losses in translation often have as much to say
about cultural projections and differences as they do about linguistic variances.

In this case, trying to translate the word is also an attempt to make sense
of the object, to understand it through one's own cultural lens. Explaining the
story behind the word, Gordon-Cumming writes that the cannibal fork was
"used exclusively for human flesh, this being the only meat that might not
be touched with the fingers" (102). This explanation builds on a substantial
tradition. The missionary Thomas Williams, with whom Gordon-Cumming
later became acquainted, provides if not the first use of this translation, then
at least the most circulated one. Williams may not have coined the translation,
but he certainly helped to crystallize it. In *Fiji and the Fijians* (1858), a comprehensive history of Fiji during the early years of missionary contact, Williams defines "*bakolo*"[6] bluntly as "dead body designed for eating" (177). Describing bokola in relation to the cannibal fork, he adds that "human flesh is
cooked and dishes or forks used in eating it are strictly *tabu* for any other purpose. The cannibal fork seems to be used for taking up morsels of flesh when
cooked as a hash" (180). Colonel W. J. Smythe, an American government of-
ficial writing roughly eight years later, likewise maintains in *Ten Months in the
Fiji Islands* that "human flesh is always eaten with forks, in this respect dif-
fering from ordinary food, which is simply taken with the fingers." He adds,
for good measure, that "whereas the Fijians reject meat if at all tainted, they

will eat human flesh in an advanced stage of decomposition" (73). This second assertion could very easily be a paraphrase of Thomas Williams's claim that "while the Fijian turns with disgust from pork, or his favourite fish, if at all tainted, he will eat *bakolo* [human flesh] when fast approaching putrescence" (180). The close resemblance across these Western accounts of Fiji suggests a sort of coauthoring: a cultural translation of the cannibal fork rather than a purely linguistic one. The common ground occupied by all these translations and definitions is the narrative of the cannibal fork (and, by extension cannibalism) as exceptional, distinct from all other modes of consumption. It is translated as "the cannibal fork" because it is specially reserved for this most savage of practices.

Except that it was not. Unsurprisingly, the long-standing translation "bokola," finally solidified in Capell's *A New Fijian Dictionary*, was not entirely accurate. The term "cannibal fork," too, then, as later scholars of Fiji have shown, was based on a misreading. A. M. Hocart, in his 1952 anthropological study *The Northern States of Fiji*, describes the term as a "misnomer." He writes that it was not simply *tabu* to touch human meat; it was *tabu* to touch food of any kind (53n1). Fergus Clunie, writing in his 1986 Fiji Museum Catalogue *Yalo i Viti*, however, remarks that Hocart's clarification did little to alter the translation. "It should have—but of course has not—been laid to rest," he laments. Amplifying the misnomer, he explains that "wooden forks of [this] type were used when eating human flesh, but not because the flesh itself— the meat of a denigrated, defeated enemy—was sanctified." Rather, he clarifies, it was considered *tabu* for chiefs and priests to touch *any* food at all. Instead, they either used this fork or had an attendant serve them the meat directly into their mouths (190). For indigenous Fijians, then, the word was wrapped in various layers of adjacent cultural meanings. The translation "cannibal fork" consolidated those meanings into one easily interpretable term. In doing so, the term lost specificity and nuance, as for Fijians this tool was so connected to the individual that many had their own proper names. Thomas Williams cites one fork in particular named "*Udroudro*," meaning, according to Williams, "a small person or thing that bears a great burden." But Williams also adds a bit of narrative embellishment to his translation, positing that this name "indicate[s] the quantity of human flesh borne on its prongs" (181).

Williams's reference to this proper name is rare, especially toward the latter half of the nineteenth century, when the translation "cannibal fork" had almost entirely replaced the original iculunibokola.[7] This might not seem strange given the audience of these writers, but leaving distinct indigenous words untranslated, because there were no cultural equivalents for them, was otherwise a fairly common practice. Thus, a word like "*tabu*" was glossed, but thereafter remained untranslated, because it could only be understood in this cultural context. "*Bokola*," too, was often only glossed, as Gordon-Cumming does parenthetically: "i.e., human bodies." It is odd, then, that this willingness to defer to the indigenous word does not extend to the compound word iculunibokola.

Providing neither the Fijian word iculunibokola nor the proper name, Gordon-Cumming writes of a cannibal fork from the Na Vatu region of Fiji, vaguely echoing Williams, that it "had a distinctive name, descriptive of the enormous work done by so small a thing" (251). Similarly, Colonel W. J. Smythe describes a Namusi priest's cannibal fork as being known "far and wide by its proper name" (73). These vague references to a "proper name" make it unclear whether they refer to a proper name like Williams's *Udroudro* or whether that proper name is the iculunibokola, the name they *im*properly translate as cannibal fork. In either respect, to keep this word in its untranslated form would mean losing the clarity of narrative; its purpose (and its savagery) would not be as immediately legible to Western audiences. This translation, then, allows the object to act as the primary marker for—and primary authentic evidence of—the savagery of Fijian culture. In representing the object through the translation "cannibal fork," these authors isolate the fork's purpose: it is a fork used specifically (and only) for cannibalism.

This misinterpretation, Nicholas Thomas contends, was hardly incidental. Imagining the cannibal fork as immediately and tangibly connected to the practice of cannibalism "provided objects which could be appropriated and handled, which did not merely represent cannibalism but which had actually been used to consume human flesh" (165). The cannibal fork, then, gives form to the abstract. It's easy to read this as a savagizing impulse, but it is also a domesticating one. Perhaps these impulses are more similar than different. Much like the cover of *At Home in Fiji*, this translation domesticates what would otherwise be a wildly unpredictable and fundamentally unreadable artifact. To return to the *At Home in Fiji*'s cover and Gordon-Cumming's "funny old cannibal fork," the translation takes the bite out of the fork. The translation turns the iculunibokola into a self-referential marker of savagery, eliding the cultural complexity of the object. It is this combination of object and translation that gives form to this otherwise unclaimable cultural practice: cannibalism.

In this way, the cannibal fork is an ideal version of what Celia Lury refers to as the "traveller's object." Distinguishing traveler's objects from tourist's objects, Lury writes in "The Objects of Travel" that traveler's objects' "ability to travel well is integrally linked to their ability to signify their meaning immanently, most commonly by an indexical reference to their 'original' dwelling" (78). These objects are thus viewed as the most authentic types of travel souvenirs. The cannibal fork "travels well" because its meaning is instantly legible and it serves to signify the most recognizable aspect of Fijian culture—at least in the minds of Westerners. The cannibal fork is metonymic of Fijian culture, but it is also the real thing. To apply Lury's formulation, "place and culture are bound together in a smooth movement through space as a consequence of practices of symbolic binding or interpretation that make themselves invisible" (78). Gordon-Cumming makes this "symbolic binding" of place and culture literal by representing the cannibal fork on, as she puts it, the "binding" of her book. This binding allows the fork to travel to Gordon-Cumming's Western audiences, and her readers become cocollectors.

Just as the prefatory note functions as a museum abstract, the cover frames the cannibal fork as a piece of art. In her analysis of modern Western displays of authentic primitive art, Shelly Errington notes in *The Death of Authentic Primitive Art and Other Tales of Progress*, "art was invented simultaneously with collecting, and the two are inconceivable without each other" (79). Errington points out that size is often a determining factor in what constitutes art. "Too small," she writes, "and the item becomes insignificant. Too large, and it becomes costly to transport and difficult to display. . . . To become art, these portable objects must be displayed, and to be displayed, they must be accommodated in a suitable space" (79). The cannibal fork lends itself to such framing because of its size and portability.

Gordon-Cumming's "fair average specimen" is perfectly housed by the book's cover, allowing it to be displayed to scale. It is this to-scale display that leads Gordon-Cumming to suggest that the cannibal fork on the cover is authentic: a "facsimile" rather than an imitation; a "specimen" rather than an illustration; a "represent[ation]" and not a re-imagining. Of course, these last two qualities are less contrastive than Gordon-Cumming seems to think, for *re*presentation is always an act of framing. As Errington puts it, "art by appropriation . . . is not born in a frame. . . . It becomes art by being framed" (84). But this framing extends beyond just the literal/representative. It is also an imaginative framing. To rearticulate Errington's framework: if it is too familiar, the object becomes insignificant. Too exotic and the object becomes strange and difficult to conceptualize. The cultural narrative of the cannibal fork is just as portable as the object itself. At least, the cultural narrative presented by Gordon-Cumming and other Western travelers is.

Western depictions of the cannibal fork thus serve to produce a version of authenticity rather than to represent it. Gordon-Cumming's cannibal fork is not simply artistic accompaniment to her literary work. The cannibal fork on Gordon-Cumming's cover is as much narrative accoutrement as ethnographic object. For, the ethnographic object is, as Barbara Kirshenblatt-Gimlet argues, "created by ethnographers." They are, she continues, "not ethnographic because they were found in a Hungarian peasant household, Kwakiutil village, or Rajashtani market . . . but by virtue of the manner in which they were detached, for disciplines make their objects" (17–18). This way of thinking about the ethnographic object suggests that authenticity is a production—it is always made rather than simply discovered and represented.[8] But such thinking also reveals how deeply embedded narrative is into ethnography. In other words, the ethnographic object is never objective. So while the cannibal fork may be a genuine object, the narrative around it is a production.

We need not doubt the veracity or authenticity of the cannibal fork on Gordon-Cumming's cover to suggest that it functions more as a narrative reimagining than as an objective ethnographic representation. Gordon-Cumming's personal sketches indicate that she had a variety of cannibal forks to choose from (figure 3.3). With the equally exotic but less culturally portable tabua lurking overhead, Gordon-Cumming's cannibal forks occupy a variety of dimensions.[9] Most of her cannibal forks are either too short or too slender to come across as impressive. Three of the forks, however, offer different features from those present in the fork on *At Home in Fiji*'s cover. The fork atop features the dramatically elongated prongs; the two forks on the bottom right have the thick, ornate, and circular handles. The fork second

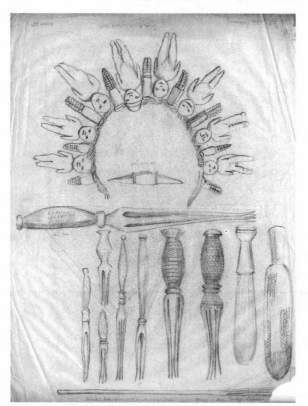

Figure 3.3. Objects from Fiji, including a necklace of human images carved from whale teeth, nine wooden forks, and two clubs. Sketch by Constance Gordon-Cumming. Courtesy of the Trustees of The British Museum.

 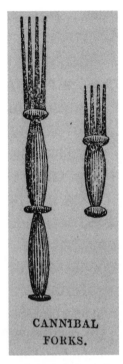

CANNIBAL
FORKS.

CANNIBAL
FORKS.

Figure 3.4. "Cannibal Forks,"
from Thomas Williams, *Fiji and
The Fijians* (1859).

to the right seems most likely to have been the model for the book's cover. It is a fitting choice: this fork features the elongated but recognizable prongs and the ornate design (though the cover fork's design is less extensive), and its dimensions are impressive but nonetheless contained. The cannibal fork on Gordon-Cumming's cover differs significantly from earlier models offered in Thomas Williams's *Fiji and the Fijians* (figure 3.4). Williams's illustrations demonstrate the range and variety of Fijian cannibal forks. Some forks have four prongs, while others have two or three; some have extensive and ornate (though undecorated) handles, while others are short or plain; some are easily recognizable as forks, while others seem more foreign. Yet, what remains consistent among Williams's samples are the general proportions between the base and the prongs. None of these samples feature the disparity between the handle and the prongs that we see in Gordon-Cumming's "fair average specimen." This is not to suggest that Gordon-Cumming's fork is "inauthentic."[10] Rather, the iculanibokola she chooses is the one that best tells a story, the one that can most easily translate to narrative. Its long tines, which, as the book's cover frames them, seem almost to extend interminably into the distance, signal a savage rapaciousness; the orbital handles and ornate designs convey both its ritualistic and artistic significance; and its familiar features exaggerated to an almost grotesque extent distinguish it from European forks.

FIJIAN FORKS AND EUROPEAN FORKS: RECOGNIZING CANNIBALISM

And yet, because of these differences, it is easy to lose sight of just how notable the similarities are. After all, the differences are apparent only because the object is so recognizable. These similarities to the European fork suggest that this production of authenticity is as much a reflection of Western culture as it is Fijian culture. The cannibal fork, with its blend of the familiar and the exotic, is as much a reflection of home as of abroad. As Terry Caesar has convincingly argued, "the writing of abroad is a writing of, and over, home" (149). For Caesar, "the traveler is always a figure framed, imperiled as soon as he [or she] goes abroad among reflections of others as well as self-reflections" (133). This way of considering travel is particularly interesting in the context of cannibalism. Framing cannibalism as a Western discourse, Peter Hulme argues in "The Cannibal Scene" that "the figure of the cannibal is a classic example of the way in which otherness is dependent on a sense of kinship denied, rather than on mere difference" (6). While Hulme's argument is focused on cannibalism in the broad sense, we can read the cannibal fork as an even more potent example of this claim. James Clifford suggests that "rather than grasping objects only as cultural signs and artistic icons, we can return to them . . . their lost status as fetishes—not specimens of a deviant or exotic 'fetishism' but *our own* fetishes" (229). The fork is, it's easy to forget, first and foremost, a marker of cultural similarity. Difference and otherness is derived only through narrativizing the fork's "savage" purpose.

That this similarity exists is rather remarkable, given that in the nineteenth century forks had only recently become popular European table tools. Bee Wilson, in *Consider the Fork*, notes that while the fork itself has a long history, this history is limited to kitchen forks, that is, forks used for the preparation of food (roasting forks and carving forks). The table fork, on the other hand, is a fairly recent invention. So, in the nineteenth century, the fork began to shift from a behind-the-scenes instrument of pure utility to being used as much for show as for purpose. Wilson reminds us, "eating with prongs is a novelty" (190). In the context of Fiji, it was a novelty shared. Sharing this novelty with supposed cannibals might well have been upsetting to missionaries and colonialists convinced of their own cultural moral superiority. Surely *their fork* was not the same as this savage instrument. After all, as Wilson writes, the Western fork emerged because it was "polite . . . less overtly violent than the knife, less babyish and messy than the spoon" (190).

But the iculanibokola, too, was a marker of refinement. This was perhaps the most vexing aspect of cannibalism for nineteenth-century travelers: within its own cultural framework, it was not a form of some imagined democratic savagery but instead a matter of "refinement" and nobility. In this way, the cannibal fork resonates with Marlow's exclamation in *Heart of Darkness* as he begins to better understand the African "cannibals" he lives and works among. "No, they were not inhuman," Marlow concedes (139). His concession, of course, is couched: "they are not inhuman" does not quite convey the same thing as "they are human." Marlow's linguistic use of double negation is visually paralleled in the cannibal fork, which, in its similarity to European forks, forces Western readers to concede "no, they were not uncivilized."

Gordon-Cumming makes this distinction in the second half of her prefatory note on "the vegetables specifically reserved for cannibal feasts." Citing Berthold Seemann's exhaustive study of Fijian plant life, *Flora Vitiensis*, Gordon-Cumming reiterates his description of one of these cannibalism-garnishing vegetables: "Bora Dina (*Solanum Anthropophagorum*)." Quoting Seemann, she writes that its berries are the "colour of tomatoes . . . and [it] is occasionally prepared like a tomato-sauce." Meanwhile, the leaves of the vegetable were wrapped around the meat and then baked on heated stones. Later in her narrative, Gordon-Cumming expands on the role of this vegetable, further connecting it to Western forms of fine dining. It is, she writes, "as essential an adjunct to *bokola* as mint-sauce is to lamb, or sage to goose" (251). Gordon-Cumming's comparisons to European-style meals speak to the surprisingly "civilized" nature of Fijian cannibalism. As her citation of Seemann suggests, Gordon-Cumming's description is not unique. In fact, Seemann pithily adds to his description of cannibal feasts that "salt is not forgotten" (176). While there are, of course, plenty of descriptions of Western descriptions of Fijian cannibalism as rapacious and undignified, there also seems to be an underlying recognition that the practice was equally defined by sophistication and civility. To be sure, there are moments during wartime where cannibalism is portrayed as taking on a much more savage dimension, but as a general practice, it is represented as much like European dining, with the finest forms reserved only for those of the highest class status.

"The Savour of Romance": Consuming Cannibalism

This desire to appropriate or, rather, to consume Fijian cannibal culture motivates Gordon-Cumming's journey to the island. Born into a wealthy Scottish family, Gordon-Cumming was one of the most prolific Victorian "lady travelers," penning narratives about her travels to Egypt, China, Hawaii, California, and more. *At Home in Fiji* was Gordon-Cumming's second major publication, but she was already a well-accomplished traveler by the time of its publication in 1881. That stated, even the well-traveled Gordon-Cumming thought Fiji the most unlikely of places for her to travel. Before her trip, her adventures were the talk of her upper-class social circle, as friends—or, as she terms them, her "aggravating acquaintances"—prodded her about where she might travel to next.

Having just returned from a half year's stay in Ceylon (now Sri Lanka) and not expecting to ever be able to travel to such a far-off land again, Gordon-Cumming would answer "Fiji," since this was "the most absurd answer that suggested itself to so foolish a question—a place known to me only as being somehow associated with a schoolboy song about the King of the Cannibal Islands" (10). An "absurd" answer, but also a perverse one, as Gordon-Cumming would well know.

Fiji had a deeply ingrained reputation as the most "savage" of Pacific islands,[11] and, as the title of Gordon-Cumming's sole frame of reference, "The King of the Cannibal Islands," suggests, the one most often associated with horrific tales of cannibalism.[12] Frustrated by the line of questioning from her "aggravating acquaintances"—likely, proper, upper-class women—Gordon-Cumming imagines herself in as inhospitable a place for a "lady" as she can think of. A brief look at the ballad that serves as her reference point provides a good sense of the perception of Fiji in the Victorian collective consciousness. "King of the Cannibal Islands" (1858) tells the story of a fictional Pacific Islands king, with the absurdly exoticized name Poonoowingkewang Flibeedee flobeedee-buskeebang, and his one hundred wives. The first fifty of his wives are roasted and eaten; the remaining fifty subsequently flee, only to be captured and have their heads cut off, while the King "laughed to see the fun." One can imagine, then, the rise Gordon-Cumming would have gotten out of these acquaintances in suggesting that she, a lady herself, would travel to Fiji.[13]

The irony of Gordon-Cumming's jest, to return to the book's cover, is that her Fiji is anything but the Fiji conjured up by this ballad. Gordon-Cumming's Fijian experience is safe, as she travels and makes her home with Sir Arthur Hamilton Gordon, the newly appointed governor of Fiji, his wife, and other friends—the "Fijian family," as Gordon-Cumming dubbed her party (11). This relative safety, Sara Mills argues in *Discourses of Difference*, was a constitutive feature of women's travel narratives, and the authors' emphasis on this subject served to suggest that "the colonised country is so much under British control that *even* women can be represented as travelling through it without the 'natives' daring to approach her" (22). However, Mills suggests that female travel writers still tended to avoid the topic of cannibalism, as "such knowledge would be 'indelicate' for a 'lady' traveller" (161).[14] Far from being too indelicate to discuss, cannibalism became an abiding topic of interest for Gordon-Cumming, despite the fact that she would never witness it firsthand. Throughout, Gordon-Cumming marvels at the incongruity between Fiji's cannibal history and her own peaceful experience. In one of many similar moments, Gordon-Cumming reflects that "it is very hard indeed to realise that the peaceful village on which I am now looking has really been the scene of such horrors as these, and that many of the gentle, kindly, people round me have actually taken part in them" (120). Later, as if sensing the judgment of her sister back home, she justifies her tales of cannibalism as her attempt to provide a "faint idea of the horrible scenes that formerly made up the simple incidents of daily life in this now quiet and lovely place" (198). Both of these passages suggest a contrast between place and people. Gordon-Cumming's reflections recall the travel narratives analyzed in chapter 2, in which the Hawaiian people are often regarded as almost undeserving of their beautiful surroundings. Now, however, the people of Fiji have been civilized, made to match their "quiet" environment. It is the Western traveler who feels he or she needs to earn the right to the landscape.

While all the members of Sir Arthur Gordon's retinue were interested in consuming Fiji's former cannibal culture, Gordon-Cumming stood out as perhaps the most curious. Alfred Maudslay, who served as Governor Gordon's private secretary, described Gordon-Cumming in *Life in the Pacific Fifty Years Ago* as a "very plain woman . . . very pushing when she wants something done, and yet one of the best-natured creatures in the world." Gordon-Cumming's unbridled enthusiasm and curiosity seems to have often made her the target of the group's chiding ridicule. Maudslay continues, "I am afraid we all tease the poor woman a good deal, but she does rise so beautifully, and besides is quite capable of taking care of herself" (85). The collector Baron Anatole von Hügel, who arrived in Fiji before Governor Gordon but later became part of Gordon's employ, provides many similar—and quite colorful—descriptions of Gordon-Cumming. Upon meeting Gordon-Cumming, he characterizes her as "certainly . . . a character—very tall, lanky, and pronounced ugly, though clever features; of exorbitant dress." This initial description seems characteristic of von Hügel's interactions with Gordon-Cumming throughout his time in Fiji. On the one hand, she is interesting and charming; on the other, she is off-putting. Put differently, she is worth getting to know if one can get past the more "pronounced ugly" aspects. One can often hear the condescension in von Hügel's journal entries on Gordon-Cumming, as in the following: "She came to lunch and expressed awful anxiety to see my collection etc. with, 'My, how, how nice, etc.' at intervals" (178). Despite her "bumptiousness" (322), Gordon-Cumming seemed to grow on von Hügel. Her enthusiasm would eventually become part of the routine of life in Fiji. On a particularly slow day, for example, von Hügel writes merely: "idle day; new house; books; pottery; Miss Gordon Cumming, etc." (296). But she never completely lost her strangeness. At other times, von Hügel would present her exuberance as incongruous and absurd: "I found Miss Gordon Cumming already disporting herself on the beach. In true character she ran along the sand waving her hands frantically and vociferating loudly, so that I thought something interesting had happened, but on landing . . . I found that it was only the exuberance of her spirits which was causing these antics" (436).

Even as von Hügel's descriptions are tinged with misogyny, he presents

Gordon-Cumming as an exceptional figure, given the standards of the time. Early in his acquaintance with Gordon-Cumming, von Hügel complains that "the lion killer [his nickname for Gordon-Cumming] nearly kills me with her loud jabber, for it is incessant and intended to be clever" (1xx). Later, he writes, "she is so different alone, all her corners and prickles disappearing and the goodliness of her sweet woman's soul coming out to perfection" (324). It is clear that von Hügel sees this more "modest" version of Gordon-Cumming as representing the proper womanly ideal. Von Hügel writes that he and Lady Gordon argued with Gordon-Cumming on the emancipation of women, with the latter two on the "conservative side and Miss Gordon Cumming on the other" (319). Her liberality had its limits, however. Both Maudslay and von Hügel critiqued her unwavering devotion to the local missionaries, particularly the prominent Wesleyan missionary Frederick Langham. Von Hügel enigmatically notes that he has heard of Langham's "'ways' (ivalavala)[15] with Miss Gordon Cumming" (434). Maudslay complains that "she travels about the country a good deal with the Missionaries, and is given not only to looking at things from their point of view, but from the ideas they have crammed her with" (85). Gordon-Cumming herself insists that the missionaries in Fiji "have shown superlative common sense in their method of dealing with native customs, discriminating between the innocent and the evil" (144). Yet on another occasion, she deplores "the unaccountable jealousy of the missionaries, and their marvellous influence with the people, which pervades all classes of white men, old residents and new-comers alike" (171). Gordon-Cumming's writing, much like her personality, presents this complex mix of liberality and conservatism, both adhering to and breaking the boundaries of the "lady's" role in colonial Fiji.

Gordon-Cumming's treatment of Fijian cannibalism is likewise difficult to pin down. While Fijian cannibalism was a source of great interest—despite scant evidence that it was indeed a widespread practice—in all early-to-mid-century accounts of Fiji, its treatment typically reflected one extreme position or the other. Missionaries, for instance, condemned Fijian cannibalism outright as savagery, while beachcombers often tended toward romanticization. This contrast is best exemplified by Mary Wallis, Gordon-Cumming's lady traveler predecessor in Fiji, and Herman Melville, whose semiautobiographical works borrowed from both written and oral beachcomber tradition.[16] Wallis traveled to Fiji alongside her husband, the American sea captain Benjamin Wallis, who figured prominently in the Fijian bêche de-mer trade. Though Mary Wallis was not directly involved with the missionary enterprise, her 1851 *Life in Feejee, or Five Years among the Cannibals* was endorsed by the famed Fijian Methodist missionary James Calvert. Wallis took this endorsement seriously, insisting that there is in Fiji "no romance, no poetry, but heathenism in its lowest state of degradation" (76). Likewise, Wallis was eager to dispel the notion of the romantic cannibal, maintaining that she "has never found a native, who . . . would say any thing in favor of their customs, but will usually say 'Yes, we are a foolish people, and our customs are foolish'" (155–56). Even Wallis's cannibals will not defend the practice.

Wallis's account may well be read as a reaction to beachcomber accounts, most pointedly, Herman Melville's *Typee* and *Omoo*, which were such sensations among the American reading public that copies of each made their way to Wallis during her time in Fiji. While Wallis praised Melville's poetic use of language, she critiqued his tendency toward romanticizing the Pacific, leading her to reflect that Melville "should never come to Feejee, for there would be some danger of his readers becoming cannibals." He would, she continues, "present the rites of heathenism and cannibalism in forms so attractive that [his readers] would be anxious to enjoy the delicate feasts" (364). In other words, Melville makes "savagery" so appealing that he could make even Fijian cannibalism—the worst of all savage South Seas practices—look good. Of course, Melville would do just that, providing the most famous apology for Fijian cannibalism in *Moby-Dick*, published the same year as Wallis's *Life in Fejee*. Melville's narrator Ishmael turns Wallis's missionary-informed critique on its head: his readers cannot "become cannibals" because they already are cannibals. Ishmael condemns self-satisfied upper-class critics of cannibalism (like Wallis), "who nailset geese to the ground and feastest on their bloated livers in thy paté-de-foie-gras." These critics, he suggests, are much worse than "the Fejee that salted down a lean missionary in his cellar against a coming famine" (326–27) "Who is not a cannibal?," Ishmael memorably concludes. Rather than making cannibalism appealing to his readers, Melville instead makes Western eating practices seem unappealing. For Melville, Fijian cannibalism cannot be seen merely as an instance of savage otherness. Fijian cannibalism serves, in this passage, as a means of interrogating Europeans' own unsavory desires.

Gordon-Cumming's descriptions of Fijian cannibalism are often a blend of Wallis's "lady"-like and missionary-endorsed condemnation of cannibalism and Melville's curiosity with cultural parallels. These similarities addressed by Melville seem to register for Gordon-Cumming in her narrative, leading her to reflect on consumptive practices at home. Yet, Gordon-Cumming often maintains the distanced tone and gendered response typical of Wallis. At one point, Gordon-Cumming, writing to her sister Nell about Fijian cannibalism, reflects on "the very ideal of a hideous nightmare." In this nightmare, she writes, each person will be visited, upon the day of resurrection, by "every animal whose flesh we have ever taken—from the chicken broth of our infancy to the present day—sheep and oxen." Gordon-Cumming goes on to list the great variety of animals one may have consumed, ranging from the everyday—rabbits, pheasants, and salmon, for instance—all the way to "whales and hippopotami, and other zoological curiosities." All these animals alike, Gordon-Cumming concludes, will demand their "pound of flesh" (250). This nightmare brings Fijian cannibalism home. The horror of cannibalism allows Gordon-Cumming to see the potential horror of all forms of carnivorous consumption. Gordon-Cumming's nightmare is framed biblically, by imagining a day of judgment. Further, Gordon-Cumming's Shakespearean allusion to "a pound of flesh" suggests equality: animal and human flesh are figured as the same thing. "Who is not a cannibal?," she seems to ask along with Melville.

But this moment of self-reflection is short-lived, as Gordon-Cumming deliberately seeks to put distance between cannibalism and European practices of consumption. The Europeans' nightmare is bad enough, Gordon-Cumming writes, but it must pale in comparison to "the horror of a similar vision in which the plaintiffs were mighty men of valour . . . claiming not a pound of flesh only, but their whole bodies!" (250). Gordon-Cumming shifts this narrative of commonality into a narrative of difference. But in so doing, she also reflects the impulse of Westerners to romanticize cannibalism, even as they condemn it. This impulse can be seen in Gordon-Cumming's poetically inflated language, which refers to cannibal victims as "mighty men of valour." Throughout her book, Gordon-Cumming seems eager to dwell on "the horror" of cannibalism. In fact, cannibalism as a witnessed ritual plays a rather insignificant—almost nonexistent, even—role in narratives like Gordon-Cumming's. Instead, these books present the Western travel narrative ritual of eagerly consuming *stories* of cannibalism. In this sense, the book's cover represents the text's only narrative instance of cannibalism.

In another striking example, Gordon-Cumming recounts the history of Bau, a small Fijian island known for its resistance to Christian missionaries and thus deemed particularly "savage," in graphic detail, seeming to relish the horror. She recounts that a "favourite phase of cold-blooded revenge and insult was to collect the bones of bodies thus eaten and reduce them to powder. Then, when peace was restored, and the tribes next feasted together, this nice ingredient was added to some favourite pudding." And then, learning of a particularly violent tribal war ten years earlier, Gordon-Cumming is shocked to find out that 260 people were killed and eaten—and they did not stop there: "They [then] proceeded to eat the pigs" (103). Gordon-Cumming's description paints Fijian cannibalism as simultaneously horrific and familiar. They desire "cold-blooded revenge," yet they have "favourite" types of meals, "nice ingredients," and their own version of "pudding." They are so rapacious as to feast on hundreds of bodies without being satiated, and yet they turn to a common and familiar source to quench their appetite: pigs.

More curious, though, is what follows her description of this horrific scene. No sooner has she finished decrying the horrors of cannibalism than she moves on to a description of her own Christmas party, a feast that includes a "roast pig on a wooden dish" and "puddings all the way from Nundiankar" (104). The pairing of these two passages, separated by no clear transition or shift in focus, is at the very least suggestive. Elements of Gordon-Cumming's cannibal horror story evocatively return in this passage: the pudding, a humiliating solvent for the bones of cannibal victims, is specially delivered from far away, leaving its "nice ingredients" a mystery; the pig, eaten in an act of rapacious cannibalism, arrives to Gordon-Cumming well presented on a wooden dish.

The juxtaposition of these scenes illustrates a deep connection between cannibalism (the ritualistic consumption of human bodies) and the traveler's consumption of tales of cannibalism (itself a ritual of Western travel to Fiji). Such a connection is also evident in Gordon-Cumming's prefatory remarks on her journey to Fiji. As with Wallis, Fiji is not just Fiji for Gordon-Cumming; it is "cannibal Feejee." While Cumming does not explicitly use this label, her introductory remarks continually frame Fiji's placeness as defined by cannibalism. She writes that "a cruise in the South Pacific has been one of the dreams of my life; and the idea of going actually to live for an indefinite period on isles where there are still a number of ferocious cannibals, has a *savour* of romance which you can imagine does not lack charm" (10, my emphasis). Gordon-Cumming's use of the word "savour" speaks to the metaphoric nature of Wallis's concern about Western readers "becoming cannibals." For to become a cannibal in this sense is to take pleasure in the idea of cannibalism, to "savour" the "romance" of danger real or imagined. Later, while exploring in the Navosa region of Fiji, Gordon-Cumming returns to this notion of the romance of cannibalism. "Half of the charm," she writes, "of wandering in these mountains is the knowledge that two years ago we should certainly have been eaten!" (72). There is a "charm," in other words, to being the consumer of cannibal culture rather than being consumed by it.

Despite its absence as witnessed practice, cannibalism continually informs Gordon-Cumming's narrative. Gordon-Cumming never observes cannibalism firsthand, but this does not stop her from providing an authentic account of Fijian cannibalism. Indeed, her approach to cannibalism is foregrounded in the cover of the text. Just as the cannibal fork cuts through the cover of the title, so, too, do Gordon-Cumming's stories of cannibalism cut through her epistolary narrative. These stories are as much catered to "home" as they are authentic accounts of "Fiji." At one point, Gordon-Cumming, as if anticipating her sister's criticism for broaching ladylike decorum, insists that she sends all these stories of cannibalism "just to give you a faint idea of the horrible scenes that formerly made up the simple incidents of daily life in this now quiet lovely place" (198). Such assertions lead Nicholas Thomas to sum up Gordon-Cumming's work as guided by the "droll, almost bizarre, motif" of being "'at home' among cannibals" ("Quite Alone in a Mountain Village" 293). But this summation misses precisely what is most "droll" and "bizarre" about Gordon-Cumming's narrative: it is only in her letters, not in real life, that Gordon-Cumming is ever "among cannibals." The romance of cannibalism pervades her narrative, even as it remains elusive in her own experience. *Tales* of cannibalism can be read as just as authentic as firsthand accounts.

"Cannibal Talk": Performing Cannibalism

Gordon-Cumming follows in a long tradition of storytelling about Fijian cannibalism, in which stories of cannibalism are taken for granted as authentic, factual eyewitness accounts. This type of storytelling is what Gannath Obeyesekere has defined as "cannibal talk." Cannibal talk, he argues, is a discourse created by Western travelers to the South Seas, one that does not prove the existence of Oceanian cannibalism but rather signifies a "Western obsession" with it (2).

Obeyesekere's *Cannibal Talk: The Man-Eating Myth and Human Sacrifice in the South Seas* (2005) builds on the groundbreaking work of William Arens's *The Man-Eating Myth* (1979). Arens attempted to show that there was no credible evidence to support the notion that cannibalism was widely practiced anywhere other than in the imaginations of Europeans. This argument set off a firestorm of debates among anthropologists, with Marshall Sahlins leveling the most fervent and sustained critiques of Arens and later Obeyesekere in publications such as "Culture as Protein and Profit," in which he argues that critical skepticism about cannibalism is nothing more than "positivist cant."[17] In a letter published by the *New York Review of Books* titled "Cannibalism: An Exchange," Sahlins went so far as to compare Arens to Holocaust deniers, accusing him of joining an emerging "pattern of enterprising social science journalism," whose goal is merely to create controversy and thus gain attention. Peter Hulme helped to bring this debate into the literary sphere, pushing scholars to consider nonfiction accounts of Oceania as textual representations rather than historical evidence. To write critically about cannibalism, Hulme argues in "The Cannibal Scene," one must, in the spirit of Paul Ricoeur, adopt a "hermeneutic of suspicious discourse, which in this case, depends upon the recognition of the genre" (25). As Hulme saw it, one must understand the Pacific travel narrative as a genre built around oral traditions of savagery rather than genuine encounters with it. Cannibal talk is just that: talk.

More recently, Victorian studies scholar Patrick Brantlinger has approached the discourse of cannibalism from a middle ground. In *Taming Cannibals*, Brantlinger poses the question: "Is this motif just the result of white racism, or does it have a historical basis?," ultimately concluding that "the answer appears to be both" (28). For Brantlinger, the idea that cannibalism is all talk relies too heavily on Pacific beachcomber narratives alone, which easily lend themselves to deconstruction.

Critics like Obeyesekere, he argues, have dismissed or ignored missionary texts, which provide a preponderance of at least partially credible firsthand accounts of cannibalism (32). His analysis of these ignored texts leads him to conclude that while one might quibble with individual accounts of cannibalism, the "cumulative record . . . is irrefutable from the standpoint of historiography; there is no countervailing body of evidence, written or otherwise" (45). In focusing on cannibalism from the Victorian perspective, Brantlinger, however, neglects to answer perhaps the more provocative question posed in Obeyesekere's *Cannibal Talk*: "Why this British preoccupation with cannibalism?" For Obeyesekere, one reason is self-evident: "Cannibalism is what the English reading public relished. It was their definition of savage" (28). This perspective turns the cannibalism debate on its head: suddenly, we are reading cannibalism from the other side of the cultural divide. For the discourse of "cannibalism" functions just as effectively—if not more effectively—for missionaries, as a means of framing one of the most potent forms of storytelling: the conversion narrative, in which "savages" are made "civilized."

Even if Obeyesekere's *Cannibal Talk* does not provide the definitive answer to the question of whether South Seas cannibalism actually existed or was purely a Western fiction, it offers an important lens through which to interpret Fijian cannibalism. While Obeyesekere proudly joins with "those who deny 'cannibalism,'" he also freely admits that "forms of 'anthropophagy'" have certainly existed in Oceanic cultures (15). The distinction that Obeyesekere draws is between practice and occurrence. Or, as he later puts it, an example of a "cannibal reaction" is not "proof that such people were 'cannibals'" (17). Instead, he argues, cannibalism is a "discourse" imposed on Oceanian people by Europeans, a discourse not of Orientalism—as Arens argued—but rather of "savagism" (1). Just as the cannibal fork provides an object to authenticate Fijian savagery, cannibal talk produces a narrative to authenticate Fijian savagery. But it was not Westerners alone who propagated the cannibal myth. Rather than trying to dispute the often absurd European fantasies of cannibalism, Oceanic peoples instead catered to those European expectations, realizing that it was a means of warding off imperial conquest.

Cannibal talk, then, was a defensive strategy. As Obeyesekere sees it, cannibal talk took advantage of the gullibility of white travelers, performing an identity that conformed to European fantasies (53). Like the cannibal fork, cannibal talk transforms conjecture into something more concrete, something to hold on to. In other words, cannibal talk authenticates Western concerns about Pacific cannibalism; it gives language to paranoia in the same way that the cannibal fork gives it form.

While Obeyesekere's argument is primarily focused on eighteenth- and early-nineteenth-century accounts, the idea of "cannibal talk," I want to suggest, evolves in the mid- to late nineteenth century.[18] For the most part, colonialization had neutralized the very real threat of physical violence and warfare between Europeans and Pacific Islanders. Cannibal talk thus becomes more ironic, more playful in the late nineteenth century. Oceanians take on the storytelling role of Jack. The cannibal-talker occupies a privileged role as storyteller; they are able to control the cultural narrative—however exaggerated or inaccurate it may be. As a local, to speak of cannibalism is to ensure that you have the interest of your audience, that you are guaranteed your own voice rather than just being spoken to or converted. Amid mass conversion and a loss of cultural identity, cannibalism stands out as "authentic," even if that authenticity is merely imagined—or seen through the eyes of others.

Indeed, if not for cannibal talk, Gordon-Cumming's narrative would feature very few moments of direct engagement with indigenous Fijians. Cannibal talk figures as the answer to Gayatri Spivak's famous question: "Can the subaltern speak?" But the answer is not the one Spivak would have expected, for this moment of speech can only be mediated through a narrative that is not produced by the subaltern herself. In other words, Fijians can speak in these narratives only if their patterns of speech conform to the already established Western narrative. In this respect, cannibal talk comes across as authentic because it is being articulated through a "native" voice. Of course, this assumption of authenticity fails to take into account how easy it is to perform a version of authenticity. The cross-cultural exchange of the beach, as articulated by Dening, becomes self-referential.

Fijians clearly sought to capitalize on travelers' desire for these faux-authentic representations of cannibalism. While in Bau, formerly regarded as a particularly savage part of Fiji[19] and now the site of a missionary stronghold, Gordon-Cumming immediately engages in exchange with the Bauian locals. From them, she obtains many "whales' teeth and carved wooden bowls." But it is from "the villanous-looking [sic] old priest" that she gets her most prized acquisitions. They are, as you might expect, "sundry cannibal forks, of carved wood with four long prongs." Gordon-Cumming's own assertion that the priest is "villanous-looking" seems to underscore the questionable nature of this exchange. Further, the fact that the priest has multiple cannibal forks to give suggests that, even if they are not forgeries, they are likely not all his own. He demonstrates none of the reluctance in parting with the forks that Seemann and von Hügel described. Instead, his prepared collection of cannibal forks indicates that he recognizes their commercial value. In fact, he seeks not to merely perpetuate this commodity but to expand it: he also offers Gordon-Cumming "large wooden spoons, or scoops, made purposely for human broth" (102). One can imagine the villainous old priest hawking his wares: "If you like cannibal forks, you'll love cannibal spoons." This is not to say that these spoons could not have been used alongside cannibal forks during the so-called cannibal feasts; but rather, at the very least, it shows an awareness that the object's value is in its story—in this case, its connection to cannibalism. Fittingly, after receiving these objects of cannibalism, Gordon-Cumming is treated to a history of cannibal warfare in Bau.

Apropos of these stories, Gordon-Cumming and her party urge a young Fijian chief to tell them about the cannibal feasts in which he surely must have taken part. Gordon-Cumming seeks to acquire some firsthand cannibal talk in much the same way she had just acquired cannibal forks. The young chief is more than happy to satisfy this desire. Approaching the most salacious topic first, Gordon-Cumming's party questions whether or not women engaged in cannibalism (surely not, the horrified party hopes), to which the young chief gleefully responds, "I'd like to see the woman who would not eat her full share!" (102). As a form of cannibal talk, this retort works on multiple levels. First, it allows the Fijian chief to take control of the narrative, to serve up a story rather than simply deny or confirm the questions from Gordon-Cumming's party. The Fijian chief relies not merely on tradition but rather on what he himself has "seen." His account is firsthand: authentic. "It's even worse than you've heard" is the implicit suggestion of his response. But more than this, the chief's response is designed to whet the appetite of his listeners, to provide a savory appetizer for more to come. It is important to note that the Fijian chief does not settle for asserting the facts alone (women engaged in cannibalism regularly), but instead frames it in specific terms of consumption (women eat their "full share"). In insisting that women eat their "full share," the Fijian chief is careful to frame cannibalism as a dining practice rather than a ritualistic one.

It is unsurprising, then, that the follow-up question from Gordon-Cumming's party pertains to the preparation and serving of human bodies. Returning to their familiar frame of reference, the party asks "whether the manner of preparing human flesh was not different from that in which pork, for instance, was cooked." Gordon-Cumming assumes he must have misunderstood the question, for he responds by declaring "Oh! there's no comparison between them—human flesh is so much the best!" (102–3). Likely picking up on nonverbal cues, the Fijian chief seems to provide them with the answer they want rather than the answer they asked for. That is to say, he understands the purpose of the question even if he does not fully understand the language. He seems to recognize that what his audience wants is not an answer but instead a performance.

Accordingly, he responds with zeal, providing them with an answer to the more salacious undercurrent of their question. They do not want him to talk about cannibalism; they want him to provide cannibal talk. The figure of the ex-cannibal is allowed to straddle both poles of Victorian desires. His cannibal past allows him to gratify his listener's desire for stories of cannibalism, while his conversion flatters their vanity for having reformed such a savage place.

It should be no surprise, then, that cannibal talk functions as an essential part of missionary conversion narratives. Across Fijian travel narratives, cannibal talk frames tales of conversion. As Gordon-Cumming writes back home: "I send you all this long story just to give you a faint idea of the horrible scenes that formerly made up the simple incidents of daily life in this now quiet lovely place" (198). These otherwise horrible stories are worth relating, Gordon-Cumming suggests, because of the contrast to present-day Fiji that they offer. Like any good conversion narrative, the more depraved one's original state, the more powerful the conversion. Tracey Banivanua-Mar argues in "Cannibalism and Colonialism: Charting Colonies and Frontiers in Nineteenth Century Fiji" that Fijian cannibal talk often served to further the interests of Western missionaries and settlers in Fiji. Building on Obeyesekere's claim that cannibal talk is a discourse of savagism, Banivanua-Mar distinguishes "cannibalism" from "Cannibalism," with the latter designating the "discourse rather than the empirical practice of cannibalism" (259). Banivanua-Mar suggests that there was much more of the capital "C" cannibalism than there was practiced cannibalism. For both settlers and missionaries and native Fijians, she argues, cannibalism was more potent as a symbol than as a practice (273). Cannibalism provided an ideal antithesis to Christianity, a clear means of identifying the depraved and savage nature of the Fijian people. In turn, this served as a forceful rationale in favor of Christian conversion and colonial expansion. Banivanua-Mar refers to this as the "harder ideological[ly] edged" counterpart to the "seaman's yarn" form of cannibal talk. This colonial form of cannibal talk, she argues, was "deployed as a strategy of dispossession" (259). In other words, cannibal talk served the interests of colonialism; it provided a tangible rationale for dispossessing Fijian culture at large. For this reason, those Fijians who were most resistant to conversion were most persistently and hyperbolically associated with cannibalism (274). Resistance, that is, was framed through the discourse of "Cannibalism." There could be no clearer representation, then, of conversion than surrendering one's cannibal fork to missionaries.

Possessing Cannibalism

James Clifford's observations on the connection between collecting objects and "collecting cultures" provide a useful framework for considering cannibal talk's relationship to the cannibal fork. In outlining his theory of the art-culture system, Clifford argues in "On Collecting Art and Culture" that "'cultures' are ethnographic collections" (230). For Clifford, "to see ethnography as a form of culture collecting highlights the ways that diverse experiences and facts are selected, gathered, detached from their original temporal occasions, and given enduring value in new arrangements" (231). Put into conversation with Banivanua-Mar's insistence that cannibal talk was "deployed as a strategy of dispossession," we might consider the cannibal fork and cannibal talk as mutually informing entities, each one authenticating the other. It is, in fact, the cannibal fork that makes this "dispossession" literal rather than merely symbolic. Often, cannibal forks and cannibal talk are collected simultaneously, with both of these things being repossessed at once.

This repossession of the cannibal fork can be seen as early as Walter Lawry's *Friendly and Feejee Islands* (1850). Upon arriving in Fiji, Lawry, a Wesleyan missionary superintendent, is greeted by a "stout cannibal [who] attempted to ascertain whether Philip Johns, one of the seamen, was fit to eat, by laying hold of his leg and turning up some of his clothing, to see how the matter stood. Mr. Hunt called out to him, and the man stared angrily at him, while Johns got into the boat. The late Chief used to salt men down, and live almost entirely upon human flesh, either fresh or salted. Through Mr. Hunt, I have procured the four-clawed wooden fork with which he used to feed himself" (92). The actions of the "stout cannibal" seem very much like the type of cannibal talk Obeyesekere identifies: more performative than instinctive. In "turning up" the sailor's pants and carefully examining his leg, the stout cannibal offers Lawry and other non-native onlookers a performance of cannibalism that is immediately legible. His actions are so exaggerated that he may as well be saying, "Look: I'm a cannibal, and I am looking for the first opportunity to eat every white man." Merely sizing the sailor up with his eyes would not be enough; it would not make his cannibalistic urges visible. Instead, he performs the act of sizing up for everyone to see. In this way, cannibal talk might be seen as what Mary Louise Pratt defines as "autoethnographic expression," wherein the "colonized subjects undertake to represent themselves in ways that engage with the colonizer's terms" (9). Knowing that this is what Fijian cannibalism looks like to colonizers, the stout cannibal plays his role. And, as Obeyesekere argues, this role was often deployed as a defensive strategy, a means of reinforcing the most threatening version of themselves. Significantly, this performance then comes to define the author's relationship to the cannibal fork.

Lawry's account mimics the relationship between the cannibal story (cannibal talk) and the cannibal object (cannibal fork). Lawry takes possession of the cannibal fork—once he has heard the cannibal tale. In other words, he consumes the "gruesome story" before receiving the object of gruesome consumption. Indeed, we can read the cannibal talk preamble as a sort of preparation, seasoning the story before Lawry delivers it to his audience. Likewise, for the Reverend John Hunt, an established missionary in Fiji, handing over the cannibal fork is more than giving a souvenir to his guest. In giving Lawry the cannibal fork, Hunt is also putting conversion on display. His mastery over the "stout cannibal" is exemplified by his mastery over the object. As Jeanne Cannizzo argues, for missionaries, cultural objects (or "fetishes") were often thought of as "trophies of . . . victories on spiritual battlefields" (163).[20] In taking possession of the cannibal fork, Lawry consequently establishes his mastery over Fijian culture. He thus provides the reader with some cannibal talk to narrativize what is now *his* cannibal fork. Not content to present the chief as engaging in cannibalism occasionally or even ritualistically, Lawry—perhaps following Hunt's lead—maintains that "human flesh" was nearly the chief's entire source of sustenance (he "live[d] almost entirely upon human flesh"). As the cannibal fork comes into the writer's possession, so too does cannibal talk.

Indeed, the language of possession is built into Lawry's account. Lawry does not receive the cannibal fork through cross-cultural exchange; instead, he "procures" the cannibal fork from his missionary guide. The word "procure" is suggestive of a legal transaction rather than a meaningful exchange. Of course, this effect is furthered by the absence of any indigenous Fijian from this transaction. This exchange is defined by the absence of risk. We would do well here to recall the Pacific possessions of the two earlier chapters: Vason enduring the pain and permanence of Tongan tattooing; A Häolé unwittingly becoming a participant rather than a mere observer of the Hawaiian hula. In fact, it is precisely because of the absence of risk that this transaction is possible. For travelers like Gordon-Cumming and Lawry, cannibalism exists *only* as talk; the cannibal fork comes into their possession *only* because it has been detached from its cultural context. That is to say, it is only cannibalism's absence that allows Lawry and others to make it present in their narratives. What is most important in these mid-to-late-century accounts of Fiji is not cultural contact but rather cultural repossession.

Sarah Bland Smythe's *Ten Months in the Fiji Islands* (1864) provides a striking example of how acquiring cannibal forks acted as a symbolic representation of cultural conversion. Like Wallis, Smythe traveled to Fiji alongside her husband, Colonel W .J. Smythe, who had been appointed by the American government commissioner of Fiji. While Smythe's narrative is primarily composed of letters home, one notable exception is a chapter that focuses extensively on Fijian cannibalism. This chapter is composed by Colonel Smythe, and it details his experience in Namusi, another region of Fiji that Westerners had deemed as notoriously savage and cannibalistic. Describing himself as "yet a novice in Fijian travel," Colonel Smythe traveled under guidance of the famed Fijian missionary Joseph Waterhouse.

Waterhouse acts as a guide not only for how to traverse the physical space of Fiji but also for how to interpret the Fijian people. In this capacity, Waterhouse takes Colonel Smythe to the home of a Namusi priest who had "formerly been a great encourager of cannibalism." Here, "at Mr. Waterhouse's persuasion he [the priest] gave up to me the cannibal fork that he possessed" (73). The clunky syntax of this sentence seems to be more than just poor writing. Instead, the awkward construction of this sentence reflects the confusing nature of the transaction. While the priest is the subject of this sentence, he does not appear as the subject before being ushered in by the adverbial phrase "at Mr. Waterhouse's persuasion." In this way, the sentence mirrors the power dynamic of this transaction: it should be the priest's fork to give, but it is Waterhouse who is positioned as in control of the object's fate. This grammatical dispossession is furthered when Colonel Smythe refers to the fork as something "that he [the priest] possessed" rather than, more simply, "*his* cannibal fork." Even this change, though, would not eliminate the ambiguous use of the possessive pronoun here. While we can assume the "he" refers to the priest, the ambiguity serves only to extend the confusion about whose possession this is in and who might therefore be able to give it away. Colonel Smythe takes possession of this fork, knowing that it has been "for generations in [the priest's] family, and was known far and wide by its proper name." And upon taking possession of the fork, Colonel Smythe likewise takes control over its history—he defines for his American audience the stories that surround that history—which includes referring to it as the cannibal fork rather than by its "proper name": *iculunibokola*. He provides his audience with cannibal talk. After receiving the utensil, Colonel Smythe's attention is drawn to various images of cannibalism: a temple with "skulls and bones" and a tree "garnished with two thigh bones, a jaw bone, a shoulder blade, and several ribs" (73–74).[21]

Gruesome enough images, but, of course, those images are supplemented with cannibal talk. The cannibal talk is offered by a chief of the town, in the form of a "short biography of the original owner of the remains" (74). In translating and presenting the chief's story as a "biography" Colonel Smythe foregrounds the story as authentic. Yet, earlier in the chapter Colonel Smythe himself notes how the most horrible stories of cannibalism ("cannibal talk") often arise from willful "slips of interpretation"—as this section of the narrative is subtitled. As an example of this, Colonel Smythe mentions how his missionary hosts proudly relate to him the story of an excursion in which they "prevented the massacre of five hundred people, whose bodies were taken to form a pile, on top of which the chief's son was to be invested with *malo*."[22] Unable to square this with what he has seen from Fijian culture, Colonel Smythe insists that this "tale appeared almost too horrible" and offered "a startling contrast with other acts of [chief] Kurunduandua" (60). Colonel Smythe implicitly sets up an opposition between "tales" and "acts," noting how much more difficult it is to accept these "tales" when one actually knows the person. It is thus "no small relief" to him when he finds out "from an undoubted authority that the number of people must have been lost in translation: it was not five-hundred lives that were saved, but perhaps one or two" (60). Perhaps a little more than just a "slip" in translation. This realization provides Colonel Smythe with relief, but it does not lead him to question more global "slips in translation." Rather, he moralizes that the sacrifice of even a single individual is "abominable, and to have prevented such an atrocity must be a proud satisfaction" (60). Despite the improbably exaggerative "slips in translation," Colonel Smythe focuses on the representative value of the story rather than the potential it has to call into question the authenticity of these exotic narratives more generally.

The facts of cannibalism were of little concern to writers like Smythe. As Banivanua-Mar puts it, "colonial writers were . . . overt in setting out not to discover or prove [cannibalism's] existence, which needed no proof, but to imagine, to see it, to describe it" (*Violence and Colonial Discourse* 24). We might well think of this distinction between "proof" and imagination as a way of describing the vexed matter of possession. For to prove cannibalism exists would be to merely "see" it as native Fijians do, but to "imagine" and "describe" it is to take possession, to "see" it the way one wants to see it. What makes Gordon-Cumming's text particularly compelling, then, is how it literalizes this re-possession at the core of Western cannibal talk. In displaying the cannibal fork on the cover of her text, Gordon-Cumming makes explicit what is suggested in earlier Western accounts of Fiji and other Pacific Islands. The cannibal fork is her possession to put on display. It does not truly function as an object of cultural exchange, nor is it a marker of personal experience. Instead, it is her possession to build a narrative around.

"At Home" with Cannibals

Collecting and displaying thus assumed a central role in Gordon-Cumming's and her companions' Fijian experience. According to Gordon-Cumming, her room and those of her companions were "like museums, adorned with savage instruments" (133). Detached from the original purpose, these artifacts, according to Nicholas Thomas in *Entangled Objects*, "express the distance of the people from their former uses. In these instances the weapons are not paraded as ugly or frightening things but are instead domesticated as mere ornaments, as innocuous relics of a former epoch which are now—but only now—available for aesthetic appreciation" (162). Thomas's emphasis on domestication is especially suggestive in the context of Gordon-Cumming's work, and it leads us back to the title of her narrative, *At Home in Fiji*. While cannibalism informs the exotic nature of the text, the concept of home anchors it in the familiar. These two opposing values, however, reinforce each other. Returning to the cover, we notice the paradoxical relationship between the fork and the phrase "At Home" in the title. The fork on the cover cuts through the cover, disunifying it, but, in doing so, it also offers a resting place for the more crucial part of Gordon-Cumming's experience of Fiji: her being "At Home" there. The cannibal fork simultaneously grounds and undercuts "home" in the text. That is to say, the ability to possess and domesticate such an object makes being "at home" possible, but it also draws attention to the colonial foundation that this home is built upon, in turn calling into question whether a European "home" could ever be built on the same soil as this "savage" place.

The dichotomy between the cannibal fork and "home" is further established through Gordon-Cumming's frontispiece, titled "Our Home in Fiji" (figure 3.5). In a way, these two images function as paired visual introductions to the text: they are the first ones the reader sees, with each image contextualized by the language surrounding it. The frontispiece, based on an original sketch by Gordon-Cumming, depicts the lush Fijian landscape and a beautiful, bustling beach.[23] Gordon-Cumming's landscape portrait places her—the artist—at a distance, allowing viewers in turn to take on the scene from a distance. This is a fitting visual introduction to the text, as it demonstrates the simultaneous embracing of, and distancing from, Fijian culture that informs her text. Such a relationship is further reflected in her written account of her painter's perch. Interested in this "new and extraordinary method of writing the mountains in colours," a group of Fijians gather around her. They were, Gordon-Cumming writes, "most courteous and quiet, and as usual my only complaint was their vile habit of incessantly spitting" (132). In this way, her painting perch mirrors the frontispiece painting: a genuine appreciation for the indigenous presence, albeit a rather passive one, is offset by cultural distancing, achieved by the distancing reference to "their vile habit of spitting." Gordon-Cumming may be "at home," but her sense of home relies on a certain level of detachment from Fijian culture.

But Gordon-Cumming's frontispiece also offers a much different, more Fijian, as it were, version of "home" than the one that dominates her text. "Home" is a central plot point in the early portion of the text, as Gordon-Cumming "hope[s] to find [their] Fijian home ready" when they arrive (25). The process of adding rooms and repairing their home's roofing drags on, forcing Gordon-Cumming and her crew to float between various Fijian

Figure 3.5. "Our Home in Fiji," frontispiece to Constance Gordon-Cumming's *At Home in Fiji.*

houses as they await the completion of their European-style home. Often, Gordon-Cumming and her party stay at Fijian homes, which "consist of only one room" and feature "comfortable, thick, clean, mats" to both lounge and sleep on (82, 77). "White men in general," she continues, "seem to consider that they are bringing their family low indeed when they adopt a purely native house as home, and mats in lieu of chairs" (77). In framing the resistance of white men to native houses, Gordon-Cumming implicitly sets up a distinction between "house" and "home." Unlike the white men who surround her, Gordon-Cumming is more willing to be a part of Fijian culture than to impose her own culture onto it. That is to say, she is more apt to find the qualities of a home within Fijian culture than to impose her own European definition onto Fijian homes.[24]

Of course, for Victorians the house was not just a place to live; it was, as Deborah Cohen argues, an "express[ion] of its inhabitant's inner self." This belief was manifested, Cohen argues, in the ubiquity of the "at home" magazine article, which was a firmly entrenched genre by the end of the nineteenth century (123). These essays presented the house as an intimate space, with each object and piece of décor reflecting the unique personality and history of its owner. Often, these essays featured an accompanying image of that particular room. Given this upper-class interest in "the home," one might expect that Gordon-Cumming would visually feature her own "home," filled with its exotic version of Victorian household gods. Instead, the one "home"

Figure 3.6. "A Chief's Kitchen," illustration by Constance Gordon-Cumming," in *At Home in Fiji.*

scene featured in Gordon-Cumming's work is of a Fijian chief's kitchen (figure 3.6). This sketch is reminiscent of Victorian "at home" photographs and sketches: wide enough in scope to take in an abundance of objects. The crucial difference, however, is that this "at home" portrait is peopled—indeed, this is the lone illustration that features Fijian people in any detail. Unlike Victorian "at home" representations, and unlike a would-be sketch of her own museum, the home's objects do not speak for themselves; the Fijian people here are intimately connected to these objects. This, of course, is much different from the cannibal fork that binds her text, detached and emptied of all context. Put into conversation, however, these different illustrations speak to Gordon-Cumming's ambivalence toward Fijian culture.

Often, Gordon-Cumming seems more sympathetic to the Fijian home than to her own European-style home. After describing why white men tend to feel Fijian houses insufficient as homes, Gordon-Cumming finds herself reluctant to agree. "Perhaps they are right," she concedes, "but I must confess to having rather a weakness for Fijian mat life." Gordon-Cumming goes on to provide what reads as a somewhat half-hearted critique of "mat life," insisting that "it tends to foster indolence; which is the bane of the islanders; and there is no denying that when you have sunk down to rest on these soft, cool, tempting mats in the semi-darkness of a Fijian house, you do feel sorely disinclined to rise thence without good cause. When this becomes a habit it is a recognized evil known as mat fever!" (77). In other words, mat life is so good it must be bad. The push and pull in this passage is characteristic of Gordon-Cumming's engagement with authentic Fijian culture. She is drawn to the romance and the charm, but she often seems compelled to dutifully resist the temptation to embrace that charm. Seen from a distance, it is charming and romantic, but get too close to it, and it is a "sin" and an "evil."

With this in mind, I return to cannibalism, recalling Gordon-Cumming's self-proclaimed romantic notions about living among "ferocious cannibals." Despite her protestations otherwise, Gordon-Cumming seems to relish this cannibal talk, enjoying the risk it represents as compared to the domestic safety of her new Fijian "home." While in "Nanduri" [Naduri], she writes that "it is a most hospitable district, and sufficiently uncivilised even for me! This morning a horrible old ex-cannibal crept close to Mr Langham, and then, as if he could not refrain, he put out his hand and stroked him down the thigh, licking his lips, and exclaiming with delight, 'Oh, but you are nice and fat!'" (210). There is an odd disconnect between the two parts of this passage: Gordon-Cumming begins by praising the "hospitable" and "uncivilised" place that she is visiting, only to relate a story in which a "horrible" ex-cannibal has his former urges awakened by the plump Wesleyan missionary Frederick Langham. Once again, Gordon-Cumming portrays her attachment to Fijian civilization as very different from the rest of her party, asserting that it meets her rather high standard ("sufficient . . . even for me") of Fijian life unspoiled by the influence of her "home" (civilization). This declaration colors the ensuing anecdote, making this story of a "horrible" cannibal seem more pleasurable than terrifying. It's clearly a funny scene. Much like Lawry's "stout cannibal" sizing up a sailor's leg, the ex-cannibal's actions here come across as comically performative; it is cannibalism writ large. Once again, it is not enough for the ex-cannibal to confess to his lingering cannibal urges; instead, he must act out those urges.

Given her excitement at the "sufficiently uncivilized" district she is describing, we can read Gordon-Cumming's portrayal and re-embellishing of cannibal talk as almost nostalgic. In other words, the story that follows seems to be evidence as to why this district is "sufficiently uncivilized even for [her]!" Gordon-Cumming's description of cannibal talk is almost voyeuristic, as she looks on and describes not a savage encounter but, in fact, a rather sensual one. The ex-cannibal "strokes" Langham's thigh, "lick[s] his lips," and shouts with "delight." In passionately commenting that Langham is "nice and fat," the ex-cannibal comes across more as courting a potential partner than threatening a future victim. It is, then, a Romantic scene in both senses of the word.

It should be unsurprising that the scene would have appeared to Gordon-Cumming this way, given her affinity for being drawn to the "charm" of precolonial Fiji. Gordon-Cumming seems to know that the ex-cannibal is not truly "horrible." Instead, she evidently relishes his playing the role of the horrible ex-cannibal. The scene is authentic in as much as it accords with Gordon-Cumming's Western-based conceptions of authentic Fijian culture. This moment thus functions as a voyeuristic peep into a precontact Pacific world. It recalls the "charm" and the "savour of romance" that inspires Gordon-Cumming to travel to Fiji in the first place. Gordon-Cumming imagines this scene in the context of past Fijian savagery, and in doing so she reflects on a former version of Polynesia as a space of risk, a space where power relations between native and colonialist are yet unsettled.

In this way, we might consider cannibal talk as more than just representing literal danger. Rather, we can read it as representative of cultural difference. For, indeed, cannibalism is cultural difference writ large. As much as the cannibal fork marks a repossession of Fijian culture, the fascination with it also represents a longing to be dispossessed. It represents, especially for Gordon-Cumming, the possibility, now lost, of surrendering one's cultural identity to another.

4

Robert Louis Stevenson's Gilbert Islands Photographs

It was a desire for surrender that drove Robert Louis Stevenson to the South Seas. If Constance Gordon-Cumming had doubts about reclining on mats surrounded by natives, Stevenson went all in. The Penguin Classics edition of Robert Louis Stevenson's posthumously published travel account *In the South Seas* (1896) features perhaps the most iconic photograph taken during the author's two South Seas cruises (figure 4.1). Surely this photograph's popularity is due to how much Stevenson looks "at home," to return to Constance Gordon-Cumming's phrase, in his exotic environs. Yet unlike Gordon-Cumming, Stevenson is at home because he has embraced island culture, not because Western culture has colonized the island. In the photograph, taken at Butaritari, a small and scarcely visited atoll in the Gilbert Islands (now known as Kiribati),[1] Stevenson occupies the foreground position, gazing directly at the camera as he lounges in the atoll's verdant forest. One of his long legs stretches out—extending past the frame of the book—and the other leg curls under it, revealing the dirt on the soles of his foot. Stevenson's unkempt hair is held in place by a garland of flowers, and his loose-fitting white pajamas billow around his thin frame. In the background is Stevenson's wife, Fanny, similarly garlanded and outfitted in all white. She clasps hands with her friend, the Butaritari dignitary Nei Takauti. Unlike Robert, both Fanny and Nei Takauti ignore the camera, gazing in opposite directions as if deliberately avoiding it. On the surface, the central narrative of this photograph is one of assimilation and immersion. Stevenson and Fanny are not mere visitors to the islands; they are inhabitants of them.

Yet for as representative as this image has become of Stevenson's South Seas experience, it is notably devoid of imagery unique to the South Seas, let alone to the Gilbert Islands atoll of Butaritari. Even the garlands—perhaps

Figure 4.1. Penguin Classics
cover (1998) of *In the South
Seas*.

the only marker of South Seas-ness in the photograph—recall Western ico-
nography, particularly Pre-Raphaelite paintings.[2] The photograph says even
less about the author's relationship with Butaritari people. Framed in the foreground, Stevenson comes across as detached from his wife and Nei Takauti.
A model image of authorial distance, Stevenson eyes the Penguin Classic's
reader, seeming to offer her or him the prospect of similarly sumptuous exotic
yet still familiar images to come. It is easy to see why Penguin would have
chosen this photograph for its cover image. It represents the highest ideal of
the South Seas traveler, bohemian and at ease in their exotic surroundings.

However, Penguin Classics does not provide the whole picture—literally.
The original photograph (figure 4.2) first appeared in Fanny Stevenson's *The
Cruise of the Janet Nichol* (1914). Here, we see not an unbalanced party of three
but instead an image of two couples: the Stevensons and Nei Takauti[3] and her
husband, Nan Tok'. The Penguin version crops out Nan Tok', which, of course,
alters the original moment of the photograph. But this cropping also affects
the formal qualities of the photograph: by cropping Nan Tok' out, Stevenson
alone becomes the focal point. In the original photograph, our eye is drawn in

Figure 4.2. "Stevensons in company with Nan Tok' and Nei Takauti, Butaritari."
Courtesy of the City of Edinburgh Museums and Galleries; Writers' Museum,
www.capitalcollections.org.uk.

different directions; our focus meanders between the various members of the
scene. Even though Stevenson, in the original photograph, technically occupies the foreground position in the photograph, his presence as a focal point is
balanced out by the mirrored posture of Nan Tok'. Like Stevenson, Nan Tok'
lounges, his back arm propping up his body. The parallelism between Stevenson and Nan Tok' serves to border in Fanny and Nei Takauti, creating two
distinct scenes of cultural exchange. Seen in its original form, it appears as
though Stevenson and Nan Tok' have been interrupted mid-conversation, as
they turn to look at the camera. In cutting Nan Tok' out of the photo, the
Penguin Classics version thus fundamentally shifts the original photographic
narrative, turning a moment of cross-cultural exchange into an idealized image of Stevenson the author.

    But beyond just focalizing Stevenson at the expense of his indigenous
friends, the Penguin Classics reframing also makes the nature of cross-cultural
exchange neater and more legible. While Nan Tok''s presence serves to create formal symmetry in the original photograph, taking him out of the photograph produces greater visual harmony. Without Nan Tok', the Penguin
Classics cover is dominated by the group's collective white outfits, but in the

original this uniformity is offset by Nan Tok"s dark lavalava. Moreover, while Nan Tok"s body position parallels Stevenson's, it does so imperfectly, his legs stretching out far past Stevenson's. His bare torso and exposed legs contrast with Stevenson's long sleeves and pants, just as Nei Takauti's exposed shoulders are thrown into relief by Fanny's modest dress.

The distinctions between the party's original photograph and the Penguin Classics appropriation of it reveal the extent to which Stevenson's South Seas photography has been decontextualized. Where the Penguin Classics version frames the author as an authoritative presence, the original suggests something more complicated. More important, such a reframing both models and advances an uncomplicated narrative about Robert Louis Stevenson's sojourn in the Pacific. It presents a version of Stevenson in control—in possession—of the South Seas. In many ways, it recirculates Stevenson's own naive belief that he was the ultimate authority on South Seas culture, that he had transcended the clichés and determined, finally, what constituted Pacific authenticity.

That stated, what the publishers of the Penguin edition get right is the centrality of photography to Stevenson's representation of the South Seas. Or, more cynically, they, like Stevenson, recognized the authenticating qualities of photography, the narrative authority that they lend to written accounts. Photography emerged, for Stevenson, as an important narrative and ideological tool, more effective than the written word alone because it was more immediate in defining the traveler's relationship with a culture or landscape. Stevenson's photographs were often preconceived or staged, designed to convey a specific narrative, much as the Penguin Classics cropping is meant to tell a particular story. Yet Stevenson conceived of photography as objective: pictures tell their own stories, he thought. Even as Stevenson saw his photography as a corrective to oppressive colonial narratives about the South Seas, it mostly functions as his own tool of colonial domination. It is merely a newly realized writing implement for the tourist.

OBJECTIVITY: STEVENSON'S AUTHENTIC SOUTH SEAS

Stevenson's first cruise, onboard the schooner *Casco*, departed from San Francisco in June 1888, arriving at the Marquesas Island of Nuku Hiva on July 20.[4] On this first cruise, Stevenson was accompanied by his mother, Margaret, his wife, Fanny, and his stepson, Lloyd Osbourne. Between June 1888 and January 1889, the Stevenson party stayed in the Marquesas, departing then to the Paumotus [Tuamotu], Tahiti, and ending in Hawaii. Stevenson's mother left after this first cruise. But the Stevenson party took on a new member, Joseph Strong, the husband of Fanny's daughter Isobel.[5] They boarded the American schooner *Equator*, captained by Dennis Reid, for the second leg of their cruise. In June 1889, they departed for the Gilbert Islands, whose atolls (Butaritari,

Mariki, Apiang, and Apemama) they hopped from until December, when they left for Samoa, where Stevenson would eventually settle and spend the final five years of his life.[6] Throughout these cruises, photography remained essential to Stevenson's literary project because he believed that photography would enable him to move past the romanticized South Seas clichés of previous writers.

In the course of *In the South Seas*, Stevenson finds all the markers of South Seas authenticity analyzed in the previous three chapters to be unsatisfying. As discussed in chapter 1, Stevenson recounts the story of a European beachcomber who, at the behest of his Marquesan lover, gets tattooed. While the Marquesan woman previously saw him as naked without his tattoos, she now views him as incongruous: "the fickle fair one could never behold him from that day except with laughter" (50). His story suggests that embodying Pacific values is impossible, no matter how much one embraces them. Stevenson recognized, too, that the Hawaiian hula had become a mere tourist marker, "which may be viewed by the speedy globe-trotter in Honolulu." It is, he continues, "surely the most dull of man's inventions, and the spectator yawns under its length as at a college lecture or a parliamentary debate" (190). To Stevenson, the hula is not only too accessible but also too transparently catered to the edification of European audiences. Likewise, Stevenson demonstrates a sophisticated traveler's resistance to curiosities, so clearly furnished for the Pacific's growing tourist market. Stevenson's "appetite for curiosities is not . . . very strong" (247). Stevenson's dismissiveness of all these period-specific Pacific traveling trends suggests that he saw himself as a new and more discerning type of South Seas traveler, one who recognized both the limits of being culturally integrated as well as the danger of fetishizing elements of indigenous culture. Photography, then, offered Stevenson a fitting avenue for capturing South Seas authenticity. The photograph at once acknowledged—indeed, produced—cultural distance while also allowing Stevenson to present unique aspects of Oceanian societies objectively, free from literary Romanticization. Or so he thought, at least.

Of course, Stevenson's photographs were inevitably inflected by his own perception of what the South Seas *should* be. They do not represent the authentic South Seas but rather reveal Stevenson's own version of what constitutes South Seas authenticity. The archive of Stevenson's Pacific photographs is vast, containing around six hundred photographic prints,[7] making it impossible to give a full account or provide a neat consensus about them in just one chapter. Accordingly, I selected photographs that are representative while recognizing the inconsistencies in terms of what Stevenson hoped to represent in his photographs. Still, this chapter revolves around narrative first and foremost; my focus is both how Stevenson writes about photography and how his photographic project informs his approach to narrative in *In the South Seas*.[8] Much like the previous chapters, the photographs figure as a narrative possession, an object imagined to distill the essence of Pacific culture. Stevenson's photographic approach, I argue, is representative of a final evolution in the genre of the nineteenth-century Pacific travel narrative. For Stevenson, photography seemed to offer a way to present to his audience the so-called real South Seas, free of the various distortions that inevitably came along with beachcomber, missionary, and imperial and colonial travel narratives. Paradoxically, however, it was Stevenson's move toward objectivity that often undermined the authenticity he sought.

While scholars have been interested in Stevenson's *In the South Seas* and its engagement with the concept of authenticity (Edmond, Farrier, Rennie, Smith), their analyses pay little attention to how Stevenson's photography fit into his project. David Farrier, for example, in *Unsettled Narratives*, simplifies Stevenson's photography as "another medium for the creation of a text of encounter" (63). In framing photography as merely "another" medium, Farrier neglects the mutually informing nature of Stevenson's narrative and visual texts. For Stevenson, photography was not merely a side hobby to his writing; rather, it was meant to be *part* of his writing. Alanna Knight's *Robert Louis Stevenson in the South Seas: An Intimate Photographic Record* (1987) was a valuable recovery project, reproducing many of the photographs that had been forgotten in Edinburgh's Writers' Museum Library. However, due to the somewhat haphazard placements of photographs in relation to Stevenson's text, the book does as much to decontexualize the photographs as it does to reclaim their significance to Stevenson's written work. Leonard Bell's "Pictures as History, Settlement as Theatre: John Davis's Photo-Portrait of Robert Louis Stevenson and Family at Vailima, Samoa, 1882" (2002) offers a model for reading Stevenson's Pacific photography within its historical context, but his analysis is independent of Stevenson's writing. The critical landscape of Stevenson's South Seas nonfiction is defined by its focus on one aspect of Stevenson's South Seas narrativizing at the expense of the other.

However, a few scholars have recently begun to close that gap, interpreting Stevenson's photography as significantly interconnected with his South Seas nonfiction. Ann C. Colley, in her book *Robert Louis Stevenson and the Colonial Imagination*, dedicates multiple chapters to Stevenson's use of photographic technology in the Pacific.[9] Colley argues that Stevenson's photographs were "a necessary complement to his writing. They were . . . a means of legitimizing or illuminating his words and of giving readers a more particularized image to consider" (117). Similarly, Carla Manfredi, whose archival research in "Picturing Robert Louis Stevenson's Pacific Phototext" has significantly resituated Stevenson's photographic project within its literary context, argues that Stevenson's "photographic practice narrows the distance between Stevenson and his photographic subject, and thus reverses the familiar expectations about colonial photography" (7).

While I agree with Colley and Manfredi that the Stevenson's Pacific photography resists familiar colonial stereotypes, I want to avoid relying on a neat
binary between Stevenson and colonial photographers. Though perhaps less
problematic than his contemporaries, Stevenson's photography was equally
invested in representing its *own* Western ideal of the South Seas. Just as important, such broad claims about Stevenson's photography necessarily overem-
phasize the uniformity of purpose and design in Stevenson's archive. I suggest,
however, that Stevenson's photographs, much like his narrative, must be conceived of not as discrete moments but rather as a whole. That is, I focus not
just on the photographs themselves as objects of exchange but instead think
about Stevenson's *use* of photography as its own form of cultural negotiation.
In tracing Stevenson's photographic endeavors, I argue that it is not until the
final part of Stevenson's trip—in the Gilbert Islands—that Stevenson begins
to abandon his own ideas of authenticity, arriving instead at a genuine interchange between himself and Oceanian peoples. More specifically, in the Gilbert Islands, Stevenson's photographic subjects are no longer just sitters but
become collaborators.

I begin this chapter by framing Stevenson's narrative approach, which he
conceived of primarily as providing "records of fact." Such a narrative approach,
I show, was informed by Stevenson's use of photography. Situating Stevenson
within the broader historical context of turn-of-the-century South Seas photography, I argue that Stevenson envisioned his photo-literary approach as providing the first truly authentic and unbiased account of the South Seas.

Analyzing first a representative photograph (and accompanying text) from
his early travels in the Marquesas, I demonstrate how Stevenson's claims to
objectivity were often undermined by his own constructed notion of what
constituted authenticity. From there, I move to the Gilbert Islands to show
how Stevenson's photography begins to change at the final location of his
cruise. I argue that these final photographs demonstrate Stevenson's eventual
awareness of the cross-cultural implications of photography. Though both Stevenson's written and photographic Gilbert Islands texts remain complicated
by Stevenson's own views of the South Seas, they represent the productive
potential of writing *within* place rather than writing *about* place. As a final
Pacific possession, then, Stevenson's photography becomes instead a shared
possession, a Western technology that Oceanian peoples can speak back to.

WRITING AGAINST TRADITION: THE SOUTH SEAS WITHOUT ROMANCE

Stevenson's intention to travel to the South Seas created an immediate buzz
within the literary world. Who better than the author of *Treasure Island* to
continue in the Romantic literary tradition of the South Seas? Surely this is

what the opportunistic American publisher S. S. McClure thought when he met with Stevenson in November 1887. McClure would commission Stevenson to write fifty letters of roughly two-to-three thousand words to be syndicated in both American and British newspapers. As Oliver Buckton writes in *Cruising with Robert Louis Stevenson*, Stevenson's compensation (£20 for each letter serialized in England and an additional $200 for American publication) would go toward funding his South Seas cruise (151). From the beginning, however, Stevenson felt constrained by McClure's commercial enterprise. The syndication of Stevenson's letters in the *New York Sun* appeared under the subtitle "Letters from a Leisurely Traveller," which, as Buckton points out, "evok[ed] a context of ease and suggest[ed] that the act of cruising was casual and pleasurable rather than pursued for profit or with literary labor as its pretext" (154). While Stevenson continued to provide McClure with letters—he needed them to fund his trip's expenses—he quickly developed much more ambitious plans, conceiving of the letters as a sort of rough draft for a book project. By 1890, near the end of his second cruise, Stevenson's concept had crystallized in his mind. He laid out his conceit to his friend and literary advisor Sidney Colvin: "I propose to call the book—*The South Seas*." Rennie notes that recognizing the boldness of his project, Stevenson concedes that it "is a rather large title, but not many people have seen more of them than I; perhaps no one: certainly no one capable of using the material" (xv). Stevenson's ambitious plans never came to fruition, as he remained dissatisfied with his ability to capture the "real" South Seas. It was only two years after his death that Stevenson's *In the South Seas* (1896) would be published, without photographs and lacking in cohesion and organization. In its published form, Stevenson's *In the South Seas* is separated into four parts, each organized around a group of South Seas islands: the Marquesas (the most extensive), the Paumotus, the Gilberts, and, finally, Apemama, the least colonized atoll of the Gilbert Islands. Cobbled together from Stevenson's published letters and unpublished drafts, *In the South Seas* is often desultory in both narrative direction and form. Where the Marquesas section is detached and anthropological, the Gilbert Island sections look much more like an author-driven travel account. Taken as a whole, *In the South Seas* demonstrates Stevenson's struggle to maintain control over his sprawling South Seas subject.

Though it may well have been true that no Western writer had seen more of the South Seas than Stevenson, his failings, as it turned out, rested precisely on his *lack* of capability of "using the material." In fact, as Robert Irwin Hillier argues in *The South Seas Fiction of Robert Louis Stevenson*, "Stevenson's retreat from optimism to despair came from the realization that his subject matter exceeded his capacity to control it" (36). Stevenson's wife, Fanny, writing privately to Colvin, worried that "Louis has the most enchanting material, and I am afraid he's going to spoil it all" (xii). Her sentiments were shared throughout Stevenson's literary circle. If Stevenson was constantly dissatis-fied with his ability to capture the "real" South Seas, those close to him were disappointed by what they perceived as a lack of charm and imagination in his early drafts and letters—surprising complaints given Stevenson's sta-tus as Victorian romanticist par excellence. But Stevenson conceived of his project much differently than his audience. Where his literary predecessors relied on Romanticism when writing about the Pacific, Stevenson was aiming for something more grounded. As Neil Rennie puts it, "Stevenson wanted to transcend the personal travel narrative. . . . He wanted, not the story of his travels *In the South Seas*, but *The South Seas* themselves" (xxv). In other words, Stevenson desired a purer form of representation. He wanted something im-possible to attain: an objective account of the South Seas from the perspective of a Westerner. He wanted authenticity. Though certainly a literary shortcom-ing, Stevenson's absence from his own text signals a well-meaning desire to decenter ethnocentric renderings of the Pacific Islands. Yet, paradoxically, this detachment itself functions as a sort of privileged space of cultural authoriza-tion, a space of only imagined neutrality. That is to say, he merely exchanged the privileged role of romancer with the equally vexed function of anthropo-logical expert.

Perhaps Stevenson's lack of presence in his initial letters can be attributed to his own critique of Western intervention in the South Seas. His writing on the Marquesas, much to the dismay of Fanny, exhibits, as Rennie notes in the introduction, Stevenson's "weakness for teaching and preaching" (xxi). In an early section titled "Depopulation," Stevenson traces the deleterious effects of missionary and colonial presence across the various South Seas Islands, ulti-mately concluding that in Polynesia "change of habit [has been] bloodier than bombardment" (34). But while Stevenson was most obviously concerned with redressing the wrongs of missionary and colonial accounts of the South Seas, he was equally wary of romanticized travelers' yarns. Though his trip was, at least in part,[10] motivated by his own literary-informed romantic notions of the South Seas, Stevenson saw his work as fundamentally different, a correc-tive to the variously biased accounts of his predecessors. Emboldened by the stakes of his own project, Stevenson aligns himself with "but two writers who have touched the South Seas with any genius, both Americans: Melville and Charles Warren Stoddard."[11] Stevenson's focus on "genius" here is suggestive of an implicit valuing of the literary, a summary dismissal of the published works of sailors, beachcombers, missionaries, and earlier travel writers. Ste-venson indirectly leagues himself with these literary exemplars. But even their works, Stevenson continues, were flawed. Melville and Stoddard were blessed with the ability to "see," "tell," and "charm," but they were not "able to hear,"

Stevenson concludes. As evidence, Stevenson points to Melville's "grotesque misspelling" of the Happa valley in the Marquesas (23). Melville, in *Typee*, had spelled it "Hapar," and his transliteration became standard within the Western world. Stevenson seems to suggest that this "grotesque misspelling" is representative of broader cultural mishearings that crystallize into reality for Western audiences.[12] For this reason, Stevenson was determined to distance himself from the romantic tradition of South Seas travel writing.

This was a continual point of frustration to Stevenson's publisher, S. S. Mc-Clure, who, looking back on the failed project, observed that "it was the moralist and not the romancer which [Stevenson's] observations in the South Seas awoke in him, and the public found the moralist less interesting than the romancer" (192). Stevenson likely wouldn't have disagreed with this assessment. As much as he admired Melville's willingness to critique the missionary project in the South Seas, he was careful to distinguish his own approach from Melville's or from the romantic traveler's tale. Sensing early on that his writing might not be meeting his readers' standards, Stevenson acknowledges that "readers of travels may perhaps exclaim at my authority, and declare themselves better informed." In response, Stevenson appeals to the authority of the local informant to validate his assessments. "I should prefer," he counters, "the statement of an intelligent native like Stanislao (even if it stood alone, which it is far from doing) to the report of the most honest traveller" (35). The "honesty" of any traveler is always in question for Stevenson, always imperfect because writers are always primarily focused on crafting narrative. What, then, did Stevenson see his work as if not a narrative? Stevenson provides an answer to that question much later in his ever-evolving letters, comparing his own mode of storytelling with that of Captain Reid, with whom Stevenson traveled on the *Equator* during the latter part of his cruise. Framing Reid as a stereotypical spinner of yarns, Stevenson maintains that Reid is an "expert romancer," who tells his stories with "the pleasing exercise of an imagination more than sailorly." In contrast, Stevenson self-assuredly refers to his own narrative mode as a "record of fact" (254). No wonder, then, that Stevenson's photography vision became central to his South Seas nonfiction.

Stevenson's Photographic Vision

What Stevenson wanted to accomplish with his South Seas writing was always in flux, but photography remained a constant throughout his changing plans. When the Stevenson party boarded the *Casco* in 1888, Colley writes, they brought along with them "an 'old broken' camera, developing equipment, and photographic plates Lloyd fitted 'as best he could'" (114). In April 1889, still unsure of how to incorporate the photography into his narrative, he proposed—rather frantically—an idea to Sidney Colvin for a book of his travels accompanied by a "fine lecture and diorama" to be presented by Lloyd Osbourne and Joseph Strong.[13] This, Stevenson hoped, would "vastly better [their] finances." Though his health was declining and Stevenson was growing increasingly homesick, he insisted that "it would be madness to come home now, with an imperfect book, no illustrations to speak of, no diorama" (275). Writing to the French author and translator Marcel Schwob in August 1890, Stevenson exuberantly declared that he was "waist-deep in [his] big book on the South Seas: *the* big book on the South Seas it ought to be and shall." He added that Lloyd Osbourne was expected to go home to "arrange some affairs" and that Schwob might expect him in Paris, where he would "arrange about the illustrations to my *South Seas*" (401).

The photographic project was in many ways the driving force of the Stevenson party's South Seas cruises, with each member playing a role in its execution. It was very much a collaborative effort, and, as such, Carla Manfredi argues in "Picturing Robert Louis Stevenson's Pacific Phototext," its "authorial entanglement challenges the [scholarly] assumptions of a nominal, uncomplicated author and a homogenous photo-literary project" (9). Lloyd Osbourne was the main photographer, though he was almost always accompanied by Stevenson, who seemed to do most of the directing and choreographing. Fanny Stevenson was often responsible for maintaining and fixing the photographic equipment, Manfredi writes, as well as organizing the photographic albums and providing captions for individual photographs (8).[14] Stevenson could not conceive of his South Seas book project without visual accompaniment. Lacking illustrations, the book was, in his mind, incomplete and inauthentic.

Even after he had all but given up on his "big book," Stevenson continued to take photographs, and he continued to think of new ways of using photography in his writing. Stevenson's interest in melding photography and South Seas history reemerged after he settled in Samoa in 1890. His initial plan was "A Samoan Scrapbook," a collaboration between himself and Joseph Strong: Stevenson would provide the narrative, Strong would be responsible for the photographs. Like so many of Stevenson's narrative/photographic endeavors, this, too, would never come to fruition. Instead, Stevenson would publish *A Footnote to History*, an account of the Samoan Civil War (1882–1892). Once again, it was not what Stevenson's reading public expected. Even Stevenson admitted that it was "not literature, you know; only journalism, and pedantic journalism. . . . There is not a good sentence in it."[15] Unanimated by the planned photographic accompaniment, *A Footnote to History*, though the only completed nonfiction work published during his lifetime, comes across as imaginatively incomplete.

Amid these failures and incomplete projects, Stevenson's "A Samoan Scrapbook" best provides some sense of what Stevenson's "big South Seas" book may have looked like—and what he hoped to accomplish through the use of photography.[16] Guiding his reader through the opening pages, Stevenson interrupts his narrative by referring to Strong's photographs. "The reader can see here for himself," Stevenson writes, directing his audience to the photographs that accompany his comments about missionary presence in Samoa (57). What is most important to Stevenson is the objectivity that these photos lend a narrative that might otherwise be seen as unreliable, merely filtered through Stevenson's own interpretation of Samoa. The photographs, he insists, are "fair, because they are simply random photographs taken with a design entirely artistic, for the effect and not the subject" (57–58). In other words, the photographs speak for themselves. They are not representations, but instead, to return to Stevenson's articulation of his narrative mode, "record[s] of fact."

Between Ethnography and Tourism: Pacific Photography at the Turn of the Century

Given Stevenson's interest in records of fact, one can see why he was so keen on making photography part of his project. In this respect, Stevenson conceived of photography in a manner typical of the late Victorian period; as Joan M. Schwartz and James R. Ryan note in *Picturing Place*, photography was "ideally suited to empiricism and the nineteenth-century passion for collecting, classifying, and controlling facts, whether in the pursuit of comprehensive knowledge or the conduct of imperial administration" (2). Of course, this belief that photography constituted empirical facts was flawed, especially so in the context of the colonial Pacific. By and large, late-colonial photography in the Pacific fell into two differently exploitative camps: first, anthropological and ethnographic photos, intent on framing the "savage" characteristics inherent in Pacific Island cultures; and, second, photographs taken for the growing tourist industry, photographs that allowed viewers to gaze upon the exotic and sexualized beauty of the Pacific. Anne Maxwell, distinguishing between these two forms of photography, writes in *Colonial Photography & Exhibitions* that "the gaze of the scientists who had photographed colonized peoples was rational and objectivist, characterized as it was by an instrumentalism that provided no opportunities for communication. The gaze of the tourist, by contrast, although no less self-enclosed, was nevertheless more subjective because it incorporated emotion" (10). But if the anthropological gaze sought to harden Pacific peoples into a category, emphasizing their savage primitivism, touristic photos emphasized what Elizabeth Edwards terms in "Negotiating Spaces" the "soft primitivism" of Pacific (115). Each had a colonial function.

Presenting Pacific Islanders as intractably savage gave purpose to colonial efforts, urging missionaries and colonists to redouble their efforts, while "soft primitivism" situated Pacific peoples as unresisting, open to the European fantasies being imposed on them. These photographic impulses can also be seen more broadly in the previous two chapters, where the desire to watch an authentic Hawaiian hula highlights soft primitivism and the horrified fascination with the Fijian cannibal fork is representative of the savagizing of Pacific peoples. Photography crystallized and gave evidence to these narratives.

It is worth tracing these trends to better understand how Stevenson's photography fits into its historical context. While Stevenson's photographs generally demonstrate a resistance to reproducing either of these broad stereotypes, they nonetheless remain informed by elements of both. Such ambivalence was common at the turn of the century. As photographic technology became more widely available to amateur photographers, the distinctions between colonial and touristic photographs began to blur. Stevenson and Osbourne's approach to photography would have inevitably been inflected by mid-century exhibition culture. Most of the photographs put on display at Victorian-era exhibitions were taken by government-sponsored photographers, a small group of specialists. However, as the camera became more accessible to the public—George Eastman's Kodak camera was patented in 1888, the "pocket Kodak" in 1895—the trajectory of Pacific photography changed. Distinguishing exhibition photography from emerging tourist photography, Maxwell contends that "exhibitions were designed to support the corporate ideologies of aggressive capitalism. . . . By contrast, photographers of colonized peoples were answerable only to the buying public" (9). A difference in kind, perhaps, but not a difference in effect, for tourist photography was just as stereotypical. The narrative that emerged in the late 1880s instead sought to frame "what remained of cultural artefacts and social practices of allegedly primitive races that were thought to be falling by the wayside in the race for survival. Unlike the objectivist images of colonized peoples' anatomy and other physical features, these photographs were executed in romantic and sentimental style" (10). This romantic style proved to be a very marketable image for tourists jaded by the Europeanization of the Pacific. Pacific women were (and still are) at the forefront of this Pacific touristic photography, implicitly yoking sexual license as enticement for Oceanian travel. As Patricia Johnston puts it in "Advertising Paradise," "rather than enabling the viewer to change places with the model, as advertisements [for other places] typically did, these advertisements encouraged the viewer to objectify the native woman as part of a travel experience the consumer might possess" (191). By the end of the nineteenth century, touristic photographic advertising had become a full-on industry. Apia, the capital of Samoa—where Stevenson would eventually settle—became a photographic hub, churning out images of "Samoan belles" that could be cheaply reproduced for postcards.[17]

This photographic commodification arose alongside the "Pacific cruise," which allowed travelers to comfortably experience the diverse and spread-out South Seas islands. Indeed, the Stevenson party's travels were facilitated by the Pacific cruise industry. And Stevenson was not alone in conceiving of photography as an essential part of the cruise. Photography allowed this new class of travelers to take part in defining Pacific culture. Michael Hayes argues in "Photography and the Emergence of the Pacific Cruise" that such photography functioned as "one of the most insidious forms of colonialism, where indigenous terrain becomes an object of representational knowledge . . . and the site for reproducing colonial relationships of power" (172). In other words, the touristic photographer is merely a subtler colonizer than their government and missionary predecessors. Hayes reads "the use of the camera itself as a signifier of Western superiority," one that demonstrates "how observation is constructed as a practice which stages a privileging of the colonizer." This creates what Hayes terms an "economy of representation," wherein tourist photography reinforces colonial power relations by creating standard representations of Pacific places (173). Pictures inform future tourists, setting a standard of representation that becomes repeated rather than complicated. For Hayes, then, the camera's touristic promise of allowing individuals to capture their own unique experience/viewpoint of the Pacific was a false ideal. Paradoxically, individual access to photography led to collectivization rather than a multiplicity of perspectives.

Hayes's interpretation of touristic photography is essential to interpreting Stevenson's photographs within a postcolonial context; however, in performing such readings, we also run the risk of decontextualizing those photographs. Elizabeth Edwards's model for interpreting Pacific photography, while avoiding presentist impulses, is useful in this respect. Building on Greg Dening's notion of the Pacific encounter as "theater," Edwards suggests that Pacific photography should be read as a "performative or persuasive act directed towards a conscious beholder." Pacific photography, in other words, represents a space of encounter, a negotiation of "the intersecting social spaces which enmesh their making and are embodied in their content" (262). Yet it will not do simply to read Stevenson's photographs in order to recover the encounter that they perhaps sought to capture. Elizabeth Edwards usefully points out that, "through the contexts of their own preservation," these photographs have also acquired ethnographic meaning (262). Thus, Stevenson's photographs are not "uncomplicated repositories," to borrow Manfredi's phrase (1), simple transcripts of a lost world, and their purity cannot be enforced by simply cutting the native out, as Penguin Classics hoped to do. As I show in the next few sections, Stevenson was well aware of this complexity and tried to marshal it for his own purposes.

STAGING AUTHENTICITY: THE PAST AND PRESENT OF THE SOUTH SEAS

While many of Stevenson's photographs come across either ethnographic or romanticizing to contemporary viewers, Stevenson himself actively sought to push against both these stereotypes. For this reason, it seems productive to read Stevenson's Pacific photographs through the lens of Dening's Pacific theater, where, for Stevenson, representation is borne out of a negotiation—or encounter—between Pacific culture in the era of colonialism and Stevenson's own ideas of what constituted authentic (precolonial) Pacific culture. Stevenson was interested in being photographed only with the nobility of the islands, and he was insistent that they dress in "native" attire, even when they had since adopted a more Western style of dress.[18] His reasons for picturing his subjects in "native" attire does not lend itself to one easy critical interpretation. In fact, this impulse is wrapped up in his critique of colonialism. For Stevenson, Polynesian culture could be seen as authentic only if it was untouched by Western influence. But, as he saw it, authenticity was not just a cultural concern but something far more serious. Stevenson theorizes that "where there have been the fewest changes, important and unimportant, salutary or hurtful, there the race survives. Where there have been the most, important or unimportant, salutary or hurtful, there it perishes. . . . There may seem, *a priori*, no comparison between the change of 'sour toddy' to bad gin, and that from an island kilt to a European trousers. Yet I am far from persuaded that the one is any more harmful than the other; and the unaccustomed race will sometimes die of pin-pricks" (34). For Stevenson, then, all Western influence was destructive, "pin-pricks" that moved Polynesian people farther away from a supposed natural state.

Shifting from native to European dress may seem superficial, Stevenson argues, but it is these seemingly superficial things that come together to form a distinct cultural identity. The comparison between the influence of alcohol and the change of attire is pointed. Missionaries often blamed beachcombers for introducing alcohol into island communities, generating a new dependence. The harm of alcohol was visible, an easy marker of what missionaries could label as degeneration. However, European-style clothing was primarily introduced by missionaries, who saw native attire—or lack thereof—as scandalous. But even some missionaries noted the incongruous effect created by Pacific Island peoples donning European clothing. The Wesleyan missionary Walter Lawry, for example, in *Friendly and Feejee Islands*, praises native Fijian modes of dress and insists that "when they try to imitate us by wearing hats or bonnets, they appear quite degraded, and sometimes ridiculous" (69). We might read Lawry in two different ways, depending on our generosity. The optimistic interpretation would be that Lawry is, despite his conservative background, exhibiting cultural deference, suggesting that Fijians should not imitate Europeans lest they lose their own cultural richness. Analyzed more cynically, however, we might see Lawry as suggesting that such superficial imitations can never make them equal to their European converters. The answer to this problem lies somewhere between the two. And so, too, for Stevenson, whose fetishization of the natural and the authentic blinds him to the possibility of cross-cultural interchange. In other words, he can see Polynesian adaptations of European sensibilities only as imitative and unnatural, never as inspired and self-motivated. While Stevenson's concern over Polynesian depopulation was certainly sincere, it was also bound up in his own romanticizing impulses. Much like the writers discussed in chapter 2, Stevenson— despite his criticism of earlier Western writers of the Pacific—arrived with romantic, literary-informed notions of what Polynesian people *should* be. His photographs, accordingly, reflect an ongoing negotiation with presenting the people of the South Seas as they are and presenting them as he imagines they should be.

It is not surprising, then, that Stevenson and his sitters often had very different ideas about what his photographs were meant to accomplish. Stevenson idealized his sitters as unaffected by photographic technology, but his sitters were quick to realize the prestige that came along with being photographed. One particularly humorous illustration of this disjunction is provided in the Marquesas section of Stevenson's *In the South Seas*. While Stevenson and Osbourne are canvassing the Marquesan village of Atuona for photographic opportunities, they are distracted by a local chief named Moipu. Stevenson writes that Moipu arrives on the scene with a "nonchalance that was visibly affected; it was plain to see that he came there to arouse attention, and his success was instant." Even before being photographed, the camera has altered Moipu's behavior; he is already performing for the camera. He is, as Stevenson puts it, a "well-graced actor." But none of this artificiality prevents Stevenson and Osbourne from giving in to Moipu's implied request. In exchange, however, Stevenson insists that Moipu "appear in his war costume" (101). Presumably, this request is motivated by Stevenson's desire that his subject look more native, to perform the version of the South Seas that Stevenson thought of as authentic. Instead, Moipu returns in a "strange, inappropriate, and illomened array (which very well became his handsome person) to strut in a circle of admirers, and be thenceforth the centre of photography." Clearly, it is not a war costume that Moipu puts on. Instead of catering to Stevenson's vision of the authentic Marquesan dress, Moipu puts on something that shows him to his best advantage, that meets the expectations of prestige Moipu's fellow islanders expect.

His rationale soon becomes clear to Stevenson when he sees the rival chief Paaaeua's jealous reaction to the show. From that point onward, Paaaeua acts as a kind of proto-photo bomber, and it becomes impossible "to get a photograph of Moipu alone, for whenever he stood up before the camera his successor placed himself unbidden by his side, and gently but firmly held his position" (102). This anecdote vividly demonstrates that Stevenson's photographic project itself gets in the way of the authenticity he seeks. The camera might have been objective, but the people's responses to it inserted their own motivations into the process. Moipu, thinking politically, knows that the camera offers a new kind of presence, while Paaaeua realizes that his absence has just as much political resonance. It creates a new system of hierarchy, even as Stevenson insists on representing the old, the one represented by the "war costume." Rather than using the camera to represent the South Seas, Stevenson incidentally ends up reconfiguring it.

Indeed, one of the surviving pictures of Moipu and Paaaeua reveals the often-staged nature of Stevenson and Osbourne's early photographs. In the photo (figure 4.3), Moipu and Paaaeua stand side by side, the former dressed in a drab and somewhat ill-fitting European-style suit, the latter in an ornate and elaborate (presumably colorful) traditional war costume.[19] The photograph announces its message even before the caption, "Moipu and Paaaeua, as the past and the present in Atuona," spells it out. It is so heavy-handed as to be almost didactic. Given Stevenson's description of what Moipu puts on the first time he's asked to appear in a photograph—the "strange, inappropriate, and ill-omened array (which very well became his handsome person)"—it is hard to imagine that this would have been Moipu's choice of attire. Far from being a "record of fact," Stevenson's photograph is putting forward its own narrative. It tells the story of two different Marquesas: the rich, culturally distinct precontact identity as opposed to the dull and familiar post-contact one. In other words, Moipu and Paaaeua are used as actors in this scene—ironic given that Stevenson himself has criticized Moipu precisely for being a "well graced actor." They perform a narrative in which they represent the past and the present. They are not the past and the present but are, as Stevenson's caption puts it, performing "*as*" the past and the present. While Paaaeua stands still, chest thrust forward, Moipu appears awkward and ill at ease. His suit pants bunch at the knees and spill out over his shoes. One of his arms hangs down stiffly, the other is positioned awkwardly at a forty-five-degree angle, the way men do when they put their hand in their suit pocket. His hand hovers outside the pocket, its fingers somewhere in between open and balled into a fist. The contrast in poses serves to narrativize the photograph.

Figure 4.3. "Moipu and Paaaeua, as the past and the present in Atuona." Courtesy of
the City of Edinburgh Council.

Paaaeua, made to represent the precontact warrior, appears proud and natural,
while Moipu looks uncomfortable and out of place, his European outfitting
incongruous to both his rival and the lush surroundings that serve as their
backdrop. As a result of this staging, both subjects become props, mere stand-
ins for Stevenson's own story about the loss of Marquesan authenticity as a
result of European influence. In seeking to distance himself from narrative in
favor of history, Stevenson incidentally constructs his own version of authenticity, ignoring the realities that push against his own interpretation.

This photographic approach thus aptly reflects Stevenson's complicated—
and often contradictory—engagement with the stereotypes produced by colonial exhibition culture. Like many colonial-era photographers, Stevenson
emphasizes what anthropologists term "the ethnographic present" (or, ethnographic present tense). The term "present" in this sense has a double meaning,
suggesting both the narrating style that frames other cultures at a sort of historical standstill—a mythical present—and a recognition of the anthropologist's literal presence in crafting these narratives.[20] In the context of colonial
photography, Anne Maxwell argues that the ethnographic present served imperial interests, "deny[ing] its subjects historical and cultural specificity" and
imposing—rather than giving voice to—indigenous perspectives. In other
words, it created a false sense of authenticity (162).

In the photograph of Moipu and Paaaeua, we see Stevenson explicitly seeking to move beyond this present tense, putting it on display beside "the past." But in doing so, Stevenson relies on the same universalism he hoped to unsettle. That is to say, Stevenson creates a monolithic "past" version of Pacific authenticity that is just as artificial a construction as the ethnographic present of colonial exhibitions. Thus, in seeking to counteract these stereotypical images, Stevenson in turn was inventing his own version of Pacific culture.

Like the colonial photographer, Stevenson often relied, both narratively and photographically, on a false construction of distance. For the ethnographic present tense, according to Kirsten Hastrup, seeks to "eliminat[e] both subjectivism and objectivism and posits truth as an intersubjective creation" (46).[21] Despite the constructed nature of Stevenson's photographs, he imagined photography—and the "factual" approach to his written narrative—as bypassing both the subjectivism of romantic writers and the objectivism of a detached ethnographer, hoping that this medium would ultimately allow him to arrive at an intersubjective truth shared between himself and Oceanian peoples.

Even in photography, Stevenson remained a storyteller. He had wanted the camera to produce objective results, uncontaminated by his presence—"pure essence," in Walter Benjamin's words. What he discovered instead was that, to paraphrase Benjamin again, "traces" of his presence "clung to the story the way the handprints of the potter cling to the clay vessel" (91–92). It was, indeed, "pure essence" that Stevenson sought in the first leg of his South Seas travels. Where Melville's *Typee* features "handprints" of Melville's own romantic imagination, much of Stevenson's *In the South Seas* was intended to be informative, reports from a detached perspective, provided with the hope that such impartial accounting would authenticate his work and put it above Melville as the standard for Western accounts of the South Seas. But if the first three quarters of Stevenson's narrative are defined by information and reportage, in the final quarter, Stevenson begins to leave behind traces of storytelling. And likewise, if his early photography seeks—unsuccessfully—to hide the handprints of those behind the camera, Stevenson's Gilbert Islands photographs leave behind traces of the Stevenson party's presence within these communities.

Butaritari, Gilbert Islands: Photography as Exchange

The final section of Stevenson's *In the South Seas*, structured around the Gilbert Islands, marks both a tonal and narrative shift in Stevenson's approach to writing about the South Seas. Rod Edmond suggests in *Representing the South Pacific* that this shift was "partly a result of increasing familiarity." But it is also the case that Stevenson had gradually divested himself of the "tropes and conventions of the dominant late nineteenth-century western discourse of the

Pacific" (167). Such an assessment, however, once again minimizes the role of Pacific places and people, instead suggesting that each unique island was merely a blank slate for Stevenson to interpret. While doubtless Stevenson's sense of the Pacific was becoming increasingly nuanced, the Gilbert Islands themselves deserve just as much credit for the shift in Stevenson's literary approach.

The Gilbert Islands (Kiribati), a chain of sixteen atolls south of Hawaii and west of Samoa and the Cook Islands, were a sort of last bastion of the pre-colonial Pacific. Less environmentally rich than their island counterparts, the Gilbert Island atolls drew little interest from traders. Missionaries, too, were reluctant to pursue the fiercely independent atolls. When missionaries finally did arrive in 1870, they encountered difficulties, since each small island functioned as its own independent kingdom.[22] Having arrived less than twenty years after missionary contact, Stevenson found the islands to be much nearer to what he expected at the beginning of his Pacific cruise. If in the Marquesas and Hawaii Stevenson was continually troubled by the feeling that he had arrived too late, in the Gilbert Islands he felt that he had arrived just in time. Stevenson notes that "in the last decade, many changes have crept in; women no longer go unclothed till marriage; the widow no longer sleeps at night and goes abroad by day with the skull of her dead husband; and, fire-arms being introduced, the spear and the shark-tooth are sold for curiosities. Ten years ago all these things and practices were to be seen in use; yet ten years more, and the old society will have entirely vanished. We came at a happy moment to see its institutions still erect and (in Apemama) scarce decayed" (156). The Gilbert Islands, in other words, were still a place of exchange and encounter, still the liminal space that typifies Dening's "beach." This moment of transition, of course, is ideal for a traveler. It's an opportunity to freely engage with local culture without having to endure any significant risks. It is, then, first and foremost, a "happy moment" for Stevenson.

It is in the Gilbert Islands that Stevenson begins to emerge as a presence with his text. In other words, the location frees him from the burden of competing authorities. Not surprisingly, the Stevenson family photographs likewise become more animated and unpredictable, less focused on ethnography and historicizing. In short, the photographs seem to capture moments of genuine encounter rather than predictable scenes. There is a sense of curiosity in these photographs to match the curiosity that finally makes its way into the narrative proper. Edmond notes that "as *In the South Seas* moves from the Marquesas to the Paumotus, and then onto the Gilberts in the western Pacific, it becomes less introspective and less inclined to sweeping generalization, more relaxed" (167). Likewise, the Stevenson party's Gilbert Islands photographs come across as more relaxed, less likely to rely on familiar

photographic tropes and elaborate staging, such as what we see in the photograph of Moipu and Paaaeua. But in recognizing this, we should remem-
ber that Stevenson's sense of relaxation was predicated on the Gilbert Islands
meeting his own standard of what the Pacific should be to the Western traveler. In other words, Stevenson is at ease because the Gilbert Islands provide
him with a type of cultural encounter and exchange that he already associated
with the Pacific. Accordingly, the narrative of Stevenson's photographs shifts
here. No longer is he interested in telling the story of the unfortunate imposition of European culture onto Pacific peoples. In the Gilbert Islands, Stevenson is intent on capturing a final moment of Western-Pacific exchange before
the Gilbert Islands, too, become just another colonial territory. And that is a
narrative in which he and his party must be included.

This shift in focus toward encounter can perhaps best be seen in a photograph not of Stevenson himself but of Joseph Strong. Taken in Butaritari—
the site of one of the liveliest sections in Stevenson's book—the photograph
centers on Strong as he takes out his false teeth in front of a gawking crowd
(figure 4.4). At first glance, we might see this photograph as merely advancing
the familiar trope of the Westerner showing off his culture's superior technology. Indeed, Strong occupies a central position both in terms of composition and narrative. The craned heads of the spectators—notably dressed in
European-style clothing and broad brimmed hats—direct our view toward
Strong, compelling the viewer to turn their head along with them. Everyone is
so fascinated with what is going on with Strong that no one acknowledges the
camera right behind him. But with Strong's back turned toward the viewer,
we can't see what they see. Our gaze, then, is directed at their gazes. We look
not at the source of their fascination but instead at their fascination itself. In
doing so, our gaze is recirculated: we turn back to Strong, whose gaze can only
be returned by the crowd.

In this way, we might think of this photograph as capturing a moment of
exchange. As central as Strong is in the composition of the photograph, his
position is, in fact, a vulnerable one. He kneels before an assembled group
of I-Kiribati, allowing them to gaze almost directly into his mouth—the
man in the middle, bends his body almost perpendicular to get an especially
good look. Their mouths open as much in awe as in sympathetic imitation
of Strong. Strong is clearly playing the showman here—as he was fond of
doing—but, in doing so, he is also putting himself on display. Strong positions
himself as a curiosity, an anthropological specimen to be studied by his interested observers. And, as much as this highlights the advancements of Western
technology, Strong also lays those advancements bare, exposing their falseness. Like a magician pulling back the curtain to reveal the secret of his trick,
Strong demystifies Western technology, letting his audience in on the secret.

Figure 4.4. "'Disbelief': Removing False Teeth." Courtesy of the City of Edinburgh Museums and Galleries; Writers' Museum, www.capitalcollections.org.uk.

Strong's false teeth work metaphorically here as a representation of the falseness produced by Western advancements; they are, in other words, a model of inauthenticity. Such exposure seems especially significant in the context of Stevenson's photographic project. Much as Strong's false teeth are mere facsimile, so, too, are Stevenson's photographs. His photographs appear to display the authentic South Seas, but that authenticity is a carefully crafted illusion. The photograph of Strong removing his false teeth, then, can be read as representative of the shifting nature of Stevenson's photographic project. In exposing the manipulation of authenticity through Western technologies, the photograph offers a subtle commentary on the camera itself. Just as Strong's exposure of his false teeth creates this moment, so, too, does the camera. In other words, this photograph achieves Stevenson's ideal of authenticity by calling attention to its own interference. It becomes not simply a unilateral photograph—one where our gaze homes in on "native" subjects—but rather a circulatory one.

Unlike earlier photographs, then, this one does not imagine the camera as passive and unmotivated. That is to say, we do not see the same staging and false construction of distance that we see in many of the earlier photographs. There is a sense of vitality to this picture. Such vitality is most clearly an effect of the crowd's craned heads and slanted bodies. Even as their response makes them come across as almost interlinked, the people within the crowd appear fluid. Instead of seeking to represent authentic Pacific culture as though from the perspective of an unbiased spectator, this photograph recognizes that interaction and exchange between cultures make up travel's authenticity. Though Stevenson is compelled to continue in his ethnographically motivated style of writing, the Gilbert Islands seem to push against such an approach. Nowhere is this more evident than in the section subtitled "Husband and Wife." Opening this section, Stevenson relies on what has become a familiar anthropological approach, focusing broadly on relations between husbands and wives within Butaritari culture. The details he provides, Stevenson concedes, "would seem to indicate a Mohammedan society and the opinion of the soullessness of women." But this, he counters, is "not so in the least. It is a mere appearance" (202). According to the generic standards set up by Stevenson thus far in *In the South Seas*, this would be the moment where Stevenson might refer the reader to a nugget of oral tradition, a story that would buttress his ethnographic theorizing. Not so in the least. Instead, Stevenson refers to his experience rather than to his imagined historical and anthropological expertise, detailing his and his wife's relationship with the Butaritari royal couple Nei Takauti and Nan Tok' discussed in the opening of this chapter.

Fittingly, the Stevensons first meet Nei Takauti and Non Tok' in what appears to be a quintessential Pacific beach encounter. It is Fanny Stevenson who first encounters the couple, and her written account of this exchange is much livelier than Robert's. Venturing—against orders—outside of their small residence, Fanny took to the beach to collect shells. Here, she writes, "a strange man and woman joined me; they were not reassuring companions, judging from their outer appearances, as they were unkempt, clad in nothing but a small fragment, each, of dirty, old gunny sack, and their faces were anxious and haggard." Despite their less than "reassuring" appearance, a wary Fanny continued to collect shells as the pair watched passively. Unable to scare Fanny off, the couple eventually took to chasing Fanny off the beach, before finally resorting to "seizing [her] by the arms, one on either side." Dragging her feet as they carried her, "the lady, evidently with a kindly feeling for my comfort, drew a clay pipe from out an enormous hole in her ear, stuffed it with a strong, coarse tobacco, lighted it, puffed a moment, and then placed it in my mouth." This proved to be just enough to pacify Fanny. When the two finally got her into town, "the man fell on his knees and offered up a fervent prayer." As it turned out, Nan Tok' and Nei Takauti were concerned for Fanny's safety, the pipe was meant to "conciliate [her] because of a supposed fiery gleam in [her] eye that disconcerted them" and the prayer was to "bless what they hoped would be a new friendship" (58–59). Stevenson recounts Fanny's experience with far less drama. As he tells it, Nan Tokʻ and Nei Takauti "took her in their charge," and "on the way, the lady drew from her earring-hole a clay pipe, the husband lighted it, and it was handed to my unfortunate wife, who knew not how to refuse the incommodious favour" (203). If Fanny's version demonstrates the risk of encounter, Stevenson's telling highlights the exchange. From this moment of uncertainty arose an intimate relationship between the two couples. We see this intimacy in the photograph that opens this chapter.

It is perhaps even more compelling that we can see the ease Nan Tokʻ and Nei Takauti felt with Stevenson in the portrait genre. In a photograph taken of Nei Takauti and Nan Tokʻ taken in their home (figure 4.5), the seated pair direct their gazes away from the camera, looking off into the distance. This was typical of many of the Stevenson party's portraits; but the gazes of Nan Tokʻ and Nei Takauti are different, animated rather than stoic. Both force their eyes up and away from the camera, with the low angle of the camera accentuating the strain, while they deliberately avoid the gaze positioned directly at them.

Figure 4.5. "Nan Tokʻ and Nei Takauti." Courtesy of the City of Edinburgh Museums and Galleries; Writers' Museum, www.capitalcollections.org.uk.

Nei Takauti looks amused, fully aware of herself looking away from the camera. Nan Tok' looks even more amused, his face seems clenched as in an effort to repress his smile. Such a look fits with Stevenson's description of him: "extremely handsome, of the most approved good humour, and suffering in his precarious station from suppressed high spirits" (203). While Nei Takauti's hands lie stiffly close to the sides, Nan Tok''s hands appear in motion, his body slightly slouched forward, failing to capture the regal pose of a chief.

This photographic portrait is unique among the Stevenson family's archive in that it comes across as at once posed and spontaneous. There is a sense of self-awareness to it, a sense that both sides of the photograph are aware that this is a moment of cultural exchange. Nan Tok' and Nei Takauti smile at the conventions of the portrait photograph even while performing them. And this sense of intimacy is not just limited to the way the couple is represented; it also extends to the relationship between the sitters and the photographer. It is clear from their relaxed poses that they are collaborators in the photographic process rather than just subjects. This is a crucial distinction. Unlike most colonial sitters, they appear nuanced and vibrant, mobile even while posing. Anne McClintock argues in *Imperial Leather* that in the context of the colonial portrait, "the immobility of the sitter conceals behind the surface of the photograph the violence of the colonial encounter" (126). Building on this claim, Anne Maxwell further suggests that the immobility of the sitters "and their inability to respond to the fantasies being imposed . . . formed the source of their disempowerment" (162). Here, we get the sense that the couple is *in* on the photo rather than merely passive objects of the photographic lens. They are empowered rather than stereotyped.

We might think of their coy smiles and relaxed postures as the "handprints" of the storyteller, in Benjamin's terminology, as evidence of the warm relationship that informs this narrative. This photograph comes across not as an attempt to portray Polynesian authenticity but rather as an attempt to authentically represent these unique individuals, as Stevenson knew them. This can be seen first at the level of setting. The couple is photographed in the comfort of their home, suggesting the intimacy that the Stevenson party shared with them. Many of the photographic props are reflected in Stevenson's narrative as well. The same clay pipe that Nei Takauti used to quiet Fanny hangs out of her mouth. Nan Tok', his chest bare, neck adorned with necklaces, sits angled in such a way to fully reveal a portrait of a European lady on the wall behind him. The photograph seems staged to reveal Stevenson's fascination with the reversal of gender roles in this relationship, a fact that Stevenson addresses head-on when he writes about Nei Takauti: "Whatever pretty thing my wife might have given to Nei Takauti appeared the next evening on the person of Nan Tok'. It was plain he was a clothes-horse; that he wore livery;

Figure 4.6. "Butaritari—Maka and Mary Maka, Kanoa and Mrs Maria Kanoa—
Hawaiian missionaries of the American Board of Missions, Honolulu." Courtesy of
the City of Edinburgh Museums and Galleries; Writers' Museum, www.capital
collections.org.uk.

that, in a word, he was his wife's wife" (203). In Stevenson's photograph, then,
the Islanders are humanized; they are distinct characters rather than mere
stereotypes.

This photograph is even more remarkable when we compare it with an
earlier Butaritari couple's portrait featuring the Hawaiian missionary couples
Maka and Mary Maka and Konoa and Mrs. Mary Kanoa (figure 4.6). In the
photograph, the two men sit rigidly on wooden chairs and look severely at
the camera, and their wives dutifully hover over them. All four subjects are
attired impeccably in European-style clothing. The whole scene feels stiff,
choreographed. The background to the picture furthers the impression of artificiality. The houses behind them, built in a traditional Oceanian style with
coconut trunks and leaves, blend in with the lush forest, suggesting a potential
harmony between nature and culture that is not extended to the people. Despite the excessive formality of the staging, there remains a degree of disorder
in the picture. The couples are similarly arranged, with the men seated and
the women hovering above them, but a stray chair to the left of Maka and
Mary and a stool in front of Maria Kanoa disrupt the parallelism. In such
a clearly staged photograph, visual disruptions should not be overlooked as

mere sloppy arrangement. Instead, they seem to be intended to heighten the photograph's narrative of the discordance between Pacific nature and European culture. The empty chair, positioned at an awkward angle, could easily have been moved out of the frame altogether. Maka and Mary Maka are positioned directly in front of the massive trunk of a tree; that tree trunk cuts between the two couples, in turn framing the clutter in front of one of the houses behind them.

Like the picture of Nan Tok' and Nei Takauti, the couples occupy a liminal space, but here that liminality is framed by Stevenson and Osbourne as evidence of inauthenticity. The couples are part of the natural Pacific world, but that world is also behind them. The liminality of the former photograph seems vivid and enriching: the portrait of the European lady behind Nan Tok', the contrast between Nei Takauti's Pacific-style shoulder-baring white dress and the Western tablecloth. Where Nan Tok' and Nei Takauti demonstrate a distinctly non-Western reversal of gender roles, the rigidity of gender roles among Maka and Mary Maka and Konoa and Mrs. Mary Kanoa is embodied in their postures. The men sit, stoic and proud, while the women stand, hands devotedly on the shoulders of their husbands and eyes averted from the camera in a show of humility. We get no sense that Stevenson and his party are intimately acquainted with these missionary couples, as they were with Nei Takauti and Nan Tok'. Nor do we get any sense of their individuality. They are, like Moipu and Paaeau, presented as props for the vitiating effects of Western intervention, the only difference being that this underlying purpose is more subtly presented.

Yet we should be careful, too, about buying into Stevenson's own distinctions between the "unnatural" post-contact Pacific world and the theoretically more intact Pacific Islands still in the midst of cultural exchange. As the deliberate staging of disorder in the portrait of the Hawaiian missionaries suggests, Stevenson was adept at using photography to do what literary narrative could not. If we praise Stevenson for emerging more strongly as a presence within Kiribati, we should also be aware that he has become more adept here at controlling his own narrative of South Seas authenticity. While the narrative of the loss of Pacific authenticity is much less clumsy and more sophisticated than in the earlier photograph of Moipu and Paaaeua, it presents a similar story, especially when viewed in comparison to the photograph of Nan Tok' and Nei Takauti. This pairing is not my own invention. Fanny Stevenson made this distinction explicit, noting that Nan Tok' and Nei Takauti were "a different sort from Maka and Mary, being natives of Butaritari and, from Maka's point of view, quite uncivilised" (4). It is the sense of being untouched by European civilization that animates the Stevenson party's interest in Nan Tok' and Nei Takauti. "Uncivilized," they are Stevenson's story to tell. In a way, they are Stevenson's story to colonize, his own Pacific possessions, rather than figures already claimed by previous writers.

APEMAMA, GILBERT ISLANDS: THE LIMITS OF TOURIST PHOTOGRAPHY

In Apemama, Stevenson finally realized his desire to take sole literary possession of an entire Pacific place. Abemama—Stevenson spells it as Apemama[23]—a small Kiribati atoll, positioned just north of the equator, was, at the time of Stevenson's arrival, "the last erect vestige of a dead [Pacific Islands] society." Stevenson, finding his romantic voice here, writes that "the white man is everywhere else, building his houses, drinking his gin, getting in and out of trouble with the weak native governments." Not so in Apemama, which is "left alone, the tourist dreading to risk himself in the clutch of Tembinok'" (204). In saying this, Stevenson establishes an implicit contrast between himself and the tourist. The tourist, as Stevenson sees it, travels only where it is safe. But the "adventurer," as Stevenson refers to himself (179), knows that risk is at the heart of travel. Stevenson frames Apemama as a "last vestige" of the authentic South Seas, a space free from Europeanization. His way of thinking takes us back to Dening's definition of eighteenth- and early-nineteenth-century Pacific encounter. The beach is once again a place of both risk and potential exchange. Stevenson writes: "In all the other isles of the South Seas a white man may land with his chest, and set up a house for a lifetime, if he choose, and if he have the money or the trade, no hindrance is conceivable. But Apemama is a closed island, lying there in the seas with closed doors; the king himself, like a vigilant officer, ready at the wicket to scrutinise and reject intrenching visitors. Hence the attraction of our enterprise; not merely because it was a little difficult, but because this social quarantine, a curiosity itself, has been the preservative of others." Stevenson knew this would not be the case much longer. He wistfully predicts that "ten years more, and the old society will have entirely vanished. We came at a happy moment to see its institutions still erect and (in Apemama) scarce decayed" (156).[24]

Yet despite the superficially dangerous nature of this encounter, the Stevenson party was well set up. Convinced that Stevenson and his party have no political designs—no "'peaking," as Tembinok' terms it—they are granted admission.[25] His terms: they were "to choose a site, and the king should there build us a town." In return, Stevenson's party would be obliged to take on the king's own cook, who would be trained by Stevenson's personal cook; the king was to always receive a dish from Stevenson's table, and Stevenson could not share with any of the king's subjects liquor, tobacco, or money, all of which they could only receive from the king himself (218). With these terms in place, Stevenson and his party established what they dubbed Equator Town

Figure 4.7. "Stevenson's Camp at Apemama. 'Equator-Town.'" Courtesy of the City of Edinburgh Museums and Galleries; Writers' Museum, www.capitalcollections.org.uk.

(figure 4.7), named after their boat the *Equator* but also a fitting name for the geographically liminal border they occupied. Comfortably situated within Equator Town, the Stevenson party was physically within Apemama but culturally outside of it, much like a modern resort. The picture of Equator Town emphasizes its proto-resort qualities. While the lush palms that overlay the town's huts create a sense of immersion within the Apemaman environment, the clearing from which the photograph is taken demonstrates the illusory nature of this immersion. It is as if the clearing were made explicitly for the purpose of that very camera angle. Taken from this distance, the photograph captures the prominence of cleared space, revealing the "town" as something akin to a dramatic set piece.

It is fitting, then, that Stevenson appears as if he were a movie director, for Equator Town offered Stevenson, finally, the chance to take control of a South Seas narrative. We can barely make out the figures, but Stevenson's long frame is recognizable: one arm akimbo, the other pointing, an image of both ease and control. Stevenson's pose epitomizes his sense of literary authority within this South Seas space. More than just an image of Equator Town, the photograph represents Stevenson as the king of his domain. Yet, in another way, this picture recalls the photograph of Joe Strong removing his false teeth. Both pictures pull back the curtain, offering an almost behind-the-scenes look at the party's experiences within Kiribati. But if the camera is in on the act in the photograph of Joe Strong, here the camera seems to only incidentally reveal the artificiality of Western pretensions. While the narrative suggests that Stevenson engaged in a more open type of exchange within Apemama than he had been involved in anywhere else in the South Seas, this photograph hints at the staged and controlled nature of that exchange. If the photograph offers only the illusion of assimilation, Stevenson's self-conscious dramatic pose in the image reinforces that whatever control one might think he had over his photo-narrative project in Apemama is a matter of wishful thinking rather than fact.

Nevertheless, scholars have been quick to buy into this illusion as well, taking for granted that the Apemama section is objectively the best part of *In the South Seas*. In his introduction to the Penguin Classics edition, Neil Rennie offhandedly says as much, calling it "the best of the four parts of the book." It is only here, Rennie argues, that we see Stevenson "no longer attempt[ing] to transcend the personal, to write The South Seas rather than In the South Seas" (xxx). Indeed, Stevenson is very much "in" this section, more so than he is in the previous ones, not only an observer but also a participant observer. Vanessa Smith similarly asserts in *Literary Culture and the Pacific* that within "the close community of Abemama, Stevenson achieves a semblance of that first contact which he has repeatedly sought" (134). Reading Stevenson's time in Abemama as "prelude to his settlement in Samoa," Rod Edmond believes that this final part of *In the South Seas* is better focused than earlier ones. Stevenson "looks more closely than before at the particularities of native lifeways and begins to experience some of the complexity of cross-cultural transaction from the point of view of a settler rather than the traveller" (168). For David Farrier, too, Abemama was the closest Stevenson came to "the possibility of engaging in reciprocal encounter" (71). Implicit in each of these assertions is the idea that there is something more authentic about this section—or, at the very least, that here Stevenson comes closest to achieving the type of authenticity he saw as essential to his South Seas experience. That is to say, taken as a whole, scholars have tended to evaluate the Apemama section on Stevenson's terms and through Stevenson's language.

Stevenson himself recognized the Apemama section as his strongest, turning to it as the selling point for his project and treating it as the account most uniquely qualified to accommodate both his narrative and his photographic interests. In 1890, pitching the project to Edward Burlingame, the editor of *Scribner's*, Stevenson tells him that he would send him "some photographs, a portrait of Tembinoka,[26] perhaps a view of the palace or of the 'matted men' at their signing, also T[embinoka]'s flag, which my wife designed for him: in a word, what I can do best for you. It will thus be a foretaste of my book of travels" (365; February 1890). Apemama remobilized Stevenson's flagging enthusiasm for his book project, providing him with untapped material. Significantly, Stevenson pitches his book no longer as his "big South Seas book" but rather as "my book of travels." Paradoxically, this shift toward the self marks Stevenson's turn toward a more genuine account of the Pacific. The pitch suggests that Stevenson is no longer claiming expertise in Pacific Islands culture but instead expertise in his *own experience* within Pacific Islands culture.

In 1894, well after Stevenson had given up on writing new material and only months before his death, he wrote to Colvin that he "read over again the King of Apemama, and it is good in spite of your teeth,[27] and a real curiosity, a thing that can never be seen again, and the group is annexed and Tembinoka dead" (August 7, 1894). Stevenson frames its merit around the scarceness of what he describes. Apemama was, at the time of his writing, unspoiled by European contact. Contrast this with his rant to Colvin about why he chose not to write about Honolulu at all: "As for telling you where I went or when, or anything about Honolulu, I would rather die; that is fair and plain. How can anybody care when or how I left Honolulu? A man upwards of forty cannot waste his time communicating matter of that indifference. The letters, it appears, are tedious; they would be more tedious still if I wasted time on such infantile and bottle sucking details. If ever I put in any such detail, it is because it leads to something, or serves as a transition. To tell it for its own sake; never! The mistake is that all through I have told the reader too much, I have not had sufficient confidence in the reader and have overfed him" (September 7, 1891). For Stevenson, writing about Honolulu has no stakes: "a man upwards of forty" should not be wasting his time writing about a place already all too familiar to Western readers. He has "overfed" those readers because Honolulu, like much of the Pacific, has already been interpreted. But Apemama is a "real curiosity." Stevenson's use of the word "real" here implicitly privileges the idea of the authentic. Only Stevenson can tell the story of this last bastion of Pacific Island authenticity. No danger of "overfeeding" the reader.

Tembinok', the King of Apemama, provided Stevenson with the type of authentic Pacific Island story he had been seeking all along. Tembinok' was Stevenson's story to tell, his own narrative possession. And, indeed, it is Stevenson's account of Tembinok' that stuck with readers. Stevenson's first biographer, Graham Balfour, remarks in *The Life of Robert Louis Stevenson*, "Who, that has read the South Seas chapters has forgotten [Tembinok's] appearance?" (257). Yet even in this section, Stevenson remains naively insistent that he is providing an objective and authentic history rather than his own narrative interpretation. Tembinok' says to Stevenson that he "look your eye. You a good man. You no lie." Turning toward his readers, Stevenson quips that this is "a doubtful compliment to a writer of romance" (218). But it is quite a compliment to a nonfiction travel writer convinced of the superior authenticity of his account. Certainly Tembinok's assessment accords with that of Stevenson's contemporary critics, who saw his nonfiction writing about the South Seas as not romantic enough. Even as Stevenson dismisses this as a "dubious compliment," he seems to highly value Tembinok's opinion, for it suggests that he is, indeed, more interested in authenticity than in the romanticism of past writers. It is only a few sentences later that Stevenson declares his writing "records of fact." As he does throughout his writing, Stevenson equates honesty with historical accuracy. Honesty means the absence of embellishment. But even as Stevenson lacks textual presence, he, much as is the case with his photography, neglects to consider the way his presence might reshape the people and places he encounters. As Rosalyn Jolly points out, Stevenson seemed to "have thought little about how the presence of the observer might affect the thing observed, how the desire to impress or please his visitors might have modified Tembinok's behavior or influenced what he was prepared to reveal to them" (46). In particular, Jolly speculates that Tembinok' may have softened some of his tyrannical behavior, keenly aware that Stevenson would be responsible for how he was perceived by the outside world.

Yet even this more critical suggestion falls into the same trap of reading Stevenson's narrative ambitions on his own terms; it imagines Stevenson's project as always his own, always imposition and never exchange. Jolly's argument might be turned around: it's just as likely that Stevenson altered his behavior in the presence of Tembinok'. Tembinok' coaxes the romanticist out of Stevenson, even as he flatters Stevenson by praising his honesty and objectivity. The critical praise of Stevenson's presence in this final section is thus misleading. In turning to this section as evidence of Stevenson's coming to embrace cross-cultural exchange, we ignore the exchange going on at the level of narrative and photography. That is to say, though we use the term "exchange," what we are really often suggesting is something more unilateral: Stevenson coming to understand Oceanian perspectives and their way of living. But exchange, of course, requires give-and-take from both parties. Rather than reading exchange merely in the events Stevenson recounts, then, we should consider the exchange occurring at the level of the artifacts he creates.

Tembinok' dominates Stevenson's photographs and narrative in much the same way that Tembinok' controls his kingdom. In this way, Stevenson and Tembinok' become cowriters—for better or for worse—of Apemaman history. Stevenson seems to imagine himself as being exempt from Tembinok's assertion, "Here in my island, I 'peak . . . My chieps no 'peak—do what I talk."

Figure 4.8. "King Tembinoka writing the 'History of Apemama' in an account book."
Courtesy of the City of Edinburgh Museums and Galleries; Writers' Museum, www
.capitalcollections.org.uk.

True, Stevenson may have the freedom to "'peak" in a way that Tembinok's
subjects did not, but it would be shortsighted to think Tembinok' does not
"'peak" alongside Stevenson. Indeed, Stevenson and Tembinok' often come
across as analogues in this section. Just as Stevenson pens his "history" of
the South Seas, Tembinok' is engaged in the writing of his own "History of
Apemama." In a photograph taken of King Tembinok' at work on his history,
we see him absorbed in his work, seemingly unaffected by both the presence
of the camera and those around him (figure 4.8). As the caption points out,
Tembinok' writes his history in an "account book," one likely procured from
the rare Western travelers Tembinok' granted access to. It is certainly an image
Tembinok' would have been fond of, framing him for the rest of the world as
both powerful and literate, taking control of his nation's history through his
mastery of Western modes of knowledge production.

In recounting this scene, Stevenson explicitly draws parallels between himself as a writer and Tembinok'. Stevenson perceives Tembinok' as a kindred
spirit, as he sees him "lying on his belly, writ[ing] from day to day the un-
eventful history of his reign." And like Stevenson, he does not respond well

to being disturbed: "When thus employed he betrayed a touch of fretfulness on interruption with which I was well able to sympathise." Tembinok's failings as a writer likewise recall criticisms made by others of Stevenson's own South Seas project: "The royal annalist once read me a page or so, translating as he went; but the passage being genealogical, and the author boggling extremely in his version, I own I have been sometimes better entertained." Like Stevenson, Tembinok' demonstrates a tendency toward the information and reportage that is the antithesis of Benjamin's storyteller. Such a fidelity to information—such an inevitably "boggled" pursuit of authenticity—bores Stevenson in much the same way as his early South Seas letters bored his readers. And yet, Tembinok' accomplishes what Stevenson fails to, for Tembinok' does not "confine himself to prose, but touches the lyre too, in his leisure moments he passes for the chief bard of his kingdom. . . . These multifarious occupations bespeak (in a native and absolute prince) unusual activity of mind" (227). It is Tembinok's control over his kingdom—both literarily and otherwise—that prevents Stevenson from controlling the narrative of Tembinok'. His mastery reflects the mastery that Stevenson himself desires.

His observant character also causes Stevenson to reflect on him as sharing an almost visual mastery of his subjects. Stevenson describes him as often taking on a look that was "wholly impersonal: I have seen the same in the eyes of portrait-painters." We can see in a photograph of Tembinok' and his adopted son this simultaneously proud and impersonal look in his eyes (figure 4.9). His military regalia once again signifies his selective engagement with European culture. Meanwhile, his gaze, proud and defiantly directed away from the camera—his hair and ascot flow back against the wind—suggests a resistance to the camera's attempt to represent him as a colonized subject. Far from being controlled by Stevenson and the camera, Tembinok' takes control of it. If we think of Stevenson and Tembinok' as analogues, it is worth considering the contrast in physical characteristics. The photographs of Tembinok' writing in his account book and of Tembinok' with his adopted son both showcase Tembinok's massive bulk. In the former photograph, Tembinok's body cuts the photograph; his head is seemingly twice the size of everyone gathered around him, his hands as big as the book he writes in. In the latter photograph, Tembinok's limbs spill out over his wooden chair as he pulls his son against his massive body. Tembinok' is a vital and unwieldy photographic subject, pushing against Stevenson's attempts define him. Even as Stevenson obsessively photographs and writes about Tembinok', he refuses to become merely Stevenson's own story to tell.

Instead, it is Tembinok' who comes to possess Stevenson's photographic gaze and narrative direction. While King Tembinok' provides Stevenson with a central character around which to frame his narrative, his obsessive focus on

Figure 4.9. "Tembi-nok[a], King of Ape-mama." Courtesy of the City of Edinburgh Museums and Galleries; Writers' Museum, www.capitalcollections.org.uk.

him decenters the people of Apemama. Tembinok' at once offers Stevenson the South Seas authenticity that he so desperately sought out and also circumscribes Stevenson's experience of Apemama. In the narrative, these people are almost completely absent; in the photographs they often come across as mere props. This propping up can be seen quite literally in a photograph Stevenson captioned "The manner in which the king is carried about" (figure 4.10). Here, King Tembinok', dressed in all white, rises proudly above the dejected group of servants carrying him. It is worth noting that while the caption frames the picture as active—the king is "carried about"—the picture itself actually interferes with the moment it is meant to be portraying. More simply, things come to a stop for the picture. The Apemaman people, shoulders collapsing under the weight of their king, look directly at the camera, but their blank expressions suggest an awareness that they are being looked past, that they are objects on display rather than performers. The dehumanization of the Apemaman people in favor of centralizing Tembinok' can further be seen in a photograph with Tembinok' and his many wives (figure 4.11). Tembinok' and his adopted son stand in the foreground, both fully attired; Tembinok''s wives all sit cross-legged, some shabbily clothed, others fully nude. In this way, Tembinok''s wives come across as one uniform whole. The picture displays not

Figure 4.10. "The manner in which the King is carried about." Courtesy of the City of Edinburgh Council.

Figure 4.11. "King Tembinoka with his adopted son—standing in front of wives." Courtesy of the City of Edinburgh Museums and Galleries; Writers' Museum, www .capitalcollections.org.uk.

Tembinok"s wives but the *idea* of Tembinok"s wives. That is to say, his wives are there merely to tell the story of Tembinok's power. So while it may seem that the Apemama section is where Stevenson begins to take authorial control of his project, it is actually where he becomes most decentered—more present within the narrative itself but less present in the creation of it.

Mesmerizing Stevenson: A Shared Pacific Possession

It is hardly any surprise that Stevenson did not make many friends outside the privileged space of the king's company. Tembinok' was not solely to blame for this. Pampered, Stevenson admits that he "saw but little of the commons of the isle." Stevenson's privilege was a source of ire for the Apemanans, who, in hushed tones, derisively referred to him as *kaupoi*, the rich man. And why not? While native Apemamans lived on what little they had, Stevenson was treated lavishly, outfitted, for example with his own royal chef. Stevenson, however, saw this unnamed cook as doing more harm than good—he felt he was lazy and incompetent. Despite Stevenson's best efforts to keep this information from Tembinok', the king finds out. It does not take long for Tembinok' to erupt. Taking out his Winchester, he fires upon Stevenson's unnamed cook. These shots, Stevenson assures the reader and perhaps himself, were only warning shots, for when Tembinok' "aims to kill, the grave may be got ready; and when he aims to miss, misses by so near a margin that the culprit tastes six times the bitterness of death." Bitter, the banished cook often skulked around Equator Town. Finally, a paranoid Stevenson chased him down, forcing him to flee. But not before Stevenson kicked him "in the place where honour lies." When Stevenson tracks the cook down again, he promises that he will not tell the king but insists, with all the boldness of a man supported by a ruthless tyrant, that next time he caught him prowling he would "shoot him on the spot; and to proof showed him a revolver" (232). This is a compelling, albeit unwieldy, metaphor for the way the white traveler's privilege inevitably interferes with local communities. While Stevenson's arrival opens up a new job for the cook, it also makes his position on the island subject to the whims of the rich traveler. In the context of his time, Stevenson was a benevolent visitor. Yet even his mercy is underlined with a threat. The space in Apemama created for the cook by Stevenson also becomes the space through which the cook becomes regulated and punished.

Despite the mix of guilt and admiration Stevenson felt for the cook, it seems Stevenson did not learn his lesson. Commenting on his lack of engagement with the "commons," Stevenson notes that local villagers used to meet with the Stevenson party at a nearby well. Unfortunately for Stevenson, while he was getting his drinking water from the well, those same commoners were washing their linen. "The combination was distasteful," Stevenson remarks, without even the marginal reflection he gives on the incident with the cook, "and, having a tyrant at our command, we applied to the king and had the place enclosed in our *tapu*." The metaphor is easier here. Stevenson is willing to interact with the common people of Apemama, but he does not want to share the same well with them. He appeals to the tyrant to support his own comfort at the expense of the local people's access to water. Even Tembinok' is at a loss for how to respond: "It was one of the few favours which Tembinok' visibly boggled about granting," and, Stevenson adds in the passage's first moment of self-awareness, "it may be conceived how little popular it made [us] strangers" (234).

Coming to realize his lack of involvement with Apemaman culture, Stevenson asked Tembinok' if his medicine men might try to cure him of a nagging cold. Stevenson's first attempt doesn't turn out so well. Eager to immerse himself in local custom, he sought out the famed Apemaman medicine man Tamaiti. But Stevenson found it difficult to lose himself in the moment, with the "irreverent sorcerer" chatting like "an affable dentist," talking of "foreign places—of London, and companies, and how much money they had; of San Francisco, and the nefarious fogs" (246). Worse yet was the "incongruous presence of Mr. Osbourne with a camera" (246–47). Staged by Stevenson as a moment of risk—he "tried vainly to lead" Tamaiti—this encounter instead becomes all too familiar: Tamaiti is more like the chatty dentist back home than the exotic South Seas sorcerer that Stevenson desires. But this moment is also disrupted by two separate intrusions of photography. The first is obvious: Stevenson's stepson and writing partner, Lloyd Osbourne, is there, as ever, to photograph the event. The second intrusion, though, comes from the other side of the lens. Tamaiti's familiarity with London companies and San Francisco fog is knowledge that was likely recirculated back to its point of origin: Stevenson. This is just the type of thing that Tamaiti would have seen and learned from a magic lantern show,[28] which Stevenson often put on for local islanders, his own form of cultural wizardry. The Tamaiti-Stevenson encounter thus encapsulates the troubled relationship between photography and authenticity throughout Stevenson's travels.

Disappointed, Stevenson turned to another medicine man, Terutaki. Terutaki seems to have taken his job much more seriously than Tamaiti did, as evidenced by the photograph of this moment of encounter (figure 4.12). Here, Stevenson seems oblivious of the camera. The photographer—presumably Osbourne—takes the photograph from a distance, several feet behind a fence that separates the photographer from his subjects. The low angle suggests that the photographer is crouched down, further attempting to render the act of photography invisible. But this low angle turns Terutaki into a towering figure. He moves toward the camera, seeming to glower at the photographer,

Figure 4.12. "Mr Stevenson being mesmerized under devil-work tree by notable devil-man named 'Terutaki.'" Courtesy of the City of Edinburgh Council.

annoyed by his intrusion. Stevenson, meanwhile, looks uncharacteristically small. His long limbs are tucked in tightly to his body. As if playing a metaphor of cultural understanding, Stevenson makes himself small. Instead of photography aggrandizing the author, it comes, finally, to diminish him. In a significant reversal of most of the pictures that include both Stevenson and indigenous subjects, it is Terutaki who acknowledges the camera and Stevenson who deliberately directs his gaze away from it.

In this moment of exchange, Stevenson is finally to put aside his imagined role as Pacific Islands cultural expert. Rather than asserting authority through his distance, Stevenson here embraces the limits of his own European modes of interpretation. Stevenson remarks, "[I] had people try to mesmerize[29] me a dozen times, and never with the least result." But with Terutaki, "at the first tap—on a quarter no more vital than my hat-brim, and from nothing more virtuous than a switch of palm wielded by a man I could not even see—sleep rushed upon me like an armed man. My sinews fainted, my eyes closed, my brain hummed with drowsiness. I resisted—at first instinctively, then with a certain flurry of despair, in the end successfully; if that was indeed success which enabled me to scramble to my feet, to stumble home somnambulous, to cast myself at once upon my bed, and sink at once into a dreamless stupor" (247). Even as Stevenson tries to give in to the moment, he finds himself "resisting," both reflexively and purposefully. Stevenson's desire to maintain bodily control, even while explicitly seeking out the loss of it, might be extended to the narrative level. Throughout his account, Stevenson seeks to possess Oceanian culture, maintaining the distance necessary to be objective in his portrayal of it. Here, however, Stevenson becomes possessed. Instead of attempting—as he might have earlier in the narrative—to rationalize his mesmerism from an objective perspective or trying to explain it through a European lens, Stevenson notes only that "when I awoke my cold was gone. So I leave a matter that I do not understand" (247). Stevenson invokes distance here, but he does so in a manner opposite to his usual approach. If the distance that dominates his narrative throughout represents a sort of anthropological objectivity, the distance in this scene is one of wonder and curiosity. He allows the narrative moment to speak for itself. Or, to hearken back to his flawed distinction between himself and Melville, he listens.

This last photograph brings us full circle, back to George Vason's Tongan tattoos with which this book opened. Much as Vason is reluctant to get tattooed until he understands that he cannot fully integrate himself into Tongan culture without them, Stevenson, too, finally realizes that he cannot claim expertise in South Seas culture without removing himself from the privileged space of the detached observer. Just as Vason turns to tattooing as a way to embody Tongan identity, Stevenson, through his mesmerism, comes—if only for a moment—to embody Apemaman ways of being. Where other photographs seek to represent Oceanian culture as if untouched by the author's presence, this final photograph demonstrates the effect the Oceanian world has on the traveler. Fittingly, then, this last Pacific possession depicts the moment Stevenson loses possession of himself.

Notes

Introduction

1. While it might be easy to suggest that the *TripAdvisor* reviewers I've looked at here are merely representative of a particularly uninformed class of tourist, I believe such ideologies are pervasive across socioeconomic status and educational level. In fact, when I went to one of the foremost conferences in the field of Victorian studies, we stayed at the Hilton Hawaiian Village and were encouraged to attend the very same type of luau performances. Unfiltered exposure to actual Hawaiian culture was limited, with the focus mainly being on the beauty of the place. Strange decisions for a conference ostensibly devoted to critiquing imperialism, colonialism, and globalization.

2. Think, in the modern context, of the Western businessman, who trades in his drab and stuffy suit in favor of the exotic prints and loose fit of the Hawaiian shirt. On the one hand, this switch represents an embrace of island culture, but, on the other hand, it is a uniform of Western distance. In short, it allows the wearer to feel both a part of and apart from the island world, close but not too close. The AMC television series *Mad Men* provocatively explores this border in the season six episode "The Doorway," as Don Draper unsuccessfully pitches a campaign for Honolulu's Sheraton Hotel. Don's pitch, which features a discarded suit on the beach with footprints leading into the water, captioned "Hawaii. The Jumping off Point," leads a confused group of executives to read the ad as morbid, as suggestive of suicide. Don tries to justify the image through Hawaiian language and mythology, but he is interrupted by an executive who protests, "I'm sorry, but this is very poetic." Don's failure here, then, is presenting a Hawaiian experience that is too Hawaiian, so much so that in this case it represents the utter annihilation of the Western subject.

3. For representative literary examples, see Vanessa Smith's *Intimate Strangers: Friendship, Exchange and Pacific Encounters* (Cambridge: Cambridge University Press, 2010) and Jonathan Lamb's *Preserving the Self in the South Seas* (2001). The historian and anthropologist Nicholas Thomas has written prolifically in this mode. The anthology *Exploration and Exchange: British and American Narratives of the Pacific, 1680–1900*, edited by Jonathan Lamb, Nicholas Thomas, and Vanessa Smith (Chicago: University of Chicago Press, 2000) offers a useful introduction to these ideas while also seeking to

expand the Pacific canon by providing excerpts from many texts that have received little critical attention.

4. We might even think of Dening's work itself as forwarding a Romanticized notion of Pacific authenticity and exchange in the eighteenth century. See Greg Dening, *Islands and Beaches: Discourse on a Silent Land* (Honolulu: University Press of Hawaii, 1980).

5. "Ellis" refers to William Ellis, a member of the London Missionary Society who was among the most influential of early Polynesian missionaries. Ellis arrived in the Pacific Islands in 1817, and while he moved through various island communities, he spent most of his Polynesian missionary career in Hawaii (at the time the Sandwich Islands). His 1829 *Polynesian Researches* (London: Fisher, Son, & Jackson) reached a wide audience and was influential in shaping Western understandings of Polynesian culture. Though Ellis's work has received less critical attention than that of Stevenson, Melville, and London, it has nonetheless been a staple within studies of missionary accounts of the Pacific. Beyond a few references in chapter 2, I do not spend much time on Ellis in this study, primarily because I do not see his work as part of the travel narrative genre.

6. Standalone studies of Stevenson, such as Rosalyn Jolly's *Robert Louis Stevenson in the Pacific: Travel, Empire, and the Author's Profession* (Surrey, UK: Ashgate, 2009) and Ann C. Colley's *Robert Louis Stevenson and the Colonial Imagination* (Burlington, VT: Ashgate, 2004), do an excellent job of historicizing the Pacific within its colonial framework, but they, too, neglect the travel accounts that came before him.

7. The same often holds true for Herman Melville. For example, Neil Rennie's *Far-Fetched Facts: The Literature of Travel and the Idea of the South Seas* (1998) jumps quickly from Melville's fictionalized travel literature to early-twentieth-century anthropologists such as Margaret Mead and Bronisław Malinowski.

8. To provide some anecdotal evidence of this elitism: when I first proposed this project, one response I received was that analyzing these works alone would not be enough, that I would have to focus on what they reveal about the literary canon. Consider writing about how these works relate to Herman Melville, was the advice. I declined. That stated, Mary K. Bercaw Edwards has done such a project beautifully in *Cannibal Old Me: Spoken Sources in Melville's Early Works* (Kent, OH: Kent State University Press, 2009). Melville's *Typee* stands as the most popular travel narrative written in the Pacific beachcomber genre. Melville, it might be stated, turned the beachcomber genre into literary art. While Melville's account of his deserting a whaling ship and absconding to the Marquesas' Nuku Hiva region is based on fact, Melville, as Edwards comprehensively shows, relied heavily on both the written and oral tradition of beachcomber narratives.

9. I do realize, of course, that these self-justifications are a generic convention of much nineteenth-century nonfiction, and that this convention often involves invocations of false humility, generally as means of directing attention away from the pecuniary interests of publication. Whether genuine or not, these statements do frame readers' experience of the text and ultimately also point us to what authors and publishers considered valuable about their books.

10. Constance Frederica Gordon-Cumming's name was presented in various ways during her life and her career. Most often, the frontispiece of her works names her as

C. F. Gordon Cumming, as in *At Home in Fiji* (New York: A. C. Armstrong & Son, 1881). Her earliest work, *From the Hebrides to the Himalayas* (1876), names her as Constance F. Gordon Cumming. Contemporary periodicals often referred to her as Miss C. F. Gordon Cumming. Her sister and female friends called her "Eka" (short for Frederica) while male companions often referred to her, at least in writing, as "Miss Gordon Cumming." Gordon-Cumming's sketches are listed in a variety of ways, including C.F.G.-C. She is now most commonly referred to as Constance Gordon-Cumming, including a hyphen that was not used during her lifetime. For consistency, I have referred to her as Constance Gordon-Cumming throughout.

11. While *Pacific Possessions* focuses largely on questioning narratives produced by Western writers, recent scholarship such as Noenoe K. Silva's *The Power of the Steel-Tipped Pen: Reconstructing Native Hawaiian Intellectual History* (Durham, NC: Duke University Press, 2017) and Kuʻualoha Hoʻomanawanui's *Voices of Fire: Reweaving the Literary Lei of Pele and Hiʻiaka* (Minneapolis: University of Minnesota Press, 2014) have reframed these conversations around indigenous Hawaiian perspectives. Focusing on the writing careers of nineteenth-century Hawaiian authors, Silva maps what she terms "native intellectual sovereignty" (9). Hoʻomanawanui's work, similarly, seeks to recover the varied indigenous literature of nineteenth-century Hawaii, including the hula (see chapter 2).

12. Adria Imada's *Aloha America: Hula Circuits Through the US Empire* (Durham, NC: Duke University Press, 2012) perceptively analyzes early twentieth-century performances and representations of the hula.

13. Fiji and Kiribati (formerly, the Gilbert Islands), two of the spaces explored in this book, are not Polynesian, but both have been inflected by Polynesian culture, and it would not have been surprising for nineteenth-century travelers to associate them with their idea of Polynesia. Fiji is Melanesian, but with an influence from Polynesian migrants and visitors. The Gilbert Islands region of Kiribati is in Micronesia. The current Republic Kiribati is located in the epicenter of Polynesia, Micronesia, and Melanesia, with islands located in all three regions.

14. See Rod Edmond, *Representing the South Pacific: Colonial Discourse from Cook to Gaugin* (Cambridge: Cambridge University Press, 1997), 16; and O. H. K. Spate, "'South Sea' to 'Pacific Ocean': A Note on Nomenclature," *Journal of Pacific History* 12, no. 4 (1997): 205–11.

15. This title was given to the work posthumously, but it was certainly inspired by Stevenson's conception of his project, which he often referred to in letters as "my big South Seas book."

Chapter 1

1. This engraving of Vason, in fact, goes against the trope of assimilation (or reassimilation) narratives, which generally feature a portrait of the character whose social normalcy is signified by their European clothing—the portrait itself is a form that further distinguishes their cultural belonging. Think, for example, of Olaudah Equiano's *The Interesting Narrative and Other Writings* (New York: Penguin, 1789) or Frederick Douglass's *Narrative of the Life of Frederick Douglass, an American Slave* (New York: Pen-

guin, 1845), both of which present their authors not as they were but as they are now, their clothing highlighting their ascension into cultural acceptance. In the context of the Pacific beachcomber, William Torrey's *Torrey's Narrative: Or, The Life and Adventures of William Torrey* (Boston: Press of A. J. Wright, 1848), which I turn to in detail at the end of this chapter, features a frontispiece of Torrey attired in European clothes, while his tattooed hands incongruously stick out. William Mariner's account (1817), presented in John Martin's *Tonga Islands: William Mariner's Account* (Tonga: Vava'u, 1991), depicts Mariner in his "Tongan costume," a costume that covers the parts of his body that were tattooed.

2. See Charles Taylor, *The Ethics of Authenticity* (Cambridge, MA: Harvard University Press, 1991), and Lionel Trilling, *Sincerity and Authenticity* (Cambridge, MA: Harvard University Press, 1972).

3. De Bry's engraving was based on a drawing of a Powhatan Indian chief done by John White, who was part of Sir Walter Raleigh's expedition to what would become the Virginia colonies. The work, of course, predates Rousseau, but so does the concept of the "noble savage," an idea popularized but not created by Rousseau himself.

4. All three authors have worked extensively with these ideas in their respective published works as well.

5. Beyond creating a beautiful estate for himself, Vason seems to have made very little use of this skill during his time in Tonga. There's poetic irony in the fact that the missionary specializing in laying down foundations is the primary reason why the mission to lay down the foundations of Christianity in Tonga failed.

6. Unless otherwise specified, all further citations refer to the 1810 edition of Vason's *An Authentic Narrative of Four Years' Residence at Tongataboo*. As this essay will discuss later, the narrative of Vason's text seems to have undergone little, if any, alteration from the 1810 to 1840 edition.

7. See James Wilson, *A Missionary Voyage to the Southern Pacific Ocean* (London: T. Chapman, 1799), for an account of how this missionary group was spread out (395).

8. The *Duff* missionaries did have "periodical meetings"; but, for the most part, they remained isolated from one another. Learning from this mistake, future missionaries dispatched to the South Seas focused on establishing their own communities within the islands.

9. Vanessa Smith has also noted the significance of this term in the context of Vason's narrative. She argues: "The notion that authorship is contingent serves to reaffirm the unity of evangelical discourse, but the desire expressed here to 'clothe' the autobiography of the fallen missionary is a post-lapsarian impulse, not just a sign of his renewed civility." Vanessa Smith, "Falling from Grace: George Vason," in *Exploration and Exchange* (2000), 160. Smith expands on this argument in *Literary Culture and the Pacific: Nineteenth-century Textual Encounters* (Cambridge: Cambridge University Press, 1998), 36–40.

10. John Coulter, *Adventures in the Pacific* (Dublin: William Curry, 1845), 216.

11. Coulter does not specify what his tattoos looked like, just that his tattooing "sufficed to mark on [his] skin the delineations and characteristics of a chief" (*Adventures in the Pacific*, 213).

12. Coulter significantly titles this section "Its [the tattoo's] Effectiveness."

13. Joanna White identifies the symbolic significance of Cabri's tattoos, as related to his social status, suggesting that "the partial facial mask indicated his title as son-in-law; a breastplate on the right breast signified his standing as a warrior; and the tattooed eye marked his membership of a specific feasting society." Joanna White, "Marks of Transgression," in *Tattoos: Bodies, Art, and Exchange in the Pacific and the West*, ed. Nicholas Thomas, Anna Cole, and Bronwen Douglas (Durham, NC: Duke University Press, 2005), 82.

14. Rutherford is cited as one of the first Englishman to put his body on display. See Leonard Cassuto, "'What an Object He Would Have Made of Me!' Tattooing and the Racial Freak in Melville's Typee," in *Freakery: Cultural Spectacles of the Extraordinary Body*, ed. Rosemarie Garland Thomson, 234–47 (New York: New York University Press, 1996). As Joanna White points out, though, Rutherford was uncomfortable being displayed but would reluctantly do so for money. See "Marks of Transgression," 87–88, and George Craik, *The New Zealanders* (London: Charles Knight, Pall Mall East, 1830), 278.

15. Neither Vason's editor not subsequent scholars have been able to provide a translation for this term. However, it seems significant that it was left in the original text without translation. Surely Vason's editor could have asked him what the term meant. Because there is no translation provided, Vason comes across as still engaged with the Tongan community. The insult, it seems, can carry weight only in the Tongan context.

16. "Mark" is the more common characterization of the tattoo in beachcomber narratives. See William Torrey, who calls it "bearing a mark" (120), in *Torrey's Narrative*; John Coulter: "mark on my skin" (213), in *Adventures in the Pacific*. See also James O'Connell, *A Residence of Eleven Years in New Holland and the Caroline Islands: Being the Adventures of James F. O'Connell* (Boston: B. B. Mussey, 1836): "My legs, back, and abdomen, were marked also" (118).

17. Alfred Gell, in *Wrapping in Images: Tattooing in Polynesia* (Oxford: Clarendon, 1993), seems, though, subject to his own logical fallacies, most notably in his uncharacteristically assumptive description of Tongan anal and genital tattooing as "sadomasochistic." Even Gell's definition of "exhibitionism" is heavily reliant upon Eurocentric analogy: he compares it to a "tan" and quips that Vason had "discovered designer beachwear."

18. Juniper Ellis, addressing Gell's assertion that Samoans usually tattooed Tongan aristocracy, notes that Vason is tattooed by Tongan tattoo artists; thus "Vason's claim that he achieved chiefly status would hence be complicated." See Ellis, *Pacific Designs in Print and Skin: Tattooing the World* (Columbia: Columbia University Press, 2008), 122.

19. It is important to distinguish the process of tattooing from the narrative account of that tattooing. Many other contemporary tattooing narratives seem to exaggerate the extent to which they were "forced." Joanna White notes that Rutherford claims to have been held down for four hours as he was tattooed, but "the moko, or Maori tattooing, borne by Rutherford on his face is usually carried out over a much longer period" (87).

20. In *Tonga Islands*, which presents William Mariner's account of the Tonga Islands, Martin similarly comments on the beautiful appearance of the tattoo, more directly

contrasting European and Polynesian skin: "On their brown skins the tattow is black, on the skin of an European it has a fine blue appearance," further footnoting that he has "seen two instances of the Tonga tattow [sic], in Jeremiah Higgins and Thomas Dawson, both of the Port au Prince. The beauty and neatness of the execution far exceeded my expectations" (396–97).

21. Martin recounts a similar incident regarding William Mariner's attempt at escape: "Mr. Mariner, without stopping to hail, on the impulse of the moment, jumped onto the main chains, and was very near being knocked over-board by the sentinel, who took him for a native, for his skin was very brown, his hair very long, and tied up in a knot, with a turban around the head, and an apron of the leaves of the chi tree around his waist" (*Tonga Islands* 260). Similarly, the captain of the ship William Torrey attempts to escape on "could hardly believe me to be [a European sailor], for the scanty allowance of clothes with which I left the wreck, had long before fallen off, leaving me entirely naked, and exposed to the sun's scorching rays; besides, my long beard and uncombed hair, rendered me in appearance scarce less than a savage" (*Torrey's Narrative* 131).

22. It is equally possible, however, that this was a denial rather than an admission. In distancing himself from their Pohnpeian meaning, O'Connell could further distance himself from insinuations that he was a willing participant in his tattooing.

23. Speaking on the Tongan tattooing tradition, Martin writes that "there are certain patterns or forms of the tattow, known by distinct names, and the individual may choose which he likes" (396); see Martin, *Tonga Islands*. Martin's nondescriptive description of "certain patterns or forms," known by "distinct" names, further illustrate the lack of connection to the material being put on the tattooed white man's body. While the recipient may choose which design he likes, Martin's description does little to suggest that Mariner has a clear understanding of what the tattoos he had chosen were meant to represent.

24. While O'Connell does, quite interestingly, describe himself as a "bird of much more diversified plumage" (*A Residence of Eleven Years in New Holland and the Caroline Islands*, 119) than before, his reference to his companion as "escaping" seems to suggest that he was less than pleased with his new "plumage." The figurative potential of this phrase, it seems to me, is offset by the surrounding language. It is for this reason that I read this phrase as more of an empty cliché/rhetorical gesture than as a means of coming to terms with the tattooing.

25. Paul Lyons notes that "Oceanians were often referred to as Indians," further arguing that "the relation of Oceanians to 'American Indians' was sensed acutely by Oceanian intellectuals and political leaders." See Paul Lyons, *American Pacificism: Oceania in the U.S. Imagination* (New York: Routledge, 2006), 30–31.

26. Martin, however, does little to illuminate the potential symbolic meanings of individual tattoos, though he does state that "certain forms of the tattow [are] known by distinct names, and the individual may choose which he likes." See Martin, *Tonga Islands*, 396.

27. Orange's personal relationship with Vason is defined only ambiguously. He claims that Mrs. Vason was "well known" to him, but his observations of Vason himself are most superficial in nature. In his introduction, Orange asserts that "every circum-

stance subsequently detailed, was taken down from Mr. Vason's mouth, and repeatedly revised in concurrence with himself" (vi). But given that there are no fundamental changes to the original narrative, it seems that Orange could only be reasserting the authority of Vason's earlier editor.

28. All passages referring to Orange's biography cite the 1840 publication of Vason's text, *Narrative of the Life of the Late George Vason of Nottingham.*

29. Thomas Nunneley's 1844 *Treatise on the Nature, Causes, and Treatment of Erysipelas* (Philadelphia: Ed. Barrington & Geo. D. Haswell, 1844) suggests that "mental anxiety frequently appeared to be a predisposing cause to the disease" (100). Nunneley's assertion seems to be reflective of contemporary perceptions about the malady.

30. See Ellis, *Pacific Designs in Print and Skin,* 49.

31. Torrey does not specify which island in the Marquesas he stayed on, though I. C. Campbell and Greg Dening suggest that it was most likely Tahuata. See I. C. Campbell, "Gone Native," in *Polynesia: Captivity Narratives and Experiences in the South Pacific* (Westwood, CT: Greenwood, 1998), 40–41, and Dening, *Islands and Beaches,* 147.

32. Torrey elaborates on the different markings, explaining that each tribe marks on a different part of the body: "These valleys are occupied by different tribes, each bearing a mark peculiar to themselves. Some bear it upon the hands, others upon the face, breast, &c. The tribe with which I was connected bore it upon the hands, wrists, and ancles. This was the largest tribe on the island, called the Teheda" (121).

33. To cite a small sampling: "Most of the hands were below when the ship fetched a lurch" (54); "most of our crew were new hands" (55); "They being in want of hands, I shipped myself as a seaman" (102); "When out to sea all hands were called and the ship's articles read, and those who had not signed them, were requested to do so at that time." Torrey's reliance on this term, of course, is not unusual in and of itself. But the phrase assumes uncanny connotations in this context.

34. I do not mean to idealize Vason or to play down the extent to which he, too, was complicit in the dehumanization of indigenous people. My primary focus is on narrative exchange and the ways in which the traveler actively engages with a different culture rather than merely observing it.

35. As this chapter has shown, we see this tendency to write over, too, in the second publication of Vason's work. Orange takes possession of Vason's narrative and, through the appended biography, reinforces that Vason was written upon—and that that writing continued to affect him up until his death. He even subtly suggests that it led to his death.

Chapter 2

1. It is unclear exactly when or how the author came to be identified as George Washington Bates, given that this name does not appear in the front matter of the original publication. Making matters even more unclear, George Washington Bates was not the author's actual name, either. In a review of *Sandwich Island Notes,* the *Polynesian* reports that they have "been distressed to learn that the gentleman is at present the inmate of a public building, where the Peter of the Place . . . knows him by neither the name above nor by that which friends and acquaintances used to recognize him. They say that

a system of enumeration prevails there, and that instead of being known and described as the Haole, or otherwise as Washington Bates, he is spoken of as NO. 97 or some similar combination of figures" (*Polynesian*, August 11, 1855, 1). I am led to speculate that George Washington Bates was the alias Baker used for the ship log. Nonetheless, this strange story of the author's namelessness lends further metaphorical resonance to his initial self-effacing pseudonym.

2. Farrier's choice of authors highlights the fact that there is no canonical author to represent these early touristic travelers. See David Farrier, *Unsettled Narratives: The Pacific Writings of Stevenson, Ellis, Melville, and London* (New York: Routledge, 2007).

3. Melville likely either owned or borrowed a copy of Wise's *Los Gringos: Or, An Inside View of Mexico and California, with Wanderings in Peru, Chile, and Polynesia* (New York: Baker and Scribner, 1849), according to melvillesmarginalia.org. While no copy of Melville's edition has been located, he writes, in a journal entry from December 1849, that he had "just returned from Mr. Bentley's . . . I also spoke to him about Lieut: Wise's book, & he is to send for it."

4. Edward Perkins's *Na Motu: Or, Reef Rovings in the South Seas* (New York: Pudney & Russell, 1854) was part of Melville's library, though it is his wife, Elizabeth Shaw Melville, who inscribed her name into and marked the copy. According to melvilles-marginalia.org, her edition features a quotation from London's *Athenaeum* "comparing Perkins and Melville . . . pasted on the flyleaf." The review opens with: "Byron's 'Island' and the 'Omoo' and 'Typee' of Mr. Herman Melville are the distinguished literary fruits of the sunny islands of Polynesian Archipelago. They have done for the islands what 'Paul and Virginia' did for the Mauritius; or 'Tom Cringle's Log' for the West Indies; or Fennimore Cooper for the Prairies." It goes on to add, much in line with the argument of this chapter, that "every place sooner or later, finds its voice,—finds somebody to paint it to the eyes of cultivated, speculative Europe—to furnish a picture of it which, according to the skill of the artist, remains its 'ideal' for generations more or less numerous" (1360). The quotation comparing Perkins to Melville is likely the following: "Mr. Perkins got traces of the Author of 'Omoo,'—which will interest admirers of a writer who is a little too fond of surrounding himself with a haze of mystery, though surely as well able as most people to bear the light of common day" (1361).

5. Upon confirming his identity, the supposed carpenter playfully maligned in *Omoo* takes issue with his representation by Melville, in particular the "insinuat[ion] that that scamp of a Long Ghost offered to do my courting for me" (323).

6. In this scene, John seems to be engaged in the production of poi. Defining taro (the root from which poi is derived), Robert Craig, in *Historical Dictionary of Polynesia* (Lanham, MD: Scarecrow, 2002), states that taro roots were "usually baked, toasted over embers, or boiled"; he adds that "in Hawaii and a few other islands, the boiled tubers are also pounded into a paste substance called poi, and eaten with almost every meal" (214).

7. The term "indolent" is as pervasive as any term within Hawaiian travel narratives. More particularly, Hawaiians are almost always described as "naturally indolent." Wise: "The Hawaiians are naturally indolent" (357). Noenoe K. Silva notes the economic motivation of missionaries in employing this term, arguing that the "myth of the lazy native" was, in fact, useful for contracting a cheap labor force to maintain plantations.

See Silva, "He Kanawai E Ho'opau I Na Hula Kuolo Hawai'i: The Political Economy of Banning the Hula," *Hawaiian Journal of History* 34 (2000): 33–34.

8. For more on Melville's storytelling infelicities. see Mary K. Bercaw Edwards's *Cannibal Old Me*.

9. The "native" friendliness of Hawaiians is emphasized throughout the travel narrative. A Häolé writes that "aloha . . . is their national word of greeting," which he defines as "love or salutation" (118).

10. See Margaret Titcomb's "Kava in Hawaii," *Journal of Polynesian Society* 57, no. 2 (June 1948): 105–71.

11. Missionaries deftly employed the rhetoric of taboo to their own advantage, repurposing it to fit with Western/Christian values.

12. Titcomb, in "Kava in Hawaii," writes that the "effect of 'awa varies according to the amount taken. In moderation, it relaxes the nerves and induces refreshing rest; taken often in large quantities it makes the skin scaly (*mahuna*), ulcerous, the eyes blood-shot and suppurated, and reduces the control of the nerves of the arms and legs. Walking is difficult or impossible. In striking contrast to the effect of alcohol, the mind remains clear until sleep comes, and emotions are unaffected. The reputation of 'awa may have suffered a little from a lack of a term that accurately expresses its effect—intoxicating, narcotic, soporific, all being peculiarly applicable to alcohol and drugs" (119).

13. While the hula was and is often translated into English as "dance," Adrienne Kaeppler argues that "Polynesian languages . . . do not have a word, phrase, or concept that precisely covers the English concept of dance. . . . Polynesian terminology for structured movement often reflects context, function, and level of formality" (7). See Kaeppler, *Hula Pahu: Hawaiian Drum Dances*, vol. 1: *Ha' a and Hula Puha, Sacred Movements* (Honolulu: Bishop Museum Press, 1993).

14. See Dorothy B. Barrère, "The *Hula* in Retrospect," in *Hula: Historical Perspectives* (Honolulu: Bishop Museum Press, 1980), 41. Kaeppler also notes the effect of Liloliho's (Kamehameha II) breaking of kapu, in 1819. Liloliho "broke sacred eating taboos by dining with women," which in turn led to a "revamping of the religious system." Kaeppler argues that because of this, the Hawaiian religious system was in a state of disorder just before the arrival of Christian missionaries (*Hula Pahu*, 2).

15. William Henry Holmes, in the prefatory note to Emerson's text, notes that "previous to the year 1906 the researches of the Bureau were restricted to the American Indians, but by act of Congress approved June 30 of that year the scope of its operations were extended to include natives of the Hawaiian islands."

16. Kaeppler regards Emerson as "largely responsible for the confusion about the 'sacred nature' of hula." Distinguishing hula from ha'a, Kaeppler argues that hula was performed in "nonsacred contexts," while *ha'a* was performed in "sacred or mourning contexts" (*Hula Pahu*, 15).

17. As Amy Ku'uleialoha Stillman notes, this is referred to in "contemporary parlance" as *hula kahiko* (ancient hula). See Ku'uleialoha Stillman, *Sacred Hula: The Historical Hula 'Āla'apapa* (Honolulu: Bishop Museum Press, 1998), 2.

18. While Hiram Bingham's *A Residence of Twenty-One Years in the Sandwich Islands*

was not published until 1848, this particular passage is dated 1821. See Bingham, *A Residence of Twenty-One Years in the Sandwich Islands: Or, the Civil, Religious, and Political History of those Islands*, 3rd ed. (Canadaigua, New York: H. D. Goodwin, 1855).

19. I have been unable to find any scholarly source that refers to Tahitian dance as *hevar*. Most likely, this refers to heiva, a Tahitian festival, part of which would be dancing. A less likely possibility is that Melville is mistranscribing "hura." See also Helen Reeves Lawrence, "Is the 'Tahitian' Drum Dance Really Tahitian? Re-Evaluating the Evidence for the Origins of Contemporary Polynesian Drum Dance," *Yearbook for Traditional Music* 24 (1992): 126–37.

20. It is unclear exactly what such an outfit might be, as he elaborates only by tautologically describing it as "just such a suit as a man chooses to wear" (126). Presumably this is a traditional European suit but worn in a less formal fashion, given that he next describes himself as looking "uncouth" and resembling a "runaway sailor." At any rate, wearing this suit is what identifies him as European. Much like the modern Hawaiian shirt—and much like the haole pseudonym—it seems to imply both belonging and separation from Hawaiian culture.

21. The author uses this scene as evidence that "there is no class of men so difficult to employ as Hawaiians."

22. The term *hula hula* is footnoted in the text as "the licentious dance," as if it were a literal translation, quite forcefully framing the English-speaking reader's conception of the hula.

23. Malinowski's *A Diary in the Strict Sense of the Term* covered his fieldwork in New Guinea from 1914 to 1915 and 1917 to 1918. Unburdened from his anthropological project, Malinowski offers personal reflections on his "life with the savages" (161), a life as "remote from [him] as the life of a dog" (167). Upon its publication, Clifford Geertz referred to Malinowksi as "a crabbed, self-preoccupied, hypochondriacal, narcissist, whose fellow feeling for the people he lived with was limited in the extreme." Christopher Herbert writes in *Culture and Anomie: Ethnographic Imagination in the Nineteenth Century* (Chicago: University of Chicago Press, 1991) that "for Malinowski, effacing his true hostility toward his subjects and replacing it with displays of empathy in the text of *Argonauts of the Western Pacific* amounted in an obvious way (obvious once we know the Diary) to an effacing of his hostility toward himself and his own ungovernable desires" (170).

24. The parameters of this discussion still persist, as evidence by Dorothy Barrère's history of the hula, "The *Hula* in Retrospect." Barrère, too, engages in the same assumptive language, ignoring the cultural bias of the term "lascivious" by conceding that there were some dances that were lascivious "by any standard." Barrère seems pained to concede that it "must be admitted . . . that such [lascivious] dances were not an innovation [one that catered to European audiences], but had commonly been performed from ancient times" (41). Instead, Barrère suggests that this form was less legitimate because less "graceful." Of course, what is implicit in her claim is that for the hula to be taken seriously it must be associated with "grace" rather than sexuality.

25. In *The Hawaiian Archipelago: Six Months Among the Palm Groves, Coral Reefs, & Volcanoes of the Sandwich Islands* (London: John Murray, 1875), Isabella Bird does not directly reference the performances she witnesses as a hula, but there seems to be reason

to believe that this synthesis of English and Hawaiian dancing is a step toward the more familiar, modern hula. Bird only directly references the hula twice in her five-hundred-plus-page account, and both of these references are hidden away in the text's appendix. Noting the "decidedly local" "features of interest" of the Hawaiian judiciary department, Bird highlights that ten people were punished for "exhibition of hula" (451). The hula is once more referenced as a sign of past debasement, as Bird describes Kamehameha V as having "transformed himself into the likeness of one of his half-clad heathen ancestors, debased himself by whiskey, and revelled in the hula-hula" (466). For Bird, Kamehameha's transformation is a sign of degeneration, a return to such ancestral evils as the hula. Bird's examples suggest how powerful the hula had become as a signifier of degeneracy.

Chapter 3

1. April 23, 1881.

2. See Edward D. Melillo, "Making Sea Cucumbers Out of Whale's Teeth: Nantucket Castaways and Encounters of Value in Nineteenth-Century Fiji," *Environmental History* 20 (2015): 449–74; and Marshall Sahlins, "The Discovery of the True Savage," in *Dangerous Liaisons: Essays in Honour of Greg Dening*, ed. Donna Merwick, 41–94 (Melbourne: University of Melbourne Press, 1994.

3. Seemann generally avoids sensationalizing Fijian cannibalism, insisting that the practice is solely a political tool of the warring upper classes, who "in order to strike terror in the enemy and the lower-classes, it is absolutely necessary for a great chief to eat human flesh" (January 26, 1861, 121). However, like most writers of the time, Seemann is quick to take secondhand accounts of cannibalism as fact.

4. Thomson credits the Wesleyan missionary Rev. Frederick Langham with establishing the best test for forgeries. "The genuine forks," Thomson writes, "are carefully finished at the root of the prongs; the forgeries have inequalities and splinters." Thomson notes that this test has been called into question but insists that he has "never known it to fail in the specimens [he has] examined" (109n1).

5. The previous translations are taken from Arthur Capell's *A New Fijian Dictionary* (Glasgow: Wilson & Guthrie, 1951).

6. The term is variously spelled "bakola," "bakolo," and "bokola." The current standard spelling is "bokola."

7. Toward the latter part of the century, the translation "flesh eating fork" is also used. This translation is equally evocative but, perhaps unintentionally, more accurate.

8. Fiji figured prominently in nineteenth-century exhibition culture. Of course, P. T. Barnum's infamous "Fejee mermaid" stands out as the most extreme example of the overexoticizing of Fijian "curiosities." So-called Fijian cannibals were also part of Barnum's tours. Beyond just Barnum, W. C. Gardenhire's "Fiji Cannibal Exhibition" promised to display not just Fijian cannibal forks, knives, spears, and clubs but also "real" Fijian cannibals. These "cannibals" were pictured as an advertisement on the front of Gardenhire's 1873 pamphlet "Fiji and the Fijians," which announces their tour throughout the United States and Europe.

9. It cannot be determined whether the forks Gordon-Cumming sketches here are all forks in her possession or if some are simply imaginings.

10. Gordon-Cumming's fork may well have been manufactured, designed to capitalize on and appeal to Western expectations.

11. Fiji, as I mention in the introduction, occupies a sort of liminal space between Polynesia and Melanesia. Geographically, Fiji is usually placed within Melanesia, but Fijian peoples and culture are of mixed Polynesian and Melanesian origin. While Fiji often was imagined by nineteenth-century writers in the same "South Seas" vein, it was, in important ways, conceptualized differently than other Polynesian spaces. Much of this has to do with racial distinctions, Fijians being darker skinned than other Polynesian peoples. This, sadly but unsurprisingly, surely informed Western notions of supposed Fijian savagery.

12. In the "Cetology" chapter of Herman Melville's *Moby-Dick: Or, the Whale* (New York: Modern Library Classics, 1992), Ishmael uses Fiji as a reference for the most savage of whales. The killer whale, he writes, "is very savage—a sort of Feegee of a fish" (155).

13. More than likely, Gordon-Cumming would not have been alone in having this ballad as her reference point. Paul Lyons notes that the ballad was "popular on both sides of the Atlantic, and [is] referred to in the first chapter of Thoreau's *Walden* and in Melville's *Typee*" (35).

14. In making this claim, Sara Mills is focused on Mary Kingsley's *Travels in West Africa: Congo Francais, Corisco, and Cameroons* (London: Macmillan, 1897). Mills argues that Kingsley's open acknowledgment of cannibalism is exceptional when compared with other "lady travelers." As the last chapter showed, however, sexuality was a much more "delicate" topic than violence when it came to Pacific travel narratives. See Sara Mills, *Discourses of Difference: An Analysis of Women's Travel Writing and Colonialism* (London: Routledge, 1991).

15. His ("i") habit, disposition, conduct ("valavala"); Capell, *A New Fijian Dictionary*, 297.

16. See Mary K. Bercaw Edwards, *Cannibal Old Me*.

17. This particular quote comes from Sahlins's 1978 review of Marvin Harris's *Cannibals and Kings: The Origins of Cultures* at https://www.nybooks.com; Sahlins has sustained this critique of Arens and Obeyesekere throughout his work. Sahlins and Obeyesekere, it seems, have engaged in a lifelong academic feud. See Marshall Sahlins, "Culture as Protein and Profit," *New York Review of Books* (November 23, 1978).

18. In *Cannibal Old Me*, Mary K. Bercaw Edwards considers "cannibal talk" as a defining feature of Melville's early semiautobiographical travel accounts. Comparing the work of Melville to popular travel accounts, such as William Endicott's, Edwards argues that much of Melville's firsthand accounts of cannibalism were based on both oral tradition (sailor talk) and the cannibal talk of popular written accounts.

19. Wallis, in *Life in Feejee, or Five Years among the Cannibals* (Boston: William Heath, 1851), referred to Bau as "the seat of cannibalism" (237). Bau's leader Cakobau later converted to Christianity, with James Calvert taking the credit, emphasizing in particular that Cakobau had renounced his supposed cannibalism. This conversion was, likely, more political than religious, a token of gratitude. Bau was in the midst of a decade-long power struggle with the chiefly kingdom of Rewa. It was the intervention

of the Wesleyan missionary–allied Tongan chief Tupou, who sent two thousand Tongan warriors to aid Bau, that would lead to Cakobau's victory. As Max Quanchi writes in *Culture Contact in the Pacific: Essays on Contact, Encounter, and Response* (Cambridge: Cambridge University Press, 1993), "Cakobau subsequently espoused the cause of British colonialism in Fiji and was the leading chief when the island group became part of the British Empire in 1874" (76).

20. In making this claim, Jeanne Cannizzo, in "Gathering Souls and Objects: Missionary Collections," is focused on African missionaries, but this passage suggests that missionaries in Oceania conceived of cultural objects in much the same way. See Cannizzo, "Gathering Souls and Objects: Missionary Collections," in *Colonialism and the Object: Empire, Material Culture, and the Museum*, ed. Tim Barringer and Tom Flynn (London: Routledge, 1998).

21. Fergus Clunie writes in *Yalo i Viti: A Fiji Museum Catalogue* (Suva: Fiji Museum Press, 1986) that "in the highlands of Vitilevu the bones of cannibalized enemies were placed as trophies on the forked branches of trees" (120).

22. A chiefly title.

23. In *Life in the Pacific Fifty Years Ago* (London: George Routledge, 1930), Alfred Maudslay was much more impressed with Gordon-Cumming's painting than her writing. Describing the latter, Maudsley writes "she can write fluently and well, and describes things she actually sees very clearly, but when she goes beyond that, and flies much higher, she fails" (85).

24. Alfred St. Johnston's 1883 *Camping Among Cannibals* (London: Macmillan and Co.) can be read as the masculine counterpart to Gordon-Cumming's *At Home in Fiji*. Where Gordon-Cumming's focus is on the domestic possibilities of travel ("at home"), St. Johnston's imagines Fijian travel through masculine terms of adventure and transience ("camping"). The cannibal fork was a subject of fascination for St. Johnston, too. St. Johnston acquires this cannibal fork not from a native Fijian, nor even from a local curiosity-dealer. Instead, he finds it right above his writing station. It sits there as if waiting for the adventurer to write about it. And write about he does, with requisite drama and Romanticism. "I think it must be, from the descriptions I have heard," he begins, slowly building the drama, "a human flesh fork." It is, he continues, "a rather shuddery sort of thing to find just as I am going to sleep, *for it is stained with use* (301–2).

Chapter 4

1. I retain the term "Gilbert Islands" when referring specifically to Stevenson's own culturally and historically formed interpretation of the space. I do this because my analysis is framed around Stevenson's interpretation. When referring, however, to the people of Kiribati, I have used the term "I-Kiribati," or referred to the particular community of each region.

2. Consider, for example, Sophie Gengembre Anderson's paintings of young girls with flowered garlands in their hair.

3. In *The Cruise of the Janet Nichol* (New York: Charles Scribner's Sons, 1914), Fanny Stevenson spells her name Natakanti. The variations in English spellings for Oceanian peoples and places is quite common. Throughout this chapter, I use the spellings origi-

nally used in Stevenson's *In the South Seas* ([1896] London: Penguin, 1998). I do this for the sake of consistency but also because Stevenson's (mis)spellings are suggestive of his imprecise understanding of Polynesia. These misspellings are themselves suggestive of limits of authenticity in Stevenson's narrative: his names are close representations of the people and places, but they are not actually those people and places.

4. Neil Rennie, "introduction," in *In the South Seas* (London: Penguin, 1998), ix.

5. Joseph Strong, an American artist and photographer, had already been living in Hawaii since 1882, with his wife, Isobel Osbourne (aka Belle Strong). In 1886, Hawaiian King David Kalākaua appointed Strong, as Stevenson describes in *A Footnote to History: Eight Years of Trouble in Samoa* (New York: Scribner's, 1892), in "the surprising quality of government artist" (62) for an American-backed Hawaiian intervention in Samoa. The Stevenson party met up with Joseph Strong, Isobel Osbourne, and their son in Hawaii. Both for his company and for his photographic acumen, Joseph Strong was asked to join the Stevenson party as they continued their South Seas cruise. Strong and Stevenson would later have a dramatic falling out, after it was discovered that Strong had an affair with a Samoan woman. His name was subsequently redacted from the posthumous publication of Stevenson's *In the South Seas*.

6. Shortly after buying property in Vailima, Samoa, the Stevenson party went on one final cruise in April 1890, aboard the *Janet Nicoll*. Fanny hoped that the four-month cruise, which visited the Penrhyn, Ellice, Gilbert, and Marshall Islands, would reinvigorate Robert, whose health was continuing to decline.

7. The photographic archive is held at the Writers' Museum in Edinburgh, Scotland. Since 1996, the Writers' Museum has digitized in high resolution almost half of these photographs, with the intention of making the entire collection available digitally. They are available via Capital Collections at http://robert-louis-stevenson.org. Additionally, the Writers' Museum made one hundred of the photographs available to Scotland's online SCRAN project ("Picturing" 2). Photographs from the SCRAN project are available for purchase, and, unlike the Capital Collections archive, are unaltered and contain the original annotations. The titles given on Capital Collections photographs are not necessarily the same as the original annotation titles.

8. My focus on *In the South Seas* solely at the expense of his fiction about the South Seas is, of course, a consideration of genre. The rigid distinction between genres is not just my own. As this chapter will show, Stevenson sought to correct the slippage between fiction and non-fiction that had become so prevalent as to turn into a constitutive element of South Seas travel accounts.

9. Beyond providing an analysis of Stevenson's photography, Colley also offers perhaps the only thorough scholarly account of Stevenson's use of the magic lantern. See Colley, *Robert Louis Stevenson and the Colonial Imagination*; and Carla Manfredi, "Picturing Robert Louis Stevenson's Pacific Phototext," *Le Répertoire de la Photolittérature Ancienne et Contemporaine* (*PHLIT*) (October 2012): n.p. Web.

10. Stevenson's declining health was the main reason he traveled to the South Seas, believing that its climate might serve as an antidote.

11. It was Stoddard who first introduced Stevenson to Pacific travel and Melville's work, around 1879 (Edmond, *Representing the South Pacific*, 160).

12. Stevenson's implicit claim that his work is more well informed than Melville's is dubious. Whatever Melville's failings in terms of Romanticizing the Nuku Hiva region of the Marquesas, he was undoubtedly more immersed in their culture than Stevenson. In his biography of Stevenson, Frank McLynn sums up this critical debate in Melville's favor: "Melville, it is said, learned about savages from life, not from books; he lived among the cannibals, as Stevenson did not, and his superiority to RLS shows in his total absorption in the Marquesas. RLS, by contrast, is accused of taking to the Pacific an *a priori* Rousseauesque notion of the noble savage, which he hoped to find confirmed; in a word, he was taking his European cultural baggage to Polynesia" (322). See Frank McLynn, *Robert Louis Stevenson: A Biography* (New York: Random House, 1993).

13. See also Carla Manfredi's *Robert Louis Stevenson's Pacific Impressions: Photography and Travel writing, 1888–1894* (London: Palgrave MacMillan, 2018). Manfredi's book was published after my manuscript was completed. I have since consulted it, and I am pleased to see that many of our interpretations of Stevenson's photographs align quite well. While Stevenson's photography works, for Manfredi, as an axis around which to analyze nineteenth-century representations of Oceania, my work focuses more on the ways Stevenson's writing and photography responds to nineteenth-century travel writing. Essentially, though, we both agree on the relevance of these photographs for understanding not only Stevenson but also the entire project of narrating the Pacific.

I am thankful to Manfredi for generously providing me with background on the photographic archive and directing me to research librarians who could aid me in accessing digital versions of the photographs.

14. Manfredi notes, however, that Stevenson and, later, his stepdaughter Belle Strong also provided some of the photographs' captions ("Picturing Robert Louis Stevenson's Pacific Phototext," 9).

15. That is not entirely true. *Footnote* opens with a lovely literary guided tour of Samoa, where Stevenson "ask[s] the reader to walk" from the western horn (Mulinuu) to the eastern (Matautu). In so doing, Stevenson continues, "he will find more of the history of Samoa spread before his eyes in that excursion, than has yet been collected in the blue-books and white-books of the world" (20–21). These beautiful descriptions do, however, indeed give way to an often tediously straightforward history of a very interesting period of Samoan conflict.

16. For a detailed analysis of Stevenson's "Samoan Scrapbook," see Carla Manfredi's "Robert Louis Stevenson's and Joseph Strong's 'A Samoan Scrapbook,'" *Journal of Stevenson Studies* 12 (2016): 4–32.

17. The use of photography in Samoa has been analyzed from various critical and historical angles. See, for example, Max Quanchi's "The Imaging of Samoa in Illustrated Magazines and Serial Encyclopedias in the Early 20th-Century" and Tiffany W. Sharon's "Contesting the Erotic Zone: Margaret Mead's Fieldwork Photographs of Samoa."

18. See Colley, *Robert Louis Stevenson and the Colonial Imagination*, 122.

19. The absence of tattooing on Paaaeua's body essentially renders the costume incomplete, further suggesting that this Stevenson and Osbourne have dressed him up according to their own idea of the Marquesan war costume.

20. As Kirsten Hastrup puts it, "by her presence in the field, the ethnographer is actively engaged in the construction of the ethnographic reality or, one might say, of the ethnographic present" (46). See Hastrup, "The Ethnographic Present: A Reinvention," *Cultural Anthropology* 5, no. 1 (February 1990): 45–61.

21. Hastrup is ultimately attempting to recover the value of the ethnographic present tense, long a source of criticism in the postmodern era of anthropology. Hastrup offers that since ethnography is "a narrative or written truth it transcends the historical moment and must, therefore, be constructed in the ethnographic present" (57).

22. See Austin Coates, *Western Pacific Islands* (London: Her Majesty's Stationary Office, 1970), 72.

23. Again, I retain Stevenson's original spelling when referencing his account of the place, as it in fact conveys an important distinction between the place and Stevenson's interpretation of that place.

24. Stevenson's prediction was accurate. In a dispatch to the Hawaiian government, published ten years later in the missionary journal the *Friend*, Rev. A. C. Walkup relays missionary progress in the Gilbert Islands: "At Apemama, a new code of laws has been published. One law is that the word 'slave' (the title given the people by the chiefs), must not be used, as there are no slaves under the British flag, and the chief must not demand any prepared food from them as heretofore. These laws have brought great relief to our Christian people. All children must attend school. Persons wishing to marry must be of age and have the permission of the king or magistrate. This island stands first on book sales this year, and ranks second in contributions."

25. Tembinok' seems to derive the term "'peak" from the English "speak." Stevenson describes Tembinok' as employing a "queer, personal English, so different from ordinary 'Beach de Mar,' so much more obscure, expressive, and condensed." Stevenson allows the readers to interpret his use of the term "peak" on their own, providing Tembinok's dialogue: "Here in my island, I 'peak. . . . My chieps no 'peak—do what I talk'" (216).

26. Stevenson's original spelling. For the publication of *In the South Seas*, it was altered to "Tembinok."

27. Presumably, Stevenson is referring to the edits Colvin made to it.

28. Stevenson mentions putting on a magic lantern show in Apemama (233).

29. In the latter part of the nineteenth century, mesmerism had lost its cachet, discredited by medical professionals. An 1873 article from the *British Medical Journal* as "passing through its decay through the customary stage of a dying delusion—the stage of fraud" (667). In referencing previous failures of mesmerism—presumably Western mesmerisms—Stevenson suggests it is the practitioners and not the practice that is fraudulent. Terutaki's Apemaman form of mesmerism, then, is authentic.

Works Cited

Arens, William. *The Man-Eating Myth: Anthropology and Anthropophagy*. Oxford: Oxford University Press, 1979.

Arista, Noelani. *The Kingdom and the Republic: Sovereign Hawai'i and the Early United States*. Philadelphia: University of Pennsylvania Press, 2019.

"*At Home in Fiji*." *Athenaeum* 2791 (April 23, 1881): 551–52.

Balfour, Graham. *The Life of Robert Louis Stevenson*. New York: Charles Scribner's Sons, 1915.

Banivanua-Mar, Tracey. "Cannibalism and Colonialism: Charting Colonies and Frontiers in Nineteenth Century Fiji." *Comparative Studies in Society and History* 52, no. 2 (2010): 255–81.

———. *Violence and Colonial Dialogue: The Australian-Pacific Indentured Labor Trade*. Honolulu: University of Hawai'i Press, 2007.

Barrère, Dorothy B. "The *Hula* in Retrospect." In *Hula: Historical Perspectives*. Honolulu: Bishop Museum Press, 1980.

Bates, George Washington. Pseud. "A Häolé." *Sandwich Island Notes*. New York: Harper & Brothers, 1855.

Bell, Leonard. "Pictures as History, Settlement as Theatre: John Davis' Photo-Portrait of Robert Louis Stevenson and Family at Vailima, Samoa, 1882." *Journal of New Zealand Literature* 20 (2002): 93–111.

Benjamin, Walter. *Illuminations: Essays and Reflections*. Ed. Hannah Arendt. Trans. Harry Zohn. New York: Schocken, 1969.

Bingham, Hiram. *A Residence of Twenty-One Years in the Sandwich Islands: Or, the Civil, Religious, and Political History of those Islands*. 1848. 3rd ed. Canadaigua, New York: H. D. Goodwin, 1855.

Bird, Isabella. *The Hawaiian Archipelago: Six Months Among the Palm Groves, Coral Reefs, & Volcanoes of the Sandwich Islands*. London: John Murray, 1875.

Booth, Bradford A., and Ernest Mehew, eds. *The Letters of Robert Louis Stevenson*. Volumes 6–8. New Haven, CT: Yale University Press, 1995.

Brantlinger, Patrick. *Taming Cannibals: Race and the Victorians*. Ithaca: Cornell University Press, 2011.

Buckton, Oliver S. *Cruising with Robert Louis Stevenson: Travel, Narrative, and the Colonial Body*. Athens: Ohio University Press, 2007.

Burton, Stacy. *Travel Narrative and the Ends of Modernity*. New York: Cambridge University Press, 2014.

Buzard, James. *The Beaten Track: European Tourism, Literature, and the Ways to "Culture," 1800–1918*. Oxford: Oxford University Press, 1993.

Caesar, Terry. *Forgiving the Boundaries: Home as Abroad in American Travel Writing*. Athens: University of Georgia Press, 1995.

Campbell, I. C. "Gone Native." In *Polynesia: Captivity Narratives and Experiences in the South Pacific*. Westwood, CT: Greenwood, 1998.

Cannizzo, Jeanne. "Gathering Souls and Objects: Missionary Collections." In *Colonialism and the Object: Empire, Material Culture, and the Museum*, ed. Tim Barringer and Tom Flynn. London: Routledge, 1998.

Capell, Arthur. *A New Fijian Dictionary*. Glasgow: Wilson & Guthrie, 1951.

Cassuto, Leonard. "'What an Object He Would Make of Me!': Tattooing and the Racial Freak in Melville's *Typee*." In *Freakery: Cultural Spectacles of the Extraordinary Body*, ed. Rosemarie Garland Thomson, 234–47. New York: New York University Press, 1996.

Clifford, James. "On Collecting Art and Culture." In *The Predicament of Culture*, 215–51. Cambridge, MA: Harvard University Press, 1988.

Clunie, Fergus. *Yalo i Viti: A Fiji Museum Catalogue*. Suva: Fiji Museum Press, 1986.

Coates, Austin. *Western Pacific Islands*. London: Her Majesty's Stationary Office, 1970.

Cohen, Deborah. *Household Gods: The British and Their Possessions*. New Haven, CT: Yale University Press, 2006.

Coleridge, Samuel Taylor. *The Rime of the Ancient Mariner* [1798]. London: Dover, 1992.

Colley, Ann C. *Robert Louis Stevenson and the Colonial Imagination*. Burlington, VT: Ashgate, 2004.

Conrad, Joseph. *Heart of Darkness*. Oxford: Oxford World's Classics, 2008.

Coulter, John. *Adventures in the Pacific*. Dublin: William Curry, 1845.

Craig, Robert. *Historical Dictionary of Polynesia*. Lanham, MD: Scarecrow, 2002.

Craik, George. *The New Zealanders*. London: Charles Knight, Pall Mall East, 1830.

Culler, Jonathan. "The Semiotics of Tourism." In *Framing the Sign: Criticism and Its Institutions*, 153–67. Norman: University of Oklahoma Press, 1998.

Curtis, George William. *Nile Notes of a Howadji*. New York: Harper & Brothers, 1851.

Dening, Greg. *Islands and Beaches: Discourse on a Silent Land*. Honolulu: University Press of Hawaii, 1980.

———. *Mr. Bligh's Bad Language: Passion, Power and Theatre on the Bounty*. Cambridge: Cambridge University Press, 1992.

Dibble, Sheldon. *History of the Sandwich Islands*. Lahainaluna, Hawaii: Press of the Mission Seminary, 1843.

Douglass, Frederick. *Narrative of the Life of Frederick Douglass, an American Slave* [1845]. New York: Penguin, 1982.

Edge-Partington, J. "56. Note on Forged Ethnographical Specimens from the Pacific Islands." *Man* 1 (1901): 68–69.

Edmond, Rod. *Representing the South Pacific: Colonial Discourse from Cook to Gaugin.* Cambridge: Cambridge University Press, 1997.

Edwards, Elizabeth. "Negotiating Spaces: Some Photographic Incidents in the Western Pacific, 1883-4." In *Picturing Place: Photography and the Geographical Imagination*, ed. Joan M. Schwartz and James R. Ryan, 261–79. London: I.B. Tauris, 2003.

———. *Raw Histories: Photographs, Anthropology, and Museums.* Oxford: Oxford International, 2001.

Edwards, Mary K. Bercaw. *Cannibal Old Me: Spoken Sources in Melville's Early Works.* Kent, OH: Kent State University Press, 2009.

Elleray, Michelle. "Crossing the Beach: A Victorian Tale Adrift in the Pacific." *Victorian Studies* 47, no. 2, Papers from the Second Annual Conference of the North American Victorian Studies Association (Winter 2005): 164–73.

Ellis, Juniper. *Pacific Designs in Print and Skin: Tattooing the World.* New York: Columbia University Press, 2008.

Ellis, William. *Polynesian Researches.* London: Fisher, Son, & Jackson, 1829.

Emerson, Nathaniel B. *Pele and Hiiaka: A Myth from Hawaii.* Honolulu: Honolulu Star Bulletin, 1915.

———. *Unwritten Literature of Hawaii: The Sacred Songs of the Hula.* 1906. Rutland, VT: Charles E. Tuttle, 1965.

Errington, Shelly. *The Death of Authentic Primitive Art and Other Tales of Progress.* Berkeley: University of California Press, 1998.

Equiano, Olaudah. *The Interesting Narrative and Other Writings* [1789]. New York: Penguin, 2007.

Farrier, David. *Unsettled Narratives: The Pacific Writings of Stevenson, Ellis, Melville, and London.* New York: Routledge, 2007.

Forbes, David. *Hawaiian National Bibliography, Vol. 3: 1851–1880.* Honolulu: University of Hawaii Press, 1999.

Geertz, Clifford. *The Interpretation of Cultures.* New York: Basic, 1973.

Gell, Alfred. *Wrapping in Images: Tattooing in Polynesia.* Oxford: Clarendon, 1993.

Goffman, Erving. *The Presentation of Self in Everyday Life.* New York: Doubleday, 1959.

Gordon-Cumming, Constance F. *At Home in Fiji*, 2nd ed. New York: A. C. Armstrong & Son, 1881.

Hanlon, David "Beyond 'the English Method of Tattooing': Decentering the Practice of History in Oceania. *Contemporary Pacific* 15, no. 1 (Spring 2003): 19–40.

Häolé, A. "*Sandwich Island Notes.* By A Häolé." *Albion* 13, no. 31 (August 5, 1854): 369.

Hastrup, Kirsten. "The Ethnographic Present: A Reinvention." *Cultural Anthropology* 5, no. 1 (February 1990): 45–61.

Hau'ofa, Epeli. "Our Sea of Islands." In *We Are the Ocean: Selected Works.* Honolulu: University of Hawaii Press, 2008.

Hayes, Michael. "Photography and the Emergence of the Pacific Cruise: Rethinking the Representational Crisis in Colonial Photography." In *Colonial Photography: Imag(in)ing Race and Place*, ed. Eleanor M. Hight and Gary D. Simpson, 172–87. London: Routledge, 2002.

Hazelwood, David. *A Fijian and English and an English and Fijian Dictionary*. London: A. Low, Marston, 1872.

Herbert, Christopher. *Culture and Anomie: Ethnographic Imagination in the Nineteenth Century*. Chicago: University of Chicago Press, 1991.

Hill, S. S. *Travels in the Sandwich and Society Islands*. London: Chapman and Hall, 1856.

Hillier, Robert Irwin. *The South Seas Fiction of Robert Louis Stevenson*. New York: Peter Lang, 1989.

Hocart, A. M. *The Northern States of Fiji*. Royal Anthropological Institute of Great Britain and Ireland, 1952.

Hoʻomanawanui, Kuʻualoha. *Voices of Fire: Reweaving the Literary Lei of Pele and Hiʻiaka*. Minneapolis: University of Minnesota Press, 2014.

Hulme, Peter. "The Cannibal Scene." In *Cannibalism and the Colonial World*, ed. Francis Barker, Peter Hulme, and Margaret Iverson. Cambridge: Cambridge University Press, 1998.

Imada, Adria L. *Aloha America: Hula Circuits through the U.S. Empire*. Durham, NC: Duke University Press, 2012.

Jarves, James Jackson. *History of the Hawaiian Islands*. 1843. 3rd ed. Honolulu: Henry M. Whitney, 1872.

Johnston, Patricia. "Advertising Paradise: Hawaiʻi in Art, Anthropology, and Commercial Photography." In *Colonial Photography: Imag(in)ing Race and Place*, ed. Eleanor M. Hight and Gary D. Simpson, 188–225. London: Routledge, 2002.

Jolly, Roslyn. *Robert Louis Stevenson in the Pacific: Travel, Empire, and the Author's Profession*. Surrey, UK: Ashgate, 2009.

Kaeppler, Adrienne. *"Artificial Curiosities": Being an Exposition of Native Manufactures Collected on the Three Pacific Voyages of Captain James Cook*. Honolulu: Bishop Museum Press, 1978.

———. *Hula Pahu: Hawaiian Drum Dances*, Vol. 1: *Haʻa and Hula Puha, Sacred Movements*. Honolulu: Bishop Museum Press, 1993.

Kingsley, Mary. *Travels in West Africa: Congo Francais, Corisco, and Cameroons*. London: Macmillan, 1897.

Kirshenblatt-Gimblet, Barbara. *Destination Culture: Tourism, Museums, and Heritage*. Berkeley: University of California Press, 1998.

Knight, Alanna. *Robert Louis Stevenson in the South Seas: An Intimate Photographic Record*. New York: Paragon, 1987.

Kuʻuleialoha Stillman, Amy. *Hula: Historical Perspectives*. Honolulu: Bishop Museum Press, 1980.

———. *Sacred Hula: The Historical Hula ʻAlaʻapapa*. Honolulu: Bishop Museum Press, 1998.

Lamb, Jonathan, Vanessa Smith, and Nicholas Thomas. *Exploration and Exchange: A South Seas Anthology, 1680–1900*. Chicago: University of Chicago Press, 2000.

Lamb, Jonathan. *Preserving the Self in the South Seas, 1680–1840*. Chicago: University of Chicago Press, 2001.

Lawrence, Helen Reeves. "Is the 'Tahitian' Drum Dance Really Tahitian?

Re-Evaluating the Evidence for the Origins of Contemporary Polynesian Drum Dance." *Yearbook for Traditional Music* 24 (1992): 126–37.

Lawry, Walter. *Friendly and Feejee Islands: A Missionary Visit to the Various Stations in the South Seas*. 2nd edition. London: Charles Gilpin, 1850.

Lévi-Strauss, Claude. *The Savage Mind* [1961]. Trans. John Russell. Chicago: University of Chicago Press, 1966.

Lindholm, Charles. *Culture and Authenticity*. Malden, MA: Blackwell, 2008.

Lury, Celia. "The Objects of Travel." In *Touring Cultures: Transformations of Travel and Theory*, ed. Chris Rojek and John Urry. London: Routledge, 1997.

Lyons, Paul. *American Pacificism: Oceania in the U.S. Imagination*. New York: Routledge, 2006.

MacCannell, Dean. *The Ethics of Sightseeing*. Berkeley: University of California Press, 2011.

———. *The Tourist: A New Theory of the Leisure Class*. 1976. New York: Schocken, 1989.

Malinowksi, Bronisław. *A Diary in the Strict Sense of the Term*. Stanford: Stanford University Press, 1989.

———. *Argonauts of the Western Pacific*. New York: E. P. Dutton, 1961 [1922].

Manfredi, Carla. "Picturing Robert Louis Stevenson's Pacific Phototext." *Le Répertoire de la Photolittérature Ancienne et Contemporaine (PHLIT)* (October 2012): n.p. Web.

———. "Robert Louis Stevenson's and Joseph Strong's 'A Samoan Scrapbook.'" *Journal of Stevenson Studies* 12 (2016): 4–32.

———. *Robert Louis Stevenson's Pacific Impressions: Photography and Travel writing, 1888–1894*. London: Palgrave MacMillan, 2018.

Martin, John, MD. *Tonga Islands: William Mariner's Account*. 1817. Tonga: Vava'u, 1991.

Maudslay, Alfred. *Life in the Pacific Fifty Years Ago*. London: George Routledge, 1930.

Maxwell, Anne. *Colonial Photography & Exhibitions: Representations of the 'Native' and the Making of European Identities*. London: Leicester University Press, 1999.

McClintock, Anne. *Imperial Leather: Race, Gender, and Sexuality in the Colonial Contest*. New York: Routledge, 1995.

McClure, S. S. *My Autobiography*. New York: Frederick A. Stokes, 1914.

McLynn, Frank. *Robert Louis Stevenson: A Biography*. New York: Random House, 1993.

Melillo, Edward D. "Making Sea Cucumbers out of Whale's Teeth: Nantucket Castaways and Encounters of Value in Nineteenth-Century Fiji." *Environmental History* 20 (2015): 449–74.

Melville, Herman. *Moby-Dick: Or, the Whale*. New York: Modern Library Classics, 1992.

———. *Omoo. Herman Melville: Typee, Omoo, and Mardi*. New York: Penguin, 1992.

———. *Typee*. New York: Modern Library Classics, 2001.

"Mesmerism." *British Medical Journal* 2, no. 675 (December 6, 1873): 667.

Middleton, Dorothy. *Victorian Lady Travellers*. New York: E. P. Dutton, 1965.

Mills, Sara. *Discourses of Difference: An Analysis of Women's Travel Writing and Colonialism*. London: Routledge, 1991.

Nunneley, Thomas. *Treatise on the Nature, Causes, and Treatment of Erysipelas.* Philadelphia: Ed. Barrington & Geo. D. Haswell, 1844.

Obeyesekere, Gannath. *Cannibal Talk: The Man-Eating Myth and Human Sacrifice in the South Seas.* Berkeley: University of California Press, 2005.

O'Connell, James F. *A Residence of Eleven Years in New Holland and the Caroline Islands: Being the Adventures of James F. O'Connell.* Boston: B. B. Mussey, 1836.

Oldman, W. O. [William Ockelford]. "Memoir No. 15: The Polynesian Curiosities of Polynesian Artifacts. Tonga, Samoa, and Fiji Groups. Installment No. 7." *Journal of Polynesian Society* 48, no. 3(191) (September 1939): 41–46.

Perkins, Edward. *Na Motu: Or, Reef Rovings in the South Seas.* New York: Pudney & Russell, 1854.

Polynesian, The. "Review: *Sandwich Island Notes,* by A Haole." Vol. XII (August 11, 1855): 1.

Pratt, Mary Louise. *Imperial Eyes: Travel Writing and Transculturation.* London: Routledge, 2008.

Quanchi, Max. *Culture Contact in the Pacific: Essays on Contact, Encounter, and Response.* Cambridge: Cambridge University Press, 1993.

———. "The Imaging of Samoa in Illustrated Magazines and Serial Encyclopedias in the Early 20th-Century." *Journal of Pacific History* 41, no. 2 (2006): 207–17.

———. "Visual Histories and Photographic Evidence." *Journal of Pacific History* 41, no. 2 (2006): 165–73.

Rennie, Neil. *Far-Fetched Facts: The Literature of Travel and the Idea of the South Seas.* Oxford: Oxford University Press, 1999.

———. "Introduction." In *In the South Seas.* London: Penguin, 1998.

Rohrer, Judy. *Haoles in Hawaii.* Honolulu: University of Hawaii Press, 2010.

Rojek, Chris. "Indexing, Dragging, and the Social Construction of Tourist Sights." In *Touring Cultures: Transformations of Travel and Theory,* ed. Chris Rojek and John Urry. London: Routledge, 1997.

Rosaldo, Renato. "Imperialist Nostalgia." *Representations* 26 (Spring 1989): 107–22.

Sahlins, Marshall. "Culture as Protein and Profit." *New York Review of Books.* November 23, 1978.

———. "The Discovery of the True Savage." In *Dangerous Liaisons: Essays in Honour of Greg Dening,* ed. Donna Merwick, 41–94. Melbourne: University of Melbourne Press, 1994.

"Sandwich Island Notes." *New Englander* 44 (February 1855): 1–19.

Schwartz, Joan M., and James R. Ryan. "Introduction: Photography and the Geographical Imagination." In *Picturing Place: Photography and the Geographical Imagination,* ed. Joan M. Schwartz and James R. Ryan, 1–18. London: I.B. Tauris, 2003.

Seemann, Berthold. "Foreign Correspondence." *Athenaeum* 1743 (March 23, 1861): 396–97.

———. *Viti: An Account of a Government Mission to the Vitian or Fijian Islands in the Years Years 1860-1.* Cambridge: Macmillan, 1862.

Silva, Noenoe K. "He Kanawai E Ho'opau I Na Hula Kuolo Hawai'i: The Political Economy of Banning the Hula." *Hawaiian Journal of History* 34 (2000): 29–48.

———. *The Power of the Steel-Tipped Pen: Reconstructing Native Hawaiian Intellectual History*. Durham, NC: Duke University Press, 2017.

Spate, O.H.K. "'South Sea to 'Pacific Ocean': A Note on Nomenclature." *Journal of Pacific History* 12, no. 4 (1997): 205–11.

Spivak, Gayatri Chakravorty. "Can the Subaltern Speak?" In *Marxism and the Interpretation of Cultures*, ed. Cary Nelson and Lawrence Grossberg, 271–315. Champagne: University of Illinois Press, 1988.

Smith, Vanessa. "Belated First Contact." In *Exploration and Exchange*, ed. Jonathan Lamb, Nicholas Thomas, and Vanessa Smith, 299–310. Chicago: University of Chicago Press, 2000.

———. "Falling from Grace: George Vason." In *Exploration and Exchange*, ed. Jonathan Lamb, Nicholas Thomas, and Vanessa Smith, 156–69. Chicago: University of Chicago Press, 2000.

———. *Intimate Strangers: Friendship, Exchange and Pacific Encounters*. Cambridge: Cambridge University Press, 2010.

———. *Literary Culture and the Pacific: Nineteenth-century Textual Encounters*. Cambridge: Cambridge University Press, 1998.

Smythe, Sarah Bland [Mrs. Smythe]. *Ten Months in the Fiji Islands*. London: John Henry and James Parker, 1864.

Stevenson, Fanny. *The Cruise of the Janet Nichol*. New York: Charles Scribner's Sons, 1914.

Stevenson, Margaret. *Letters from Samoa: 1891–1895*. Ed. Marie Clothchilde Balfour. New York: Charles Scribner's Sons, 1906.

Stevenson, Robert Louis. *A Footnote to History: Eight Years of Trouble in Samoa*. New York: Scribner's, 1892.

———. *In the South Seas*. 1896. London: Penguin, 1998.

———. "A Samoan Scrapbook." *Sophia Scarlett and other Pacific Writings*. Ed. Robert Hoskins. Auckland: AUT Media, 2008.

St. Johnston, Alfred. *Camping with Cannibals*. London: Macmillan and Co., 1883.

Taylor, Charles. *The Ethics of Authenticity*. Cambridge, MA: Harvard University Press, 1991.

Thomas, Nicholas. *Entangled Objects: Exchange, Material Culture, and Colonialism in the Pacific*. Cambridge, MA: Harvard University Press, 1991.

———. *In Oceania: Visions, Artifacts, Histories*. Durham, NC: Duke University Press, 1997.

———. "Quite Alone in a Mountain Village." In *Exploration and Exchange*, ed. Jonathan Lamb, Nicholas Thomas, and Vanessa Smith, 292–98. Chicago: University of Chicago Press, 2000.

———. "Von Hügel's Curiosity." *HAU: Journal of Ethnographic Theory* 1 (2011): 299–314.

———. "Objects of Knowledge: Oceanic Artifacts in European Engravings." In *Empires of Vision: A Reader*, ed. Martin Jay and Sumathi Ramaswamy. Durham, NC: Duke University Press, 2013.

Thomson, Basil. *South Sea Yarns*. London: William Blackwood, 1894.

Tiffany, Sharon W. "Contesting the Erotic Zone: Margaret Mead's Fieldwork Photographs of Samoa." *Pacific Studies* 28 (Sept./Dec. 2005): 19–45.

Titcomb, Margaret. "Kava in Hawaii." *Journal of Polynesian Society* 57, no. 2 (June 1948): 105–71.

Torrey, William. *Torrey's Narrative: Or, The Life and Adventures of William Torrey.* Boston: Press of A. J. Wright, 1848.

Trilling, Lionel. *Sincerity and Authenticity.* Cambridge, MA: Harvard University Press, 1972.

Twain, Mark. *Roughing It.* Hartford, CT: American Publishing, 1872.

Urry, John, and Larsen, Jonas. *The Tourist Gaze 3.0.* Lancaster, UK: SAGE, 2012.

Vason, George. *An Authentic Narrative of Four Year's Residence in Tongataboo.* Ed. Samuel Piggott. London: Longman, Hurst, Rees, and Orme, 1810.

———. *Narrative of the Late George Vason of Nottingham.* Ed. James Orange. Derby: Henry Mozley, 1840.

Von Hügel, Anatole. *The Fiji Journals of Baron Anatole Von Hügel, 1875–1877.* Ed. Jane Roth and Steven Hooper. Suva: Fiji Museum, 1990.

Walkup, A. C. "Report of Tour in the Gilbert Islands." *Friend* 57, no. 6 (June 1899): 42–43. Web. Hawaiian Mission Houses Digital Archives.

Wallis, Mary Davis. *Life in Feejee, or Five Years among the Cannibals* [By a Lady]. Boston: William Heath, 1851.

———. *The Fiji and New Caledonia Journals of Mary Wallis, 1851–1853.* Ed. David Routledge. Suva: Institute of Pacific Studies, 1994.

White, Joanna. "Marks of Transgression." In *Tattoos: Bodies, Art, and Exchange in the Pacific and the West,* ed. Nicholas Thomas, Anna Cole, and Bronwen Douglas. Durham, NC: Duke University Press, 2005.

Williams, Thomas, and James Calvert. *Fiji and the Fijians* (2 vols.). Ed. George Stringer Rowe. London: Alexander Heylin, 1858.

Wilson, Bee. *Consider the Fork: A History of How We Cook and Eat.* New York: Basic, 2012.

Wilson, James. *A Missionary Voyage to the Southern Pacific Ocean.* London: T. Chapman, 1799.

Wise, Henry Augustus. [Harry Gringo] *Los Gringos: Or, An Inside View of Mexico and California, with Wanderings in Peru, Chile, and Polynesia.* New York: Baker and Scribner, 1849.

Index

Abemama, 129, 131. *See also* Apemama

anthropophagy, 89. *See also* cannibalism

Apemama: in context of Gilbert Islands, 121; as part of Stevenson's cruise, 109; Stevenson family's camp there, 130–31; Stevenson's romanticization of, 129; Stevenson's spelling of, 129. See also *In the South Seas*

Arens, William, 88, 89

Arista, Noelani, 4, 47–48

At Home in Fiji. See Gordon-Cumming, Constance

Authentic Narrative of Four Years Residence in Tongataboo, An. See Vason, George

Balfour, Graham, 132

Banivanua-Mar, Tracey, 92–93, 96

Barnum, P. T., 29, 153n8

Barrère, Dorothy, 52–53

Bates, George Washington. *See* Häolé, A

Bau, 86–87, 90–91, 154–55n19

beachcomber narrative, 5–7, 16–17, 21–22, 32, 39–40, 44, 49–50, 84–85, 89, 106–7, 144n8, 146n1, 147n16

Bell, Leonard, 107

Benjamin, Walter, 120, 126, 135

Bingham, Hiram, 54–55

Bird, Isabella, 63–64, 68, 152–53n25

bokola, 74–76, 81, 153n6. *See also* cannibalism

Brantlinger, Patrick, 88–89

Buckton, Oliver, 109

Burlingame, Edward, 131–32

Burton, Stacy, 43

Butaritari: in photograph of Joseph Strong, 122–24; Nan Tok' and Nei Takauti in photographs, 102–4, 126–28; Stevenson's impressions of in *In the South Seas*, 124–27

Cabri, Jean-Baptiste, 17–18, 147n13

Caesar, Terry, 80

Calvert, James, 84

cannibal fork: curiosity collecting of, 68–73 155n24; illustrations of, 64–66, 77–79; missionary accounts of, 92–96; as Pacific possession, 66–67; translation history, 74–76

cannibalism: Gordon-Cumming's accounts of, 85–88, 90–92, 100; Gordon-Cumming views on, 71–72, 81–84, 85, 100–101; as a discourse, 8–9, 66–68, 80, 88–90, 92, 96; Herman Melville views on, 84–85; in relation to cannibal fork, 65–68, 75–76, 80; scholarly debate about, 88–90

cannibal talk, 8, 67, 88–96, 100–101, 154n18; *See also* Obeyesekere, Gannath

Cannizzo, Jeanne, 94

Capell, Arthur, 74–75
Cary, William, 69
Casco, 105, 111
Clifford, James, 73, 80
Clunie, Fergus, 75
Cohen, Deborah, 98
Colley, Ann C., 107–8, 111
Colvin, Sidney: Fanny Stevenson letter
    to, 109–110; Robert Louis Stevenson
    letter to, 109, 111–12, 132
conversion narratives: Fjian, 89, 92, 94;
    Vason's *Account* as, 7, 28–29
Cook, James, 55, 68
Coulter, John, 6, 16, 17, 29, 146n11,
    147n16
Cuckoo clock, 29–30
Culler, Jonathan, 7, 13, 23, 38
curiosity collecting, 68–70, 86, 106, 121

DeBry, Thomas, 13
degeneration, 66, 116, 152–53n25
Dening, Greg: account of Peter Hey-
    wood's tattooing, 20–21; the beach,
    4, 14–15, 70, 90, 121; *Mr. Bligh's Bad
    Language*, 4, 14–15, 20–21, 56
Diary in the Strict Sense, A (Malinowski),
    152n23
Dibble, Sheldon, 53–54
Douglass, Frederick, 145–46n1
Duff, 7

Edmond, Rod, 107, 120–21, 131
Edwards, Elizabeth, 113–15
Edwards, Mary Bercaw, 144n8, 151n8
Ellis, Juniper, 21, 22, 24, 27
Ellis, William, 39, 144n5
Elleray, Michelle, 21
Emerson, Nathaniel B., 52
Equator, 105, 111
Equator Town, 129–31, 138
Equiano, Olaudah, 145–6n1
Errington, Shelly, 77

Farrier, David, 5, 39, 107, 131
Footnote to History, A, 112 (Stevenson)

Gardenhire, W. C., 153n8
Geertz, Clifford, 59, 92–93
Gell, Alfred, 17, 19
Gilbert Islands, 9, 102–3, 108–9, 120–29
Goffman, Erving, 38
Gordon, Arthur Hamilton, 70, 82
Gordon-Cumming, Constance: on can-
    nibal forks, 64–66, 70–72, 74, 76–78,
    81; on cannibalism, 82, 85–94, 96,
    100–101; illustrations and sketches,
    78, 97–99; reasons for traveling to
    Fiji, 5, 68, 81–82; travel companions'
    comments on, 83–84; as travel writer,
    10–11, 68, 81–82

Hanlon, David, 24–25
Häolé, A: account of hula ceremony,
    2, 36–37, 55–62; contemporary re-
    views of *Sandwich Island Notes*, 37; in
    contrast to beachcombers, 44–49; as
    pseudonym, 8, 37, 149–50n1
Hastrup, Kirsten, 120
Hau'ofa, Epeli, 9–10
Hayes, Michael, 115
Hazelwood, David, 74
Heart of Darkness, 81
Herbert, Christopher, 62
Heywood, Peter, 20–21
Hill, S. S., 41–42, 55–56
Hillier, Robert Irwin, 109
Hocart, A. M., 75
Ho'omanawanui, Ku'ualoha, 52, 145n11
hula: A Häolé's account of, 36–37,
    55–62; Edward Perkins' account of,
    49–51; formal elements of, 51–53;
    as marker of authenticity, 38, 43,
    49–50; Mark Twain's comments on,
    62–63; missionary restrictions on,
    52, 54–55, 63; nineteenth-century
    Western descriptions of, 53–56; as
    pacific possession, 37–38, 64, 94, 114;
    in response to American imperialism,
    62; as tourist marker, 38, 106;
    sexualization of, 39, 51, 53, 58–59,
    62–63; Stevenson comments on, 106

Hulme, Peter, 80, 88
Hunt, John (Rev.), 93–94

iculanibokola, 74–76, 79–80. *See also* cannibal fork
Imada, Adria L., 51, 59, 62
imperialist nostalgia, 49
In the South Seas (Stevenson): Apemama in, 131–41; Butaritari in, 120, 124–30; Gilbert Islands in, 9, 102–3, 108–9, 120–129; Marquesas in, 22, 109, 117, 121; Penguin Classics edition cover, 102–104; photography in, 106–107, 109; scholarly commentary on, 131–32

Jarves, James Jackson, 53, 62
Johnston, Patricia, 114
Jolly, Rosalyn, 133

Kaeppler, Adrienne L.: *"Artificial Curiosities,"* 68; *Hula Puha*, 51–52
Kalākaua, 62
Kanoa and Mary Kanoa, 126–28
Kapihenhui, [M. J.], 52
"King of the Cannibal Islands, The," 82
Kingsley, Mary, 154n14
Kiribati, 9, 102, 155n4. *See also* Gilbert Islands
Kirshenblatt-Gimlet, Barbara, 77–78
Knapman, Claudia, 68
Knight, Alanna, 107
Kodak camera, 114

Langham, Frederick, 74, 84, 100
Lawry, Walter, 93–94, 100, 116–17
Lindholm, Charles, 12
London, Jack, 5
London Missionary Society, 7, 15–16
Los Gringoes. See Wise, Henry Augustus
luau, 1–3
Lury, Celia, 76–77
Lyons, Paul, 4, 28, 40, 42, 52

MacCannell, Dean: front and back regions, 38, 50, 55, 59; staged authenticity, 38

Mad Men, 143n2
magic lantern shows, 139
Maka and Mary Maka, 126–29
McClintock, Anne, 126
McClure, S. S., 109, 111
McLynn, Frank, 157n12
Malinowksi, Bronislaw, 61–62, 152n23
Manfredi, Carla, 107–8, 112, 115, 157n13
Mariner, William, 15, 25, 148n21
Marquesas Islands, 105–6, 108, 110, 117
Martin, John, 25, 148n21, 148n23
Maudslay, Alfred, 83–84
Maxwell, Anne, 113, 119
Melillo, Edward D., 69
Melville, Herman, 5, 16, 84–86, 110–11, 141, 150n3, 157n12; *Moby-Dick*, 85–86, 154n12; *Omoo*, 40, 56; personal library of travel narratives, 150nn3–4; *Typee*, 16–17, 40, 45–46, 56, 85, 111, 120
Mesmerism, 139–41
Middleton, Dorothy, 68
Mills, Sara, 82
Moipu, 117–19

Namusi, 94–95
Naduri, 100
Nan Tok', 103–5, 124–26, 128–29
Narrative of the Life of the Late George Vason of Nottingham. See Vason, George
Navosa, 87
Nei Takauti, 102–5, 124–26, 128–29
"Noble savage" trope, 12–13, 20, 42
Nuku Hiva, 105

Obeyesekere, Gannath, 8, 67, 88–90, 93. *See also* cannibal talk
O'Connell, James, 23–26, 29, 14n24
Orange, James, 28–29, 148–149n27
Osbourne, Isobel, 105, 156n5
Osbourne, Lloyd, 105, 111–12, 114, 117–19, 139

Paaaeua, 117–19
Pacific Islands: historical context of term,

9–11. *See also names of individual islands*

Pacific possessions: comparison of chapter's examples, 94; definition of, 4; Stevenson's Apemama photographs as, 129

Partington, James Edge, 72

Paumotus, 105

Perkins, Edward, 3, 5–6, 40–42, 49–51, 53, 150n4

photography: colonial photography, 113–14, 119; Stevenson's views on, 106–8, 111–13, 120; tourist photography, 114–15

picturesque, 10; in context of Hawaii, 42–44

Polynesia, historical context of term, 9–11. *See names of individual islands*

Port au Prince, 15

Pratt, Mary Louise, 4–5, 93

Reid, Dennis, 105, 111

Rennie, Neil, 107, 110, 131

Resaldo, Renato, 49

Ricoeur, Paul, 88

Roughing It (Twain), 47–48, 53, 62–63

Rousseau, Jean-Jacques, 12, 157n12

Rutherford, John, 17, 19, 32, 147n14

Sahlins, Marshall, 88

Samoa: Stevenson's settling in, 106–7, 131; Stevenson's writing about, 112–14

"Samoan Scrapbook, A" (Stevenson), 112–113

Sandwich Island Notes. See Häolé, A

Savage, Charlie, 69

Schwob, Marcel, 112

Seemann, Berthold Carl, 71, 81, 90, 153n3

Silva, Noenoe K., 52, 54–55, 145n11

Smith, Vanessa, 5, 16, 29, 131, 143n3

Smythe, Sarah Bland, 94–96

Smythe, W. J., 74, 76, 94–96

Spivak, Gayatri, 90

Stevenson, Fanny, 102–5, 109–10, 112, 124, 126, 128; *The Cruise of the Janet Nichol*, 103

Stevenson, Robert Louis: on Herman Melville, 110–1; and photography, 9, 105–8, 111–13; and Nan Tok' and Nei Takauti, 103–5, 124–26, 128–29; and Tembinok, 129, 132–39. See also *In the South Seas*

Stillman, Amy Ku'uleialoha, 52–53

St. Johnston, Alfred, 155n24

Stoddard, Charles Warren, 110–11

Strong, Joseph, 105, 112, 122–24, 131, 156n5

tabua, 66, 69, 78

Tamaiti, 139–41

tattooing: in beachcomber narratives, 16–17; Māori tattooing, 17–18; Marquesan tattooing, 17–18, 22–25, 106; Pohnpeian tattooing, 23–26; Tongan tattooing, 7, 17, 19–20, 26–27, 68

Tembinok', 129, 132–39

Thomas, Nicholas, 66, 68–70, 96–97

Thomson, Basil, 72

Titcomb, Margaret, 151n10, 151n12

Tonga: missionary endeavors in, 15; warfare in, 29. *See also* Tongan Tattooing

Torrey, William, 30–35

TripAdvisor, 1–3

Twain, Mark, 47–48, 53, 62–63

Vason, George: arrival in Tonga, 15–16; comparison to James O'Connell's tattooing, 23–24; in frontispiece to *Narrative of the Life of the Late George Vason of Nottingham*, 12–14; in New York, 26–27 return to England, 28–29; his tattooing, 7, 14, 17, 19–22, 26–27 von Hügel, Baron Anatole, 70–71, 83–84, 90

Wallis, Mary, 84–85, 94
Waterhouse, Joseph, 95
"Weroan or Great Lorde of Virginia, A" (DeBry), 13

Whippy, David, 69
White, Joanna, 32
Williams, Thomas, 74–76, 79
Wilson, Bee, 80
Wise, Henry Augustus, 2, 5, 40, 42–43, 57, 150n3
Writers' Museum in Edinburgh, 156n7